For the Camden Public Library

Good sailing to all borrowers!

Roger C. Taylor

Good Boats

Good Boats

ROGER C. TAYLOR

INTERNATIONAL MARINE PUBLISHING COMPANY
CAMDEN, MAINE

Copyright © 1977
by International Marine Publishing Company
Library of Congress Catalog Card Number 77-70205
International Standard Book Number 0-87742-076-9
Typeset by A & B Typesetters, Inc., Concord, New Hampshire

DEDICATION

To the memory of Captain Conant Taylor, U.S. Navy, my father, who showed me the difference between a good boat and a lousy boat.

Contents

Preface

You should be warned from the outset that this is a highly subjective book. I have been prejudiced on the subject of boat design since an early age and am now old enough so that often I may unwittingly confuse prejudice with Good Taste, or, worse yet, with Truth. Of course such confusion on my part will not matter greatly to you, who, I trust, will bring your own judgment to bear on the boat designs presented on the following pages and on my remarks about them. Doubtless you will be able to decide for yourself what constitutes a good boat.

In the process, I hope you will learn more about your own boat design prejudices. The key to choosing the "right boat" is perhaps self-knowledge more than it is expertise in naval architecture.

I hope, too, that the book will show you something about how to interpret boat plans, that it will even demonstrate a bit of basic seamanship here and there, and that it might perhaps go so far as to expand your boating vocabulary a bit. (I can guarantee, for example, that you'll be sick and tired of being told what wonderful things vangs are before you are through.)

But, of course, the primary purpose of this book is simply a way for me to share with you my favorite boat designs, hopefully for your pleasure and enjoyment.

None of the boat designs in this book is very recent. There are two reasons for this:

1. A good, new, cruising boat design is hard to find. Under the powerful influence of a style created by the racing rating rules, today's designers often turn out lousy cruising boats in the belief that good cruising boats won't sell any more.
2. Most people who are looking for good boat designs are aware of the few good new designs that are advertised or described in the boating magazines, but many folks are unaware that there are plenty of good, old designs that merely want dusting off to be worthy of consideration for building to today.

At any rate, here are thirty-six boat designs I like. As I say, I hope you will like them too; prejudice welcomes company.

A second warning you deserve is that the way in which this book has been published borders on incest. The author is also the president of the publishing company and is frankly seeking to realize a life-long dream: signing his own royalty checks.

All of these designs have already been presented in articles that appeared between mid-1972 and mid-1975 in the *National Fisherman*, that wonderful marine newspaper, published right across the hall from my office. I want to thank Dave Getchell and everyone who works on the *National Fisherman* for printing my design articles each month and for presenting them so well. The Prologue is reprinted from the late, great *Skipper* magazine of Annapolis, Maryland, and the Epilogue is reprinted from *Yachting* magazine.

The biggest thank you I want to say is, of course, to the designers whose work appears in the book. It is more their book than mine, and whatever value the book may have will be due to their artistry, common sense, and seamanship.

I want to thank the publishers and photographers whose names appear at the ends of the captions for their permission to reproduce the plans and photographs in the book.

Finally, I want to thank the readers of the *National Fisherman* who have written me commenting on the designs they have liked. They have caught me up on many a mistake and have given me much additional information about many of the designs, and I have used their knowledge to make the book more accurate and interesting than it otherwise would have been. Without the enthusiastic response of *National Fisherman* readers, there would have been no book.

ROGER C. TAYLOR
Rockport, Maine

Prologue — Tacking the *Mahoskus*

When I was seven years old, my father taught me to sail. His method of instruction and the training vessel used were, to the best of my knowledge, unique.

My father was a retired naval officer who had been to sea in almost every kind of craft, large and small, good and bad. As early as the time of his graduation from the Naval Academy in 1906, someone wrote of him in that year's "Lucky Bag" that he could "sail over Niagara Falls in a teacup without shipping a drop."

He expected all of his children to sail their various craft among the coves of the Pawcatuck River without shipping a drop, either, whether we were working the Rhode Island or the Connecticut shore of the stream. We were all just supposed to be born sailors.

The spring I turned seven I was told I would sail the *Mahoskus* that summer. Her captaincy, even to a boy of seven, seemed a dubious honor. Seven feet long and square ended, she had no more than twenty-four inches extreme beam.

The *Mahoskus* had been designed and built by my father as an experimental craft. The idea was to see if a flat-bottomed boat could be made to go to windward without benefit of either centerboard or leeboards. When I was instructed on how to put her in commission, I was told not to bother getting the rudder down from the boathouse rafters; I wasn't to be allowed any such convenience during my first summer in command.

It was with heavy heart that I sanded and sanded and sanded on the rough bottom planking of the *Mahoskus* that spring. How I longed for rainy days. Admittedly, I hadn't much seagoing experience, but I'd seen a lot of boats out of water, and I knew a dog when I saw one. I couldn't understand how a homemade, pointed sail with bamboo fishing poles for mast and boom was going to drive that cranky hull anywhere. And to windward? Even supposing I could get her along on a steady course heading up reasonably close to the wind, how, without a rudder, would I ever swing her round from one tack to the other?

Repeated requests to be allowed to spend the summer with a chum in central Vermont brought looks of scorn from older brothers and sisters, and caused an expression of indescribable horror upon my father's countenance.

I applied red-lead and putty to the seams where the cross planks on the bottom met each other. A brilliant scheme to be a bit casual with the putty knife, in hopes that some of the wider seams never would swell up tight, had to be discarded almost as soon as conceived. I saw at once that such work would never pass inspection.

Each day of fair weather brought me a day closer to going sailing, and I still had no solution in mind for tacking the *Mahoskus*. The inside work went all too quickly. My father was a bit frugal with boat supplies, and, being the youngest, I was last in line for inside paint. When the remains of this and that had been stirred together and carefully mixed with just the right amounts of turpentine and linseed oil, the coffee can held a pink sauce. I had thought that my barometer had sunk as low as it could go, but as soon as I saw the pink paint, I realized that despair could go deeper. The paint was applied to the innards of the *Mahoskus* without enthusiasm.

Launching day came. Much to my secret delight, the *Mahoskus* filled to the gunwales as soon as she was overboard and had to be towed to her berth at the dock by my brother in his dory. He had a dory with a centerboard, a real mast and boom, a jib as well as a mainsail, and a steering oar that worked in a stern notch. I was told not to worry or to look so sad; my boat would be all swelled up and tight as a bottle in a week.

I had to pump the *Mahoskus* every morning with a big galvanized lift pump. Every morning she filled back up, but each day it occurred at a distressingly slower rate. After five days, only a trickle came in. Then, two days after that, she stayed dry.

I had spent the time in between pumping and making sure she was filling again in surveying the body of water where I was to try to navigate my charge. It was known as Creep Mouse Cove to us, although it was called Babcock Cove on the chart. The cove was several hundred yards long by a hundred wide, and opened onto the Pawcatuck River to the northwest. With high trees coming to the water's edge on each side, the winds were usually light and variable. My oldest sister said the only way to sail in the cove was to trim the sail halfway in, head where you wanted to go, and wish your way along. I wasn't sure I knew just how to do that.

One day my father said I was to start sailing. While we were stepping the mast and unfurling the sail, my father carefully explained the theory of the *Mahoskus'* hull form so that I would have no difficulty sailing her. It seemed that, to get maximum resistance to being blown sideways, you were supposed to keep the boat heeled over so she had just two inches of freeboard on the lee side. It was explained that this was done by shifting one's weight across the boat as necessary. The objective was to keep her lee side well down in the water so its long, flat surface would dig in and keep her from making leeway. If I trimmed her on an even keel, I was told, she would drift off and go out of control.

I was to steer by shifting my weight forward and aft. If I crept forward, the boat's bow would go down, and the stern would go up and blow off to leeward, thus turning the boat. If I eased my weight aft a little, exactly the opposite effect was supposed to take place.

Of course I had an alternate method of steering

if I wished. I had the main sheet to hold and use for trimming the sail in or out, just as I pleased. I was told that if I trimmed the sail in, it would tend to steer the boat up into the wind, and that if I slacked the sheet out, it would tend to steer the boat off the wind, but that the former reaction, the heading up, was a stronger and surer one than the latter, the heading off. I think it was this part that confused me most.

It was now revealed that my duties in the *Mahoskus* would be twofold: learning to sail; and running a series of experiments to determine, further than had already been ascertained, the practicality of the vessel's design. I was, at any rate, to concentrate on getting the *Mahoskus* to windward.

I was to be pushed off from the dock "to see what you can do with a gentle, dry northwester," and was to steer, heading as close to the wind as I could, for the opposite shore of Creep Mouse Cove. After I reached that shore, I was to tack and head back across the cove, still sailing close on the wind. Upon regaining the near shore, hopefully at a point to windward of the dock, I was to head downwind. Then, while my father measured off the distance made good to windward along the shore, I was to round up in the lee of the dock and make a landing. This all sounded complicated enough, but what worried me most was the lack of instruction on the subject of tacking. Although that maneuver had been uppermost in my mind for a long time, I didn't dare inquire as to how it was to be performed.

Without further ceremony, the *Mahoskus* and I were cast off from the dock. I trimmed in my sheet, hung on to it grimly, sat sort of amidships but a little to leeward to heel her over, and hoped for the best. The *Mahoskus* slowly gathered way.

On the run across the cove, I was quite busy keeping her heeled over just right and trying to steer. I remember looking back at the dock once and seeing my father walking along the shore toward the point to which he expected me to return. Mostly the boat would head up into the wind because I got my weight too far forward. Then I would have to scurry aft to get her going again, trying to remember to keep her heeled down at the same time. It wasn't a very smooth thing, but we were making progress and hadn't yet been blown off to leeward and gone out of control. I wondered just how it would be if those two things did happen.

We approached the opposite shore. I still had no idea how to get the *Mahoskus* around onto the other tack. I had just decided that such a vessel couldn't be tacked, and had resigned myself to running her straight ashore with whatever consequences might follow, when my father's voice came booming across the water with, "Walk up round the mast!" I hesitated momentarily before carrying out this unorthodox order, but then, seeing the shore coming on fast, as the *Mahoskus* was going strong at the moment, I leaped for the bow. I landed forward in a heap, the bow went almost under, and the stern spun round smartly. "Now go aft," com-

manded the voice. As I crawled aft to grab the sheet again, the *Mahoskus* settled down on her new tack, just as she was designed to do. We were headed back across the cove, and it looked as if we would make a little to windward!

From that minute on, the rest of the summer, the *Mahoskus* was under control. She was a bit cranky now and then, especially in a fluky breeze, but she was never impossible. I was glad then I had not gone to central Vermont. Under the stern and expert supervision of my father, the little boat taught me many lessons.

The *Mahoskus* was broken up some years ago. She was not a bad training ship. She had no centerboard or leeboards and no rudder, but there was a lot of learning packed into her twenty-four inches of extreme beam. It's sad to know she's gone.

1/ The Cogge Ketches

Length on deck: 50 feet 4 inches
Length on waterline: 42 feet 6 inches
Beam: 13 feet 11 inches
Draft: 7 feet 6 inches
Sail area: 1,480 square feet (four lowers)
Designers: Douglas P. Urry and F. Wavell Urry

After I had arrived at the ripe old age of fourteen, I was allowed to explore the closet of my father's study on the third day of a northeaster, the day when the continued restrictions of his children's youthful energies made it mandatory that my father secure peace at any price. He knew that my being allowed into that particular place would have the desired effect on me, but, being an orderly man, he was a bit wary, I think, of my going through his neat stacks of old boating magazines.

He had the issues from 1926 right up to the then-current 1945 numbers. It was tremendously exciting to pull out a stack I had not yet explored and look through them for the first time, knowing not what fantastic schooner or ketch might lie in wait on the next page. For I was a naval architect in those days and was intensely interested in discovering "good" boat designs, separating them from the many "lousy" boats whose plans were published.

A "good" boat had to be well proportioned in hull and rig; she could be rugged or dainty, but she had to please the eye. Any ugliness was sufficient reason for the epithet "lousy boat," with perhaps a "too high-sided" or "not enough sail" thrown in.

The "good" boats were pored over, studied, and absorbed; dimensions and sail areas were ingested beyond mere memorization. The vessel under examination would be imagined sailing in a variety of conditions, and the rig would be shortened down mentally, or light sails would be set to suit the full extremes of wind. Sometimes the route and weather conditions of some actual cruise would be applied in imagination to a newly discovered "good" boat, to both test and enjoy her abilities. Maybe a rolling run from Block Island to Cuttyhunk in a busting sou'wester would be remembered, and the new discovery would have to make the same run on the same day to see how she behaved.

Of course there was always a little editing that had to be done on even the best boats. I never tampered, however, with the hull. If the counter was too heavy for the bow, it was no use pretending she was finer aft than she really was. It was no good wishing that a flat sheer line cocked up nicely. If you had to make basic changes like that, you just had a "lousy" boat—and that was that.

There was one piece of editing I used to do, though, that came very close to hull-tampering. Every now and then I'd come across a boat I

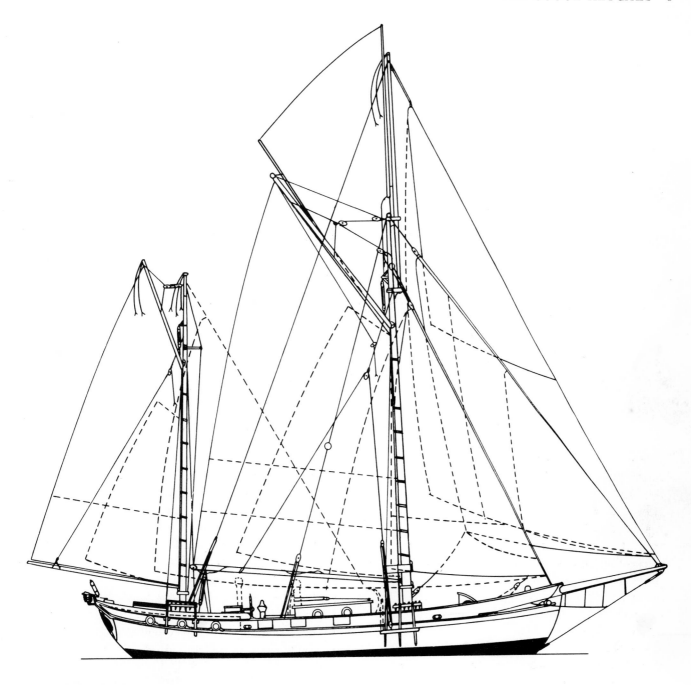

The Urry brothers' 50-foot version of the Cogge ketch, third of the type they designed, but the first one I discovered. (F. Wavell Urry)

really liked, except that it was obvious she didn't have enough lateral plane to do really well to windward. In a case like that, I'd just shut my eyes and stick in a centerboard right down through the keel without changing another thing.

Most of the changes required were either to the rig or to the interior arrangement, and these were limited to minor modifications. A traditional three-headsail rig might have to become a more

modern double-head rig if the jib topsail shown were ridiculously small. More often, topmasts, or at least club topsails, were added to bald-headed, gaff-rigged boats. Or, down below, a huge head taking up most of the best part of the boat would have to be relegated to the fo'c's'le to make room for a really decent chart table.

A standard design change at the easily pure age of fourteen was the instant removal of all

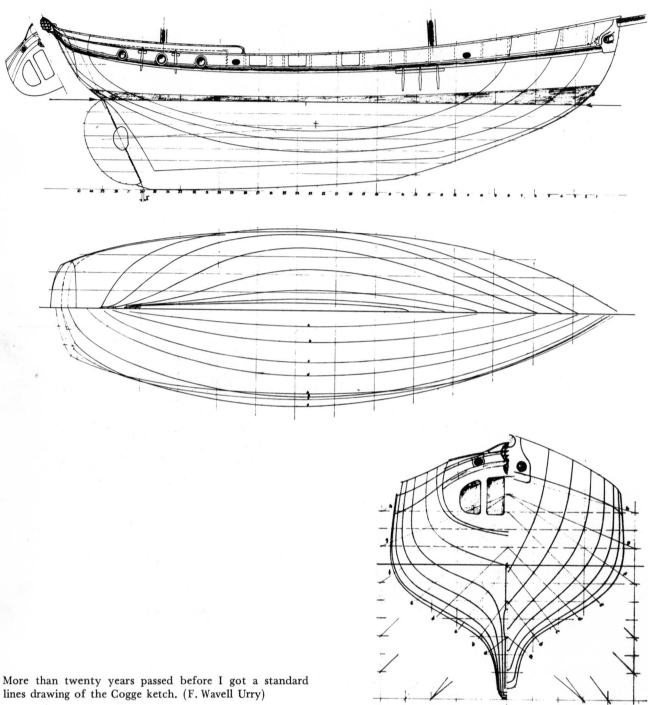

More than twenty years passed before I got a standard lines drawing of the Cogge ketch. (F. Wavell Urry)

engines, and then the more deliberate determination of the use for the space gained. It was always particularly pleasant to close up the propeller aperture.

There was one issue of *Yachting* that I used to keep returning to. It was November 1927. In it was the most wonderful boat I'd ever found. She was labeled, "A 50-footer of the Cogge type,"

and then it said in smaller print, "Something between the intriguing *Nonsuch* and the *Coggette.*"

The first time I saw this design, it was quickly obvious that here was a good boat. The Cogge ketch, as I termed her, was designed by Douglas P. and F. Wavell Urry. She was 50 feet 4 inches long on deck and 42 feet 6 inches on the

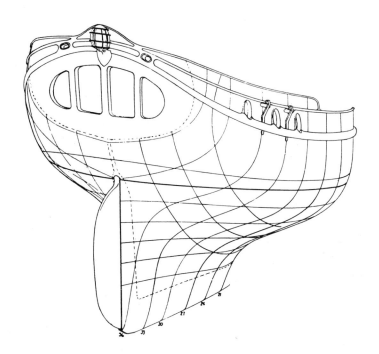

Left: This is the perspective lines drawing that appeared in the November, 1927, issue of *Yachting*. (*Yachting*, November, 1927)

Below: The 50-foot Cogge's arrangement plans. (*Yachting*, November, 1927)

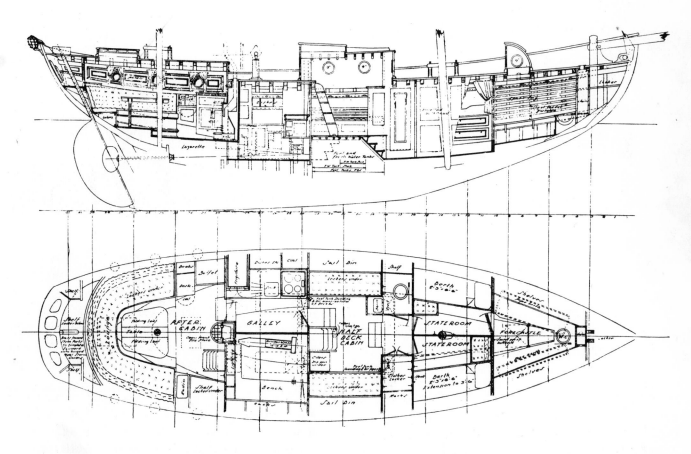

water, with a beam of 13 feet 11 inches and a draft of 7 feet 6 inches. She carried 1,480 square feet of sail in her four lowers.

Her hull was well balanced, with high ends, a bold sheer, and nicely curved, short overhangs. She looked able. And, most exciting of all, she had a raised poop and a great cabin with a fireplace and stern windows! She carried a boat on

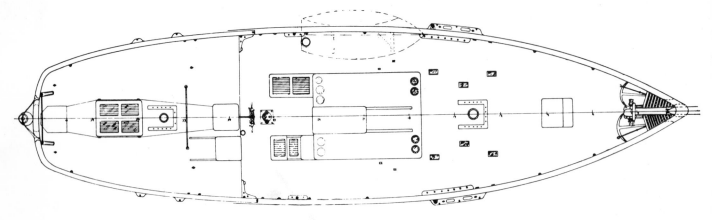

Above: The 50-footer's deck plan. (*Yachting*, November, 1927)

Right: A model of the 50-footer built by William Kinsella of Greenwich, Connecticut. (William Kinsella)

deck and had a substantial deckhouse amidships. Here was a great find, a boat that clearly deserved much scrutiny.

It took some time to take in this design and come to some real appreciation of the vessel. The lines, unfortunately, were shown only in perspective, from the quarter. The drawing did show the shape of the stern, with its windows and its quarter ports, and that was the most unusual, and therefore hard-to-visualize, part of the vessel. The exact shape of the bow had to be imagined. She was shown with white sides and a nicely sheered boot top. I always thought of her, though, with darkly oiled planking, a coppered bottom, and the rubbing strake and rails picked out in royal blue, with the whole set off by some gilt scroll-

work around the hawse forward, around the quarter ports, and, of course, above the stern windows and just below the lantern, where her name would be richly carved. What with her channels to take the main shrouds, the net under the well-steeved bowsprit, and the booby hatch over the fo'c's'le, she certainly looked the true little ship.

The sail plan showed both main and mizzen trysails, each with a short gaff that could be hoisted on the throat halyard alone—a sensible-looking arrangement. The mizzen gaff was not too long, a typical failing in gaff-rigged ketches. There was a balloon forestaysail, an extremely handy and useful cruising sail. There were two jibs smaller than the working jib, and the smaller of these looked modest enough to stand some real breeze. The huge, light jib topsail looked efficient, either on or off a light air. She was clearly designed for offshore cruising, but she didn't look slow.

On deck, she had handsome gratings by the bowsprit, and the deck plan showed two anchors stowed neatly by the post. There were fife rails at the masts and pin rails around the decks. I always did approve of belaying pins in a boat. You could work her rigging without climbing on houses, tripping over deck fittings, or trying to pull on a level with your toes. Her wheel looked made to stand up to, yet the box was high enough so you could sit down on it and still see forward. And there was the stern lantern.

Below was the wondrous great cabin with, as the article said, "the stern windows looking out on the foaming wake, the cheerful fireplace and the broad lounge or transom seat surrounding the table on three sides." I noticed a flush hatch in the great cabin sole, leading below to the lazarette. I assumed this hatch would be hidden by a carpet so the lazarette could be used for piratical purposes. The galley was well aft, where the motion would be least, and handy to the great cabin. The deckhouse would serve admirably for chart work, the head was out of the way, and there was a good-sized fo'c's'le. I gave the latter over to sails, rigging, spares, tools, paint, and naval stores for the topsides.

It was apparent that any editing done on the Cogge ketch ought to be done with great care and deliberation. Here was a rare, fine vessel; perfunctory changes were neither wanted nor deserved.

First, of course, the engine was removed. That made room for the best stateroom in the ship, opening into the galley passageway. The fuel tanks were purified and filled with fresh water. With the shaft and wheel removed, the aperture was sealed and faired. Ahhh.

On deck, the dinghy stowage turned out to be less than entirely satisfactory. It was a tight squeeze between the boat and the house, and when driving into a big, steep sea, carrying sail to push her through, that boat was a worry on the starboard tack for fear a freak sea would pick her out of her lashings. So she came right in on deck in way of the mizzen on the port side. Somehow,

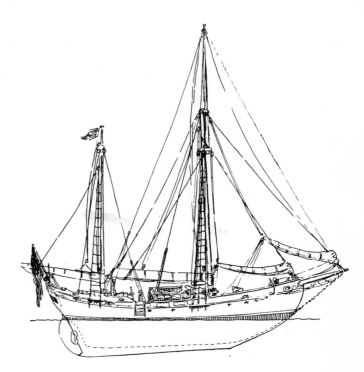

The Urrys' sketch of the original Cogge, the *Nonsuch*, 56 feet on the waterline. (*Yachting*, June, 1925)

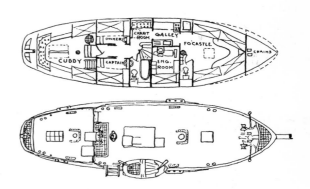

The Urrys' sketches of her deck layout and arrangement below. (*Yachting*, June, 1925)

in the process, she became a slightly longer double-ender, and there appeared lashed in the port mizzen rigging a spar that doubled as boat derrick and boat boom.

Aloft, the two running backstays on each side were brought to a single tackle making down at the break of the poop, so there would be only one backstay tail to set up when tacking. To simplify the tacking drill further, the staysail was

A pen-and-ink of the *Nonsuch* full-and-by, drawn by F. Wavell Urry. (*Yachting*, June, 1925)

THE CUDDY, LOOKING AFT

Wavell Urry put his dream of the great cabin of the *Nonsuch* on paper. (*Yachting*, June, 1925)

cut down a little, given a club and a traveler, and thus made self-tending. This change was carried out with reluctance, since it made the rig less perfect in the name of mere handiness.

The club topsail was stowed away in the fo'c's'le, the clubs being lashed in the starboard waterways on the poop; this sail was saved for showing off in a prolonged calm. In its place, a working thimble-header with hoops on the topmast was bent on, fisherman style. This meant rattling down the main shrouds so you could go

Wavell Urry's drawing of the *Nonsuch* at rest. (*Yachting*, June, 1925)

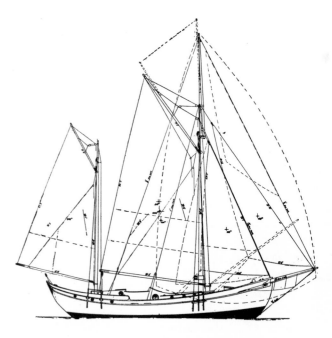

The sail plan of the 42-foot *Coggette*. (*Yachting*, February, 1926)

aloft to furl or loose the sail, a not unwelcome requirement.

Another show-off sail was added, a huge ballooner that filled the whole fore triangle and then some. And, for the trades, a squaresail and raffee were put aboard. The yard was mounted on a gooseneck just above the forestay, and the

Point of View,— 5'1" from Stemhead; 60° on Starb'd Bow; 1'-6" below W.L. Plane.

The *Coggette*'s lines in perspective from the bow ... (*Yachting*, February, 1926)

... and from the stern. (*Yachting*, February, 1926)

squaresail was rather high cut in the center of the foot so it would clear the forestay. The sail never chafes when full, but it does have to be brailed up in a very light air or calm.

Lastly, a favorite piece of rigging was rove off, a single-part vang leading from the end of the main gaff through a block at the mizzen truck and down to the deck. This keeps the gaff from sagging off and controls the shape of the mainsail. It has one drawback: when the sail is being set or lowered, the vang is slack unless specially tended, and, if the vessel is pitching into a head

The *Coggette*'s interior arrangement plan. (*Yachting*, February, 1926)

sea, it may wrap itself around the mizzen mast-head. This possibility was an excuse for putting ratlines on the mizzen.

I had taken the Cogge on only a few trial sails

Wavell Urry's sketch of the *Coggette*'s cockpit and quarterdeck arrangement. (*Yachting*, February, 1926)

and was one day inspecting her plans yet again, when, for the first time, I read the text with the plans carefully. I suddenly realized what was meant by, "Something between the intriguing *Nonsuch* and the *Coggette*." These were apparently two similar vessels by the same designers, one bigger and one smaller than my Cogge. I kept admiring the fifty-footer and wondering what her sisters were like.

We lived close enough to the Mystic Marine Museum, as we called what has become the Mystic Seaport, so that I used to visit it often. Once, in 1948, I went there to see Carl Cutler, the wise and patient curator, to ask his advice about a school research paper I was supposed to write.

In the course of the conversation, I mentioned my interest in the Cogge's sister ships, and that remarkable man turned up a magazine that pre-dated my father's collection, and there was the smaller Cogge ketch, the *Coggette*, a forty-two-foot version of the design. I've never been more tempted to steal. A hurried survey of the *Coggette*, however, was all I could accomplish on that occasion. I carried away only a confused mental image of a rather pinched version of the boat with which I was so familiar.

It was 1964 when I finally obtained a copy of the *Coggette* article from the Mystic Seaport Library. I also discovered that the "intriguing *Nonsuch*" had been described in a 1925 article, and the Seaport was kind enough to send a copy of that article too. The *Nonsuch* turned out to be the original of the type. She was fifty-six feet long on the waterline.

Now, having multiplied my dozen-plus years by three, I could at last study and compare all three Cogge ketches. No longer a naval architect by profession, I had, nevertheless, retained a lively interest in that art, and my early prejudices about engines and other features of yacht design had, with advancing age, deepened into fetishes.

Over the years, I had yanked hundreds of engines out of published boat designs, to their great improvement. Yet I had found fewer and fewer boats worth the editorial process. Thus it was with relish that I returned to the Cogge and her two sisters. Since my opinions had strength-

A 55-foot ketch designed by Chester A. Nedwideck in 1932. Though she was presented in *The Rudder* as "extraordinary" and "novel," we can guess at her inspiration. (*Rudder* Magazine, © December, 1932, Fawcett Publications, Inc.)

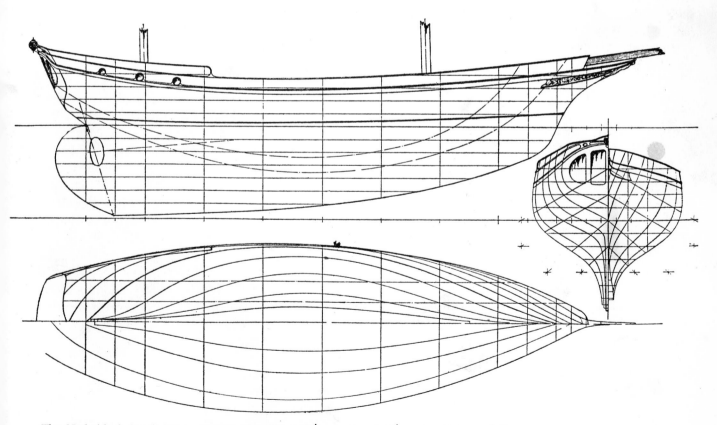

The Nedwideck ketch has a waterline length of 44', a beam of 15', and a draft of 8'6". Her sail area in the four lowers is 1,471 square feet. (*Rudder* Magazine, © December, 1932, Fawcett Publications, Inc.)

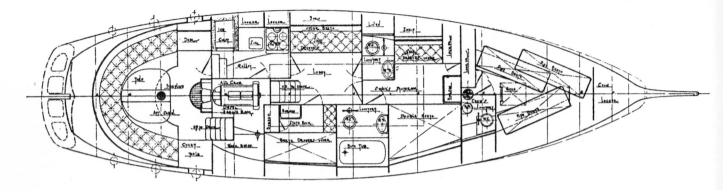

The accommodation plan of the Nedwideck ketch. The perfect proportions of the Cogge ketches are missing in this design, and it is presented only as an interesting sidelight. (*Rudder* Magazine, © December, 1932, Fawcett Publications, Inc.)

ened, rather than merely changed, I found, of course, that my early editing of the fifty-footer stood up beautifully. Inspection of the new Cogge ketches in my possession showed, furthermore, that the same minor modifications as had been applied to the fifty-footer would be desirable in her relatives.

Looking at the big *Nonsuch* and the little *Coggette*, I found it apparent that these design-ancestors of the fifty-footer were more extreme than she was. They had lots more sheer than the fifty-footer—almost, but not quite, too much. Although only sketches of the *Nonsuch* were shown, these gave a good idea of her shape.

For the *Coggette*, two perspective lines drawings were presented, one from the bow and one from the quarter. Her dimensions were: length on deck, 42 feet; length on the waterline, 34 feet; beam, 12 feet; and draft, 6 feet 8 inches. The two additional articles greatly enriched my Cogge ketch resources, but I still did not have a standard lines drawing for any of them.

An attempt to track down such drawings led in 1967 to the information that F. Wavell Urry was in Vancouver, B. C. A letter of inquiry to him brought a nice reply and a set of drawings of the fifty-footer, including standard lines. These showed her hull to be beautifully proportioned and faired.

Perhaps the most interesting new information yielded by the additional articles was a clue to the origin of the Cogge type. Douglas P. Urry, serving in the North Sea in 1916, was reading an old book of voyages while off watch. A phrase, "the Cogge *Thomas*," caught his eye. His imagination began to play with this simple reference to an old, obscure vessel. Douglas Urry surmised she might have been a seventeenth-century northern European trading ketch.

He corresponded with his brother, F. Wavell Urry, about this fleeting vision of an old boat. Those letters, their yarning, and the sketches sent home to Vancouver gave substance to their conjurings after the war.

The Urry brothers sorted out the characteristics of their own Cogge and by 1925 had designed the *Nonsuch*. Her name, aptly chosen for a unique vessel, became all too literally appropriate, for her construction was beyond their means, and she has remained to this day a dream ship.

An attempt to scale down the design to an affordable size produced the *Coggette*, but the Depression kept her, too, from being laid down.

The third Cogge design, the fifty-footer, was drawn for an admirer of the type. But she, too, was never built.

So the Cogge remains a dream, elusive to her designers and her admirers, who may, like me, have sailed many miles in her. Her handsome hull, her regal rig, even her foaming wake watched through the stern windows, seem almost real. Perhaps they may one day become so.

2/ The *Cresset*

Length on deck: 40 feet
Length on waterline: 31 feet
Beam: 10 feet
Draft: 6 feet 6 inches
Sail area: 1,045 square feet
Designers: Douglas P. Urry and F. Wavell Urry

The traditional gaff-rigged cutter, with her five working sails, plumb bow, and long, fine counter, makes a handsome vessel indeed.

The *Cresset* seems well named, for she does light the way when it comes to cutter design, in my opinion. She's the handsomest cutter I know of.

This pretty boat is another creation of the Urry brothers, who created the Cogge ketch designs described in the preceding chapter.

The distant heritage of the *Cresset* is perhaps in the English pilot cutters, but she is really pure Urry. Those two gentlemen certainly knew the art of forming a shapely hull and putting in a good-looking, wholesome rig. The English look of a short overhang forward and a long one aft appears out of balance to some American eyes, but the form does seem to produce a boat that somehow looks both able and delicate. And the long bowsprit helps balance her up.

Some of the plumb-bowed cutters were so fine forward that they lacked buoyancy in the bow and tended to pitch rather heavily in a head sea. I recall seeing the old *Nebula*, near the end of her long career, working into just a moderate seaway and burying her bow in every sea right down to the rail. The *Cresset* might be a bit "pitchy" too,

but this would not be excessive, for she has some fullness in her forward sections.

Her lines look sweet and fair throughout. She has a bit of hollow in the waterlines forward, quite hard bilges for stiffness, and a handsome tumblehome to her midsection that gives her an able look—and rightly so, for it would tend to keep the lee rail out of the water.

In the best cutter tradition, the *Cresset* has plenty of draft, and a hull that should foot well to windward and go where she looks. Her long, straight run flowing into the counter should give her a good turn of speed, yet the counter is steeved up high enough so that there shouldn't be too much danger of being pooped in a following sea. Her generous rudder and moderately cutaway forefoot should make her highly maneuverable, even in a light air.

The *Cresset*'s length on deck is 40 feet; she is 31 feet long on the waterline, with a beam of 10 feet and a draft of 6 feet 6 inches.

The Urry brothers worked out her design in a year of spare time in 1926 and 1927. She was built by George F. Askew in 1928 and 1929, with the Urrys doing the interior work and the spars and rigging. They also designed and built a nine-foot dinghy for her.

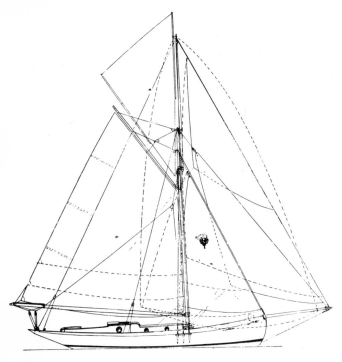

The *Cresset*'s traditional cutter rig is well proportioned, efficient, and versatile. (*Yachting*, July, 1930)

Her keel is 10 inches by 20 inches; the frames are 1½ inches molded, 2¼ inches sided on 9-inch centers. The frames were put in on 4½-inch centers for four feet in the way of the mast. Her floors are 2½ inches sided and 10 inches deep. Her planking is 1⅜ inches and the deck is 1½ inches.

An unusual feature of her construction is an extra set of U-shaped frames running from bilge stringer to bilge stringer in a single piece down across the floors. These are the same size as the regular frames and are bolted in as sister frames. Where they curve down across the top of the floors, the floors have been cut out in an arc to receive them. This construction would keep the garboards from wringing, and it has the effect of doubling the frame size below the waterline.

The *Cresset* is planked with British Columbia yellow cedar on oak frames. Her stem- and stern-posts are Australian gum. Cypress was also used in the boat. Her trim is teak.

The *Cresset*'s cutter rig is certainly a fine example of what this rig should and can look like. With her five working sails set, she has plenty of sail area for light going; there are big, light headsails that can be set in addition. Yet, when shortened down to her close-reefed mainsail, reefed forestaysail, and a spitfire jib, her rig would be snug indeed. I'd like to see a third deep reef available in the mainsail and a tiny jib that could replace the working jib. Some of the sail plans of English cutters show as many as four

Her lines show a hull a man could enjoy looking at for a long time. (*Yachting*, July, 1930)

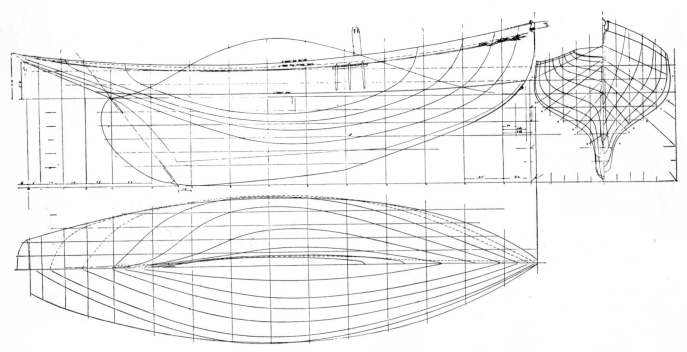

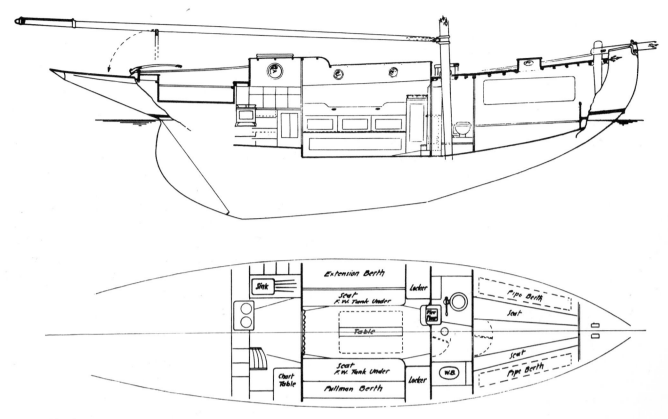

She has a common arrangement plan but with some well-thought-out modifications. (*Yachting*, July, 1930)

small jibs of varying sizes, all smaller than the working jib.

The English practice was to reef spars as well as sails in heavy going. Their topmasts could be lowered and housed right alongside the lower mast, and their bowsprits could be run in on deck. When these spars were heavy and the vessel tended to dive into a head sea, it was undoubtedly necessary to reduce the pitching moment by bringing in these spars. It would not be so in the *Cresset*. Incidentally, one advantage of the separate topmast is that if it should carry away, it leaves the lower part of the rig intact.

The *Cresset*'s sail area of 1,045 square feet is divided up as follows: mainsail, 500; forestaysail, 140; jib, 145; main topsail, 145; and jib topsail, 115.

Her mainsail is nicely shaped for efficiency. The clew is far enough abaft the peak for the sail to set nice and flat for windward work; that is, with the sheet trimmed in hard, the pull aft on the leech would keep the gaff from sagging off to leeward. Her jackyard topsail certainly reaches up where the wind blows; its head is about fifty-five feet above the water.

That balloon forestaysail can be poled out for a heavy-weather spinnaker that is under good control and easy to jibe over. Her big spinnaker would be double-luffed today, for ease in jibing. With a modern spinnaker set on this boat, she'd

The *Cresset* working to windward in a light air. (She also happens to be crossing the finish line to win the first race she entered, one of many victories.) (*Yachting*, July, 1930)

just have to go like a scared cat. But there would be no horsing around with those topmast backstays with the spinnaker set in any breeze at all. A few seconds' delay in setting up could result in a fair-sized lash-up.

The *Cresset* was bored for a shaft, but no engine was installed, at least for the first few seasons. It was found that a dinghy with an outboard, lashed alongside as a tug, could shove her along at an honest three knots in a calm. I used to see Martin Kattenhorn use this tactic to get in and out of the harbor in his engineless forty-four-foot schooner, *Surprise*, when there was no wind. It worked fine. An outboard motor designed for the purpose with a large, low-pitch wheel and reduction gear would improve this kind of towboat work considerably. The great advantage is that the engine is out of the boat for increased safety and ease of maintenance.

In a sort of premonition of the doghouse, the Urry brothers widened and heightened the after end of the *Cresset*'s cabin house. This was to allow the floor of the galley to be raised so it could be wider, and also to give plenty of light and air to the galley. The companionway is off-center, so traffic flows past the cook rather than colliding with him, and there is a skylight in the house adjacent to the companionway. Quoting the designers: "To paraphrase a well-known saying, some skylights leak all the time and all skylights leak some of the time, so the placing of the sink directly under the skylight is the crowning master stroke of this design."

The full-width head is a good arrangement. While its use may temporarily restrict traffic fore and aft, its transformation from the usual torture chamber into a respectable compartment is well worth that little inconvenience.

The short cabin house ending abaft the mast is, of course, old-fashioned. But, in my opinion, the deck space gained around the mast and forward is more valuable than full headroom in the head and fo'c's'le. The headroom under the beams at the mast step in the head is five feet.

In cool climates, the open fireplace in the cabin would be a wonderful thing; hopefully, its chimney would take the chill off the "throne."

Upon seeing my article on the *Cresset* in the *National Fisherman*, John F. Dore of Seattle wrote me, "I had the *Cresset* for a very short period of time in Vancouver. She was a witch in light airs and a strong, reliable vessel in dirty weather. The former owner, a Standard Oil tanker skipper, told me he layed to in a full gale under staysail alone for three days and made considerable distance to windward without much trouble."

The *Cresset* is now owned by Gerry Palmer of Vancouver, who has had her since 1957. He reports that her rig was changed to Marconi in about 1938. He wrote me, "In twelve to fifteen knots [wind strength] she can just about hold a new C & C 35 to windward."

All in all, the *Cresset* is a fine example of the cutter type. She might well be worth emulating today. She wouldn't be cheap to build, for she is a fancy vessel; no doubt she would be more expensive than some of her modern counterparts. It would be a joy to sail her, because she would always do well for herself under any conditions.

The *Cresset* is still going strong, now with a Marconi rig, under the ownership of Gerry Palmer of Vancouver. (Gerry Palmer)

3/ The *Prospector*

> Length on deck: 42 feet 7 inches
> Length on waterline: 38 feet 6 inches
> Beam: 12 feet 6 inches
> Draft: 6 feet
> Sail area: 1,200 square feet
> Displacement: 19 tons
> Designer: The Concordia Company

The ketch *Prospector* was so named because her owner used to prospect for gold in Canada. But the name seems appropriate in another sense, because the vessel herself looks well able to seek her fortune in any corner of the world.

She was designed by William Harris of the Concordia Company of Boston, later of South Dartmouth, Massachusetts. The boat was built in 1937 at Scott's Yard in Fairhaven, Massachusetts. Shortly before she was to have been launched, both yard and boat burned.

The *Prospector*'s iron keel was saved and another *Prospector* was built to the same design, this one in the backyard of the owner in Fort Lauderdale, Florida, in 1940. She was built of southern woods, with an acana keel, madeira for frames and deck beams, and longleaf yellow pine for planking. Her fastenings are galvanized boat nails, and she is fitted with iron chain plates.

The *Prospector*'s length on deck is 42 feet 7 inches; her length on the waterline is 38 feet 6 inches; her beam is 12 feet 6 inches; and her draft is 6 feet. She displaces 19 tons. Her sail area is 922 square feet in the four lowers, with 403 in the mainsail, 225 in the mizzen, 116 in the forestaysail, and 178 in the jib. Her main topsail adds another 115 square feet, and the jib topsail has 157 square feet. The six sails total just under 1,200 square feet.

Her power plant is a 56-h.p. Gray that drives her at 7½ knots at 1,400 r.p.m.

On the second *Prospector*, the mizzenmast was moved aft of the cockpit, and the sail was made jib-headed and reduced in size. This allowed a bigger mainsail with more drive, and one that would set better with its longer boom. A doghouse over the forward end of the cockpit was also added to the design.

This is a boat that seems to be an almost perfect example of the motto, "Moderation in all things." She is moderately sharp at bow and stern, yet she is quite beamy and burdensome. She should have a moderately good turn of speed. Her sail plan is moderate, her draft is moderate, her forefoot is cut away to a moderate degree, she has bilges that are neither hard nor slack, and she has a moderate amount of tumblehome and a moderate hollow in her garboards.

The lines are fair and easy throughout, and the diagonals are unusually fair. There is just a little hollow in the waterlines both forward and aft. Her transom is shapely, and it has enough deadrise not to drag. It is raked moderately to provide lift without spanking in a following sea.

The *Prospector's* sail plan is broken into small, easily handled sails that can be set in many combinations to meet the variety of conditions encountered when cruising. (*Rudder* Magazine, © July, 1942, Fawcett Publications, Inc.)

Her rig is mighty handy for cruising. She would balance well under mainsail and staysail, though probably sail even better with mainsail and jib. She should also do well under mizzen, forestaysail, and jib.

Of course she would profit by my favorite piece of rigging for gaff-rigged ketches and yawls, a vang from the end of the main gaff through a block at the mizzen masthead and down to the deck. This simple piece of rigging brings the mainsail under perfect control for trimming. And if a boat were to be built to this design with the original sail plan, it would be a good idea to peak up the mizzen a bit higher to make it set better on the wind.

Her loose-footed sails are interesting. They are

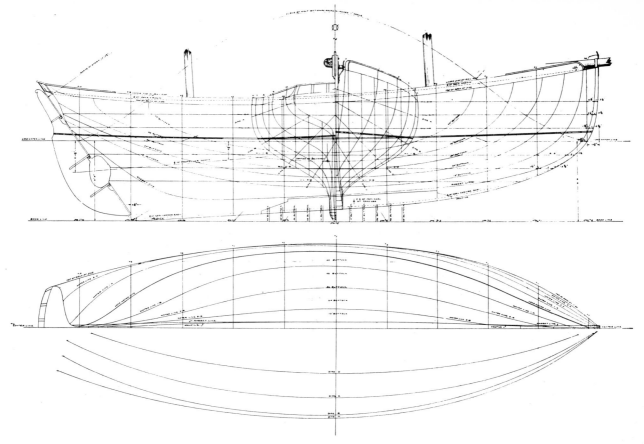

Above: Her lines show a fair, easy hull whose every characteristic is moderate. (*Rudder* Magazine, © July, 1942, Fawcett Publications, Inc.)

Below: The *Prospector*'s layout is conventional until you get aft to her fine, big engine room. (*Rudder* Magazine, © July, 1942, Fawcett Publications, Inc.)

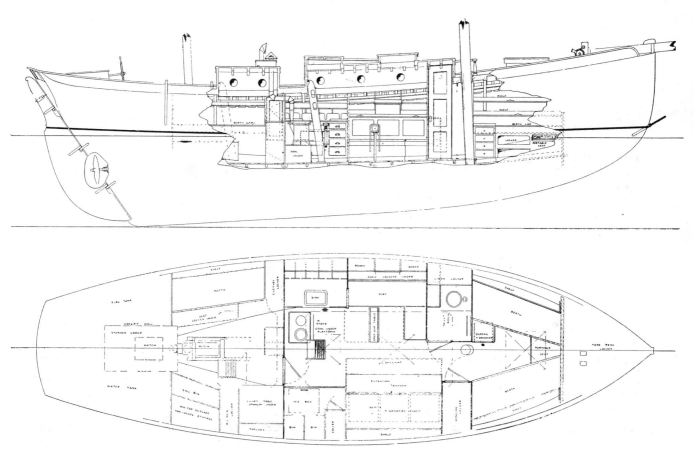

Above: On the wind with her topsail set, the *Prospector* makes a handsome picture. (*Rudder* Magazine, © May, 1942, Fawcett Publications, Inc.)

Below: Slipping along under power at Fort Lauderdale. (*Rudder* Magazine © January, 1943, Fawcett Publications, Inc.)

somewhat easier to reef, and set a bit better than sails that are laced to booms along the foot. There is far more strain at the clew, however, when the sail is loose-footed, and for cruising, I'd rather see the strain distributed along the boom with a laceline. Notice on the sail plan that the forestaysail is self-tending even though it is loose-footed. The photo of the *Prospector* sailing shows that a club was added to the sail when the vessel was rigged.

Her jib and jib topsail are good-sized sails that would really pull. Her jib is set flying and is tacked to a bowsprit traveler, English-style. Note that the bowsprit is offset to starboard of the stem. It might be as well with the jib set flying to remove the jib stay and give her double forestays. With this rig, the jib could be lowered in light weather and a big jib topsail, filling the whole fore triangle, could be set. With no jib stay, such a sail could be passed around the forestay rather readily when tacking. And the double forestays would be handy when changing from the working forestaysail to a light weather balloon forestaysail, or vice versa.

The running backstays on the topmast would only have to be set up when the topsails were

set, of course, or to steady the bare topmast when the vessel was driving into a steep head sea.

A big mizzen staysail could be set on this boat, though this is a sail that's useful only on a fairly narrow range of reaches; it always seems that whenever you want to get out the mizzen staysail, the wind is always either just too far ahead or just too far aft for the thing to pull well. Not believing the wind could really be quite that perverse, you set the sail anyway, in hopes it will draw—and then wish you hadn't. Then down it comes again, convincing the helmsman that the whole thing is a plot to keep him from seeing where he is going. The sail can give a nice free ride on rare occasions, though, and is probably worth carrying against such lucky possibilities. Of course the real way to beat the mizzen staysail into submission would be to take it out into the middle of the ocean and then spend a week with the sail set on just the right point of sailing—never mind the course steered.

The *Prospector's* layout below is straightforward and practical, with a big engine room aft that includes a chart table and plenty of headroom, working space, and storage space, and forward, a standard accommodation plan for four people. The spare bunk in the engine room would probably become a catchall for gear; besides, who wants to sleep in the engine room?

She has a Concordia smokehead fitted to the top of the galley stove pipe, and the claim is that these well-designed smokeheads always draw and never blow smoke back into the cabin, no matter which way the wind is coming from.

Above: Her cockpit is well protected by the doghouse, she has plenty of space on deck, and her forestaysail halyard needs setting up. (*Rudder* Magazine, © May, 1942, Fawcett Publications, Inc.)

Below: The *Prospector* showing off her shapely underbody. (*Rudder* Magazine, © January, 1943, Fawcett Publications, Inc.)

All in all, the *Prospector* looks to be a fine seagoing cruising boat. Her gear and rigging are simple enough to be repaired miles from the nearest boatyard, so she seems well adapted for the independent life of going wherever her master may think the prospects look good.

4/ The *Maud*

> **Length on deck:** 41 feet 9 inches
> **Length on waterline:** 34 feet 6 inches
> **Beam:** 11 feet 4 inches
> **Draft:** 6 feet 8 inches
> **Sail area:** 1,100 square feet
> **Designer:** William Fife

It seems curious, until the reason is explained, that under her most famous owner, the British ketch *Maud* apparently had no captain. The English yachtsman, Claud Worth, owned her, along with C. D. Marshall, for several years following their purchase of the vessel in 1906. Mrs. Worth was generally aboard the boat with the owners.

Worth wrote: "*Maud* had no commander. We three who formed her regular crew had sailed together so often that the work of the vessel had become almost automatic. For example, in setting the topsail, it was always the same man who hoisted the sail while the other took charge of the sheet and tack; the man who first cleaned the motor ever afterwards held himself responsible for keeping it bright and spotless; in entering a harbor, or in getting underway, Mrs. Worth took the helm and we others attended each to his own part of the work forward. This division of labor had grown up as a habit, without any express agreement."

Must every vessel have a captain? Of course the general rule is that she must, but there are those rare instances where two people of equal seamanship ability may run a boat together for so long that, as in the case of Worth and Marshall in the *Maud*, they tacitly agree as to who shall do what and how the vessel shall be managed. A tough decision with time to mull it over would be arrived at jointly after discussion. In an emergency, either would obey instantly and without question the direct order of the other.

We used to cruise two-handed in an old Nat Herreshoff Buzzards Bay fifteen-footer. My shipmate and I thought pretty much alike on how to do things around the water, and we got to the point where there needed to be little or no talk about the handling of the boat. Whoever was steering expected certain things out of the other fellow, and vice versa. I guess before a cruise we must have discussed whether we were going down-east or up to the westward, but that was about all. The only serious argument we ever had was one time, after a long, tedious day's sail, when we almost came to blows over exactly what was the only acceptable way to make a line fast to a cleat. Speaking of which, I'd best belay all this philosophy and get back to the *Maud*.

Designed and built by William Fife of Fairlie, Scotland, in 1899, she was originally named the *Acsenov*. The *Maud* is, in my opinion, a fine cruising vessel for four people, although from the above, it is clear she could be handled by fewer.

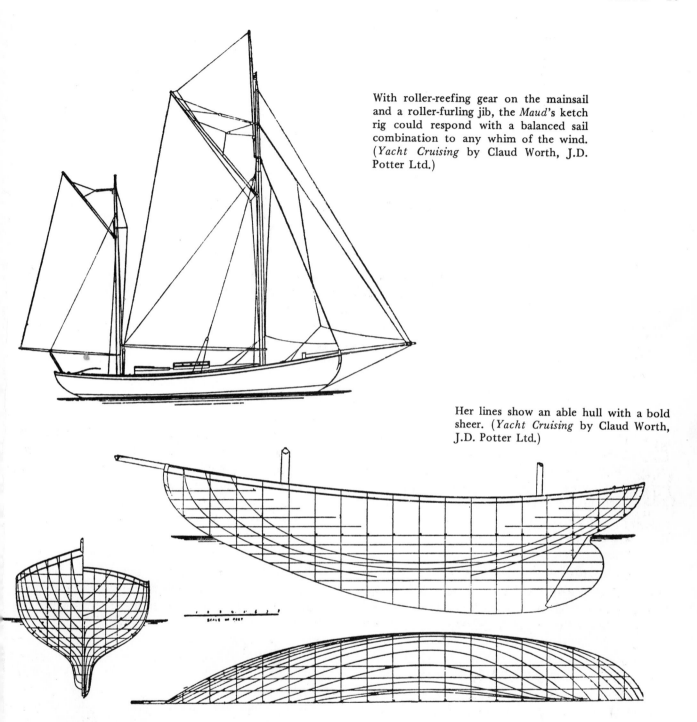

With roller-reefing gear on the mainsail and a roller-furling jib, the *Maud*'s ketch rig could respond with a balanced sail combination to any whim of the wind. (*Yacht Cruising* by Claud Worth, J.D. Potter Ltd.)

Her lines show an able hull with a bold sheer. (*Yacht Cruising* by Claud Worth, J.D. Potter Ltd.)

Worth and his wife sometimes went off in her by themselves.

The *Maud* is 41 feet 9 inches long on deck, with a waterline length of 34 feet 6 inches, a beam of 11 feet 4 inches, and a draft of 6 feet 8 inches. Her sail area is 1,100 square feet. She carries seven tons of ballast outside on her keel and two tons inside. She was built with oak frames and pitch-pine planking.

The *Maud* has a pert look to her. Her hull should be dry, but it would probably have a rather lively motion. She is a deep-bodied boat with a run that is almost, but not quite, too steep. Fife, the great Scottish designer, just gets away with producing a very able boat that is not slow.

Her stern would be more graceful if it were drawn out a bit, but I prefer the rather short,

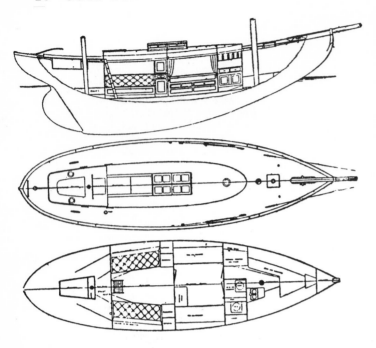

Left: The *Maud* has plenty of deck space and good visibility for the helmsman, but perhaps more attention should have been paid to her cockpit and galley. (*Yacht Cruising* by Claud Worth, J.D. Potter Ltd.)

Right: Close-hauled in a light breeze. Note her nicely setting, vertical-cut sails and the heft of the main boom for roller reefing. (*Fore and Aft Craft and Their Story* by E. Keble Chatterton)

cocky stern as being more in harmony with the rest of the design.

She certainly has considerable sheer. The sheer line appears to be accentuated in the profile view by the shapes of the stem and stern profile curves. To my eye, at least, she seems to have more sheer in the profile drawing than in the drawing of the sections, especially aft. In any event, she looks to be a stiff, able boat, one that would be at her best in rough water and one that would have no bad point of sailing.

The *Maud*'s ketch rig is certainly versatile. She would balance well under main and staysail, or with both headsails and the mizzen, or under forestaysail and a reefed mizzen. She has a roller-reefing mainsail (with Woodnutt's screw gear) and a roller-furling jib (with Wykeham-Martin roller rig). Her roller-reefing mainsail adds to the flexibility of a rig that already has many combinations.

She has masts of Norway spruce, and a main boom of Oregon fir that is 5½ inches in diameter for rolling up the sail.

The peak halyards on both the main and mizzen are relatively high on the masts to get a good lead, and their strain is offset by the pull of

the jib on the main and of the jumper stay on the mizzen. The jib's pull would be available whether or not the sail were rolled up, but it would be lost if the furled jib were taken down for any reason.

An interesting rigging detail is that the main upper peak halyard block is shackled to a horse running horizontally one-third of the circumference around the after side of the mast, so that the block never puts a wringing strain on the mast.

The *Maud* has a squaresail, with its yard hoisting on a jackstay by the forestaysail halyards.

Most Americans would prefer a club on the forestaysail to make it self-tending, though there is no doubt the sail would set better as shown in the sail plan. To prevent her gaffs from sagging off, it might be well to vang the main gaff to the mizzen masthead and peak up the mizzen gaff more.

Claud Worth installed in the *Maud* a Seal kerosene motor with an off-center shaft and a two-bladed, feathering propeller. The motor develops 2½ h.p. and drives the boat in a calm at nearly three knots. "We wanted something which would move the vessel in a calm just a little faster than two men with sweeps," Worth wrote. The tiny engine is evidently tucked away beneath the floor of the sail room ("We would not spoil the sail-room") under the bridge-deck.

It would be a joy to work on deck in this ketch with her low house and wide decks. The helmsman would have good visibility forward, even with the boat's 8½-foot dinghy stowed upside-down over the skylight.

The boat does need a bigger cockpit, unless she were to be used solely for shorthanded work. I would like to see her house shortened up aft to make way for a good-sized, deep, watertight cockpit just forward of the mizzenmast. The headroom robbed from the after end of the after cabin and from the sail room would be little enough payment, in my opinion, in return for a really comfortable cockpit for four people. The after cockpit could remain as is for the helmsman. You spend a lot of time on deck in a little vessel.

The English think nothing of cooking in the fo'c's'le without standing headroom. I'd prefer to put the galley under the forward end of the house where the head is, so you could stand up to the stove and sink. But no matter how she was arranged inside, the *Maud* would, I think, be an admirable and able cruising vessel in which up to four people could make anything from puddle-jumping runs along the coast to long passages offshore.

Claud Worth sailed the *Maud* round Great Britain in the summer of 1908 and described the cruise (and the *Maud* herself) in his book, *Yacht Cruising*. In seven weeks, the ketch called at many ports and sailed about 1,250 miles.

The *Maud* lying to her buoy. Who wouldn't want to climb on board, stow his gear, make sail, cast off, and let her fill away for a trip?

Worth wrote of the *Maud*'s performance: "She was as handy as a gimlet, and would wriggle through a narrow channel like a Una boat. At sea she was light and easy to steer on all points of sailing. She proved weatherly for a ketch, and an exceptionally safe sea-boat. With wind against tide in shallow water she was rather unnecessarily playful, and at sea her peculiar motion proved rather tiring on a long passage. But she would be almost incapable of shipping heavy water."

5/ An Alden Ketch

Length on deck: 32 feet
Length on waterline: 27 feet 1 inch
Beam: 9 feet 10 inches
Draft: 5 feet 6 inches
Sail area: 656 square feet
Designer: John G. Alden

Did you ever hanker after a little sailing vessel that would really be well suited for a variety of tasks—from hauling driftwood scrounged off an island beach with a good little skiff, to being mother ship for a dory with a longline trawl, to being a Good Samaritan salvage vessel for boats in trouble, to being a diving tender, to taking care of a fleet of small sailboats? I think this able-looking ketch, designed by John G. Alden in 1911, would fill the bill. She is a workmanlike cruising boat, in my opinion.

The ketch was built at Sandusky, Ohio, for Captain Richard McKean. He wanted a boat for whitefishing in Lake Superior, and the boat was designed to carry up to 5,000 pounds of fish. McKean had fished out of Gloucester, and he specified a Gloucester fishing schooner type of hull, but he wanted her rigged like a local Great Lakes ketch.

He got a wholesome hull. The diagonals are sweet and fair, showing a nice model. She is stiff and able and could be driven quite hard, including lugging sail to windward in a breeze. She also is handy and maneuverable, with her forefoot considerably cut away and a big rudder well aft. It's true she might be a bit "pitchy" (as the old-timer would say of a boat he thought would hobby horse in a head sea), judging by the steep rise of her forebody buttocks and with the weight of her mainmast so far forward. She was built on 2-inch by 1½-inch frames and planked with 1¼-inch oak. All her ballast was carried inside.

She certainly has plenty of deck space, a great joy in a boat. She can easily carry a dory or peapod on deck, and the main boom makes a handy boat derrick. She has a seven-inch rail all around. The foredeck is as cramped as that of a catboat, of course, but the working anchor can be kept out of the way slung under the bowsprit. If her tasks require some complicated ground tackle work, this should be done over the stern. Her heavy anchor can be stowed in the bottom of the hold for ballast and can be handled easily by the main boom. A boat like this, which cries out to be used in all manner of challenging situations, ought to have a 100-pound, old-fashioned anchor on board, so the master knows he can keep her where he wants her under almost any adverse conditions.

The ketch has no power, but if absolutely necessary, an engine could be installed amidships with the wheel in an aperture on the centerline, but with the motor placed off-center just enough

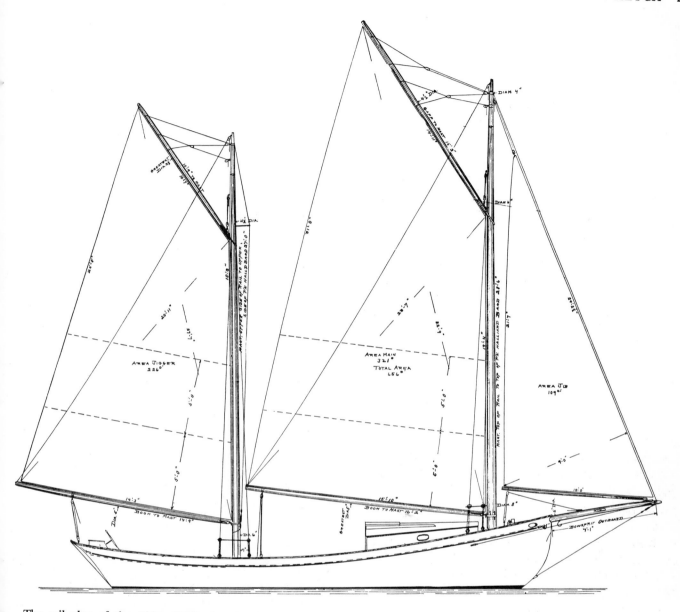

The sail plan of the Alden fishing ketch shows a practical rig that would balance well under mainsail alone and sail like a reefed catboat. Or, under jib and reefed mizzen, she would handle nicely in heavy going. (*Rudder* Magazine, © 1911, Fawcett Publications, Inc.)

so the shaft would clear the mizzenmast. With this arrangement, the motor would be positioned to port of the centerline to counteract the twist of the right-hand-turning propeller.

With the engine to port and the propeller on the centerline, the boat would tend to turn to the right. The right-hand-turning propeller, turning clockwise when viewed from aft, would tend to walk her stern to the right, thus turning the boat to the left. The reason for the slight turning force applied to the boat by the direction of rotation of the propeller is that the propeller's

blades give more push in the deeper water at the bottom of their swing than they do in the shallower water at the top of their swing. The push to the right imparted to the stern by a given blade at the bottom of its swing is a bit more than the push to the left imparted to the stern by the same blade at the top of its swing.

The quarters for two may look snug, but it should be remembered that whatever space there is can be devoted entirely to living. With so much stowage space aft, there is no reason why any boat gear, spares, or staples should ever find their

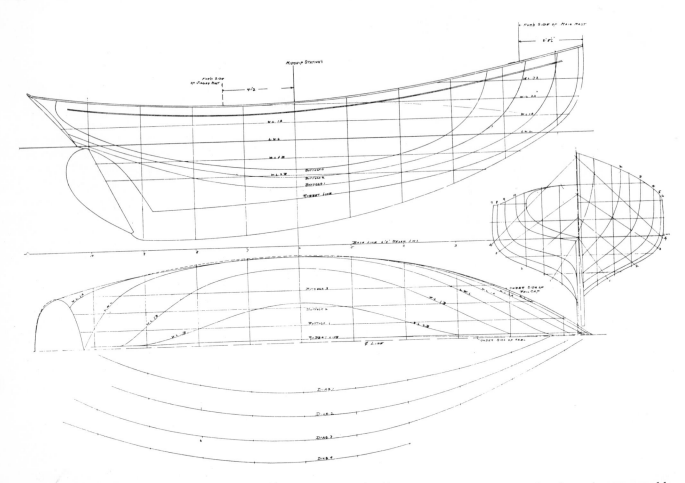

Above: The ketch's lines show her to be stiff and able, and, with her forefoot cut away, handy and maneuverable. (*Rudder* Magazine, © 1911, Fawcett Publications, Inc.)

Below: Her deck and arrangement plan shows a cabin that appears cramped, but with so much stowage space aft, it could be devoted entirely to living. (*Rudder* Magazine, © 1911, Fawcett Publications, Inc.)

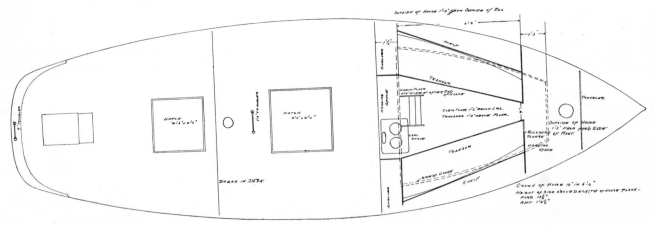

way into the cabin to compete with people for space. Headroom in the cuddy is 5 feet 6 inches. McKean lived aboard her eight months of the year.

The rig of the ketch looks eminently practical if you don't mind reefing the mizzen, and there's no reason anyone should mind such good sailorizing work. She can balance well under mainsail alone and sail like a reefed catboat. Or she can go well in heavy going under jib and reefed mizzen.

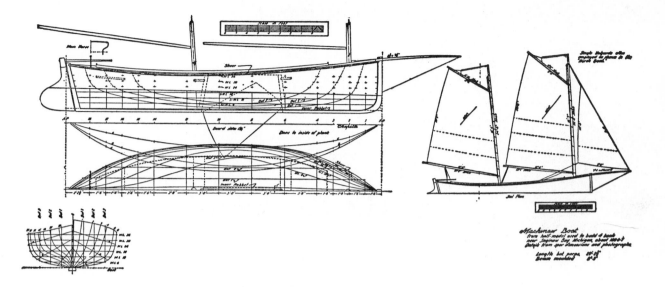

The Lake Huron Mackinaw boat, or Collingwood skiff, a local type of open double-ender, was one ancestor of the ketch. The other was the Gloucester fishing schooner. (*American Small Sailing Craft* by Howard I. Chapelle, W.W. Norton & Company, Inc., © 1951. Reproduced with the permission of the publisher.)

The self-tending jib is most handy; the only thing to do when tacking is to put the wheel over.

The ketch naturally needs the usual main vang led to the mizzen masthead, and she needs her mizzen gaff peaked up more.

A main topsail set on a tall club would make a useful light sail. So would a balloon jib that could be poled out when running off. Such a sail is particularly handy on a single-head-rigged boat, because it can be jibed across so easily.

The ancestor of this boat, as far as her rig is concerned, is the Lake Huron Mackinaw boat, or Collingwood skiff, a local type of open double-ender from twenty-six to thirty-five feet long developed for fishing. Some of these craft were sprit-rigged instead of gaff-rigged, and, until 1882,

according to Howard I. Chapelle, had no bowsprits or jibs. They were characterized by two major sails of almost the same size.

By pure coincidence, rather than through any connection that can be shown, the rig of this ketch is nearly identical to that of the fifty-five-foot pearling "luggers" that were still sailing out of Broome, Northwest Australia, in 1930. These were handsome and able vessels that tended divers on long cruises to the pearling grounds well offshore.

Looking back on the design of this little Alden ketch, one can't help but think what fun she would be to knock around the coast in, and perhaps even make a little money with, whether pearling, fetching-and-carrying, or fishing.

6/ The *Fundulus*

Length on deck: 36 feet
Length on waterline: 31 feet
Beam: 10 feet 2 inches
Draft: 5 feet 2 inches
Sail area: 650 square feet
Designer: William H. Hand, Jr.

It blew a moderate gale out of the southeast all night on the coast of Maine not long ago, and looking out over Penobscot Bay at first light you could just barely make out through the gray scud the whiteness of the tops of most of the waves as they rolled over and foamed on their march up the Bay.

It wasn't blowing all that hard, but as the first gale of the winter, it was impressive.

Whenever I see rough water like that, I always begin wondering how various boats I know, either through sailing them or studying their plans, would behave out there. The Beaufort scale says, under "Action of Fishing Smack" for Force 7, "Remains in harbor, or if at sea, lies to," but it is always tempting to imagine putting out in a modest-sized craft under such conditions to see what she will do. The temptation of indulging in such vicarious voyages is particularly hard to resist, in that they involve neither danger nor discomfort.

Looking out on what the southeaster was doing to the Bay that early morning, one vessel that came to mind as a candidate for beating out through those seas to Matinicus Island was the thirty-six-foot ketch *Fundulus*, designed by William H. Hand, Jr., more than sixty years ago.

With a single-reef down all around, she would have worked to windward in that seaway in reasonable comfort and speed and with great style.

This ketch was built by the Greenport Yacht Basin and Construction Company at Greenport, Long Island, New York, in 1913. She is 36 feet long on deck, with a waterline length of 31 feet, a beam of 10 feet 2 inches, and a draft of 5 feet 2 inches. Her sail area is 650 square feet.

The *Fundulus*, later named *C. D. B.* [?], and, still later, *Cynosure*, is quite reminiscent of the John G. Alden ketch described in the preceding chapter. The *Fundulus* is a bit more sophisticated. Incidentally, she was thought to be one of Bill Hand's very best designs by another John G., John G. Hanna.

The *Fundulus* would make a fine long-distance cruiser for two people, in my opinion. She is a bit under-rigged for my taste, but she was designed for safety and comfort rather than for speed. None of her owners ever claimed she was a fast boat. One said she would do seven knots, but no more, under ideal conditions, and that going to windward in a fresh breeze and rough sea, she would make a good 2¾ knots to windward. He said she was "not close-winded," but only made a half

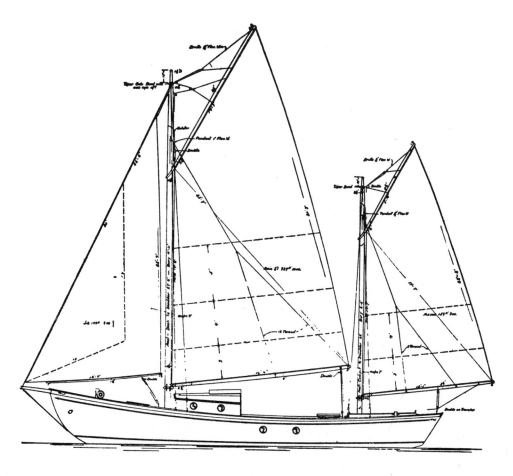

Above: The *Fundulus* is a handsome, able ketch that would make an admirable long-distance cruising boat for two. (*The Rudder Treasury* edited by Tom Davin)

Below: Her ends are well balanced and buoyant; she has a reputation for dryness in rough water. (*The Rudder Treasury* edited by Tom Davin)

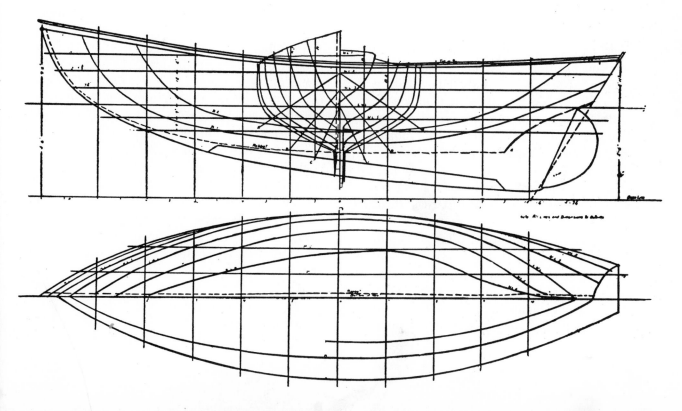

point of leeway at the most. I would guess that she would be sailed about six points off the wind when full and by and would thus make good a course of perhaps 6½ points off the wind. All of this indicates a reasonable, but not outstanding, performance, as far as speed is concerned. (As the *Cynosure,* she came in fifth out of eight boats in the 1930 St. Petersburg-Havana Race.)

Where the *Fundulus* comes into her own is in the comfort department, especially in a rough sea. Comfort in rough water in a small vessel is a relative thing, of course, but it implies at least a rather strong feeling of security and confidence in the boat on the part of her people, a reasonably easy motion, and reasonable dryness on deck. These things the *Fundulus* can certainly provide.

In a head sea, such as the one I was subjecting her to during that early winter sail, her buoyant bow and fine stern let her lift her head easily. It would take quite a big breaking sea to smother her bow. Nor would she bury her nose or take undue water over the stern when running or broad-reaching in a steep sea. The deep drag to her keel, combined with her moderately cut-away forefoot, would keep her from wanting to broach when hard-pressed off the wind.

The ketch's midship section shows plenty of sail-carrying power to make up for only a modest bearing aft; her stern is almost like that of a dory.

The *Fundulus* has, I think, an exceedingly handsome bow. The details of bowsprit length and angle of steeve, point of attachment of the bobstay, and position of the hawse pipe have all been drawn just right by Bill Hand. This is a good example of the artistry of designing a boat. That bow looks just the part for what the ketch was designed to do. It gives her an able look that tips off the observer as to her performance at sea. (Of course I must say that to eliminate chafe, I'd rather run the anchor line through a big block lashed to the end of the bowsprit than through that hawse pipe.)

It was said, with some pride, that the *Fundulus* seldom needed reefing. I guess my reaction to that is that such a statement probably indicates she needs more sail. Certainly for summer coastwise cruising, she could be given a longer bowsprit and bigger jib, main topsail, and a somewhat bigger mizzen.

There is no quarrel with the handiness of her rig. To tack, roll the wheel over. To shorten down for a squall, or make a run in a real breeze, take the mainsail off her. To work her around the harbor, or make a run in a strong breeze, sail her like a catboat with mainsail alone.

The main topping lift probably would be handier rigged in the usual style to the mainmast rather than to the head of the mizzenmast. What should be rigged to the head of the mizzenmast, of course, is my favorite piece of rigging, a vang. She probably should have a boomkin so you could reach the clew of the mizzen without nearly throwing yourself overboard.

The seven-eighths-length club on the jib is a good rig. It lets the sail set better than with a full-length club, yet it can be self-tending. It would need lazy jacks to keep the sail off the deck when rounding up to a dock or anchor, or when picking up the home mooring with its inevitable coating of slime after being away on a cruise. The storm jib should be set farther up the headstay than shown in the sail plan. A good light sail for the ketch would be a big, high-footed, overlapping jib, with a pole to wing it out when running.

Bill Hand gave the *Fundulus* an unusual and most practical arrangement. Her open deck amidships, at the widest part of the vessel, gives a sense of spaciousness and a working area seldom found in a boat of this size. It could be used for carrying a dinghy on deck.

She has a snug steering cockpit abaft the mizzen, but perhaps the highlight of the arrangement is the placement of the head just forward of the mizzenmast with a hatch to the deck. When the head is used as a head, it does, to be sure, have the confinement of only sitting headroom. But it would probably be used as a second cockpit more than as a head. What a great place for the helmsman's watchmate to stay warm and dry, yet instantly handy to the deck and near enough to the wheel for conversation. If a bit of spray or rain got below into the compartment, what matter? It would be a great place to stand and watch her go—as long as you remembered where to put your feet. A "cockpit" seat hinged to the after bulkhead of the little compartment might make sense.

The sleeping cabin is private, not too sunny for

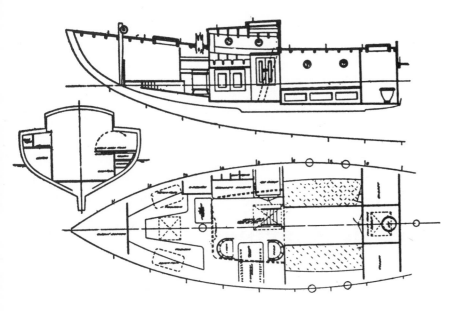

The ketch's arrangement is unusual, but practical, with real chairs in the saloon, a private, quiet, sleeping cabin complete with portholes, and a head compartment that could double as an admirable auxiliary cockpit. (*The Rudder Treasury* edited by Tom Davin)

the off-watch during the day, and it has all the headroom needed for sitting up in bed and reading or drinking the morning mug-up. It should be a quiet place.

There is full headroom under the short trunk cabin, which houses a galley and saloon combined. The chairs are a real luxury afloat. A chair is a lot more comfortable to sit in than is a bunk to sit on. These ought to be fastened down, of course, but they ought to be turnable, so you could swing them around to different positions and lock them in place. Facing the table, as shown, is fine for eating or playing cribbage in harbor, but you'd want to be able to face the chairs to starboard when eating a meal below at sea with the boat heeled over on the starboard tack, and you'd want to be able to face to port when in the same situation on the port tack. It's no fun trying to hold yourself in a chair that's trying its best to tip you out of it, especially if you are trying to eat at the same time.

The ketch has opening ports in both the hull and trunk cabin. I wonder how much real ventilating is done by these opening ports facing athwartships. You used to see them open in the topsides of big yachts at anchor with rounded metal scoops projecting out from their after semi-circles trying to catch a little air and send it in. This boat has three hatches to let air in aft and out forward, and I doubt if the opening portholes add much to the circulation. I'd prefer to have them fixed in place and plenty strong. Opening or fixed, the ones in the sleeping cabin would be a joy. It's great to be able to wake up and look

out at the water from a porthole by your bunk. The only time I've ever been able to do it (except in my patented "high" bunk in the skipjack I had) was in an eighty-eight-foot schooner. Those bunk ports are a nice touch in this design.

The *Fundulus* was used by several owners cruising between Nova Scotia and Cuba and into the Gulf of Mexico. She may still be going, for all I know. The people who did this cruising were unstinting in their praise of the ketch. They particularly commented on her good behavior in rough going. One owner wrote: "With the exception of rare occasions when curling seas have slopped over her rails, she has shipped green water on but one occasion, a memorable night when we thrashed to windward against a snortin' no'ther in the Gulf of Mexico under full sail, at a time when able fishing smacks ran under the beach and anchored. Our decks would have been virtually dry that night had we furled the mainsail."

The same owner also commented on her ability to run inlets on the New Jersey shore in breaking seas. Here is his description of running Barnegat Inlet one time: "Owing to the course of the narrow channel through the bar, it was impossible to hold her dead stern-to when a huge comber roared down upon us. Down the forward slope of that hill of water she raced at a pace which backed her sails against a fresh breeze! Yet she showed no tendency to broach or disobey her helm and crossed the bar with only a little spray on her after deck."

7/ Chapelle Sharpies

In the depths of the Great Depression, Howard I. Chapelle introduced a series of articles in *Yachting* magazine on workboats that he considered suitable for pleasure use with these words: "In these days of depleted bankrolls, 'cheap' yachts are a matter of importance to most of us." While the bankroll is merely a historical curiosity to many, we could certainly understand and agree with Chapelle's statement today if we substituted some such phrase as "purchasing power" for "bankrolls."

Chapelle's series was an admirable one, covering such craft as catboats, Friendship sloops, pinkies, Bahama sharpshooters, Gloucester sloop boats, fishing schooners, and pilot schooners. But he began with the simplest craft of all, the New Haven sharpie, a type developed in the late 1850s from the flat-bottomed sailing skiff. The New Haven sharpie, built to serve the Long Island Sound oyster fishery, is probably the thoroughbred of the type. But sharpies also came into use on the Chesapeake Bay, up and down the Carolina Sounds, and in the waters of Florida, the West Indies, and the Great Lakes. These boats fished, carried mail and cargo, went sponging, and even did a bit of smuggling here and there.

A significant modification to the sharpie was introduced in 1878, when Thomas Clapham, building sharpies at Roslyn, Long Island, New York, gave his boats a little deadrise in the bow and stern, though he left the bottom flat. The resulting partially vee-bottomed sharpies, used mostly as pleasure boats, were known as Roslyn or Nonpareil sharpies.

One of the basic rules in building a sharpie was that the width of the bottom should be one-sixth of the length on deck. The boats were built with from 3½ to four inches of flare per foot of depth amidships, with less flare if speed was a primary consideration, and more flare if seaworthiness was a key objective. Sharpies were always light-displacement craft, with low freeboard and strong sheer. It was thought that with the boat floating with her normal weight aboard, the heel of the stem should be just out of the water. (This rule was not followed from the Chesapeake Bay south; Bay watermen always built their skiffs and sharpies so they would float with the heel of the stem just underwater.) The sharpie always had a long, flat run. She has a light rig with a low center of effort.

The sharpie is an extremely simple type of craft, yet one that will give excellent performance with intelligent use. A Pentagon systems analyst would describe a sharpie as "very cost effective." A builder of sharpies of a century ago would have found the phrase meaningless, but he understood the principle involved. It was simply to develop a craft that could accomplish more work per dollar expended on her than could any other.

The "intelligent use" part simply has to do with the fact that the sharpie lacks ultimate stability. She cannot be driven but must be

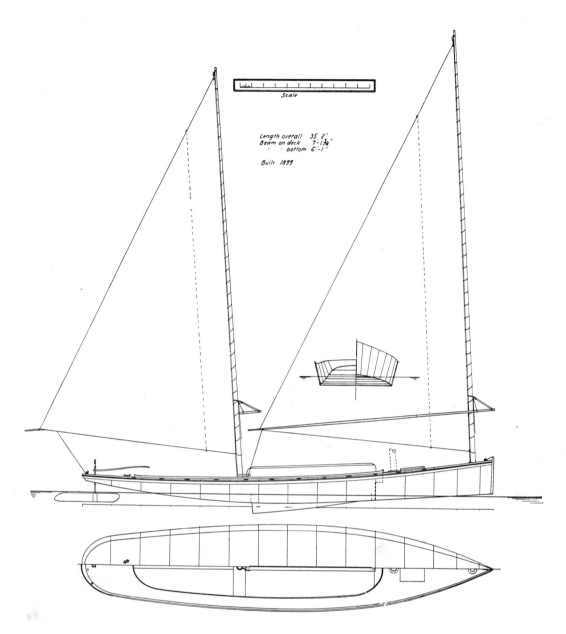

Length overall 35. 2
Beam on deck 7-1¾
" bottom 6 -1
Built 1899

Scale

Lester Rowe's sharpie of 1899 was considered by Howard Chapelle to be a fine example of the type. (*Yachting*, May, 1932)

shortened down in a breeze. Her rig is designed very much with her stability problem in mind. The masts are unstayed and are very flexible, so that they will bend to the gusts and spill wind out of the sails. They are not strong enough to exert enough force to tip the boat over. But they will break before she capsizes.

Being flat-bottomed, sharpies pound more than most boats do, but as they heel, the pounding is reduced. A sharpie is not the ideal boat for a long, hard thrash to windward, nor for lying at anchor in a small chop. The former problem can

be avoided by not using the boat on a schedule that demands getting somewhere on a given day regardless of wind or weather. The second problem usually can be solved by using the sharpie's advantage of shoal draft to slip into smooth water close to shore or snuggle right up onto a protected beach.

Of course the sharpie depends on her centerboard for lateral resistance and maneuverability. She may have one long board of about one-third the length of the boat, or two shorter boards, one forward and one aft. Her lee chine also

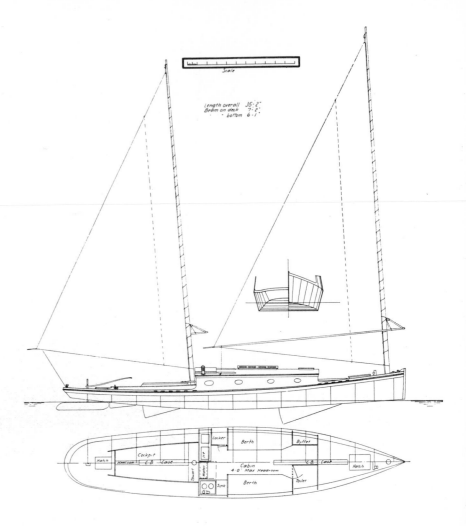

Length overall   35·2°
Beam on deck   7·2°
"   bottom   6·1°

Chapelle designed this sharpie yacht to follow closely the model of the Rowe sharpie. The sides of her house extend to the rail. (*Yachting*, May, 1932)

provides considerable lateral resistance, and she can work to windward and maneuver with surprisingly little board lowered when necessary.

The sharpie's centerboard trunk or trunks lend strength to her backbone, which typically consists of a log keelson made up of three two-by-eights on edge. As traditionally built, she had wide side planks, usually three or four strakes to a side, of 1½-inch white pine. Her bottom was always cross-planked, usually with 1½-inch yellow pine. The bottom planks were fastened both to the sides and to a chine log. A sheer clamp was used, and instead of frames she had cleats running between it and the chine log.

The sharpie rig is very simple, with few parts, all easily made, and little in the way of gadgets. The sails are reefed vertically, with a brail or lace-line used to hold the unwanted bunt to the mast. Some sharpie sails have a vertical batten at the reefing line, thus using the same reefing principle

developed by the Chinese, but rotated ninety degrees. With sprits extending the clews of the sails, it is desirable to have the masts rotate when the boat is put on the other tack, so some builders have installed mating brass plates on the mast heel and mast step.

The first sharpie plan shown is that of a thirty-five-footer built by Lester Rowe in 1899. Howard Chapelle, who drew the plans, felt that this was a very fine example of the type, and I certainly agree with him. Every line is a fine, fair sweep; she would probably look like a sissy if it weren't for her bold plumb bow. Her length on deck is 35 feet 2 inches, her beam is 7 feet 2 inches, and her draft is one foot.

The second sharpie shown is a yacht designed by Chapelle based closely on the Rowe thirty-five-footer. The dimensions of the two craft are nearly identical, but Chapelle has deepened the stern a bit and increased displacement slightly to

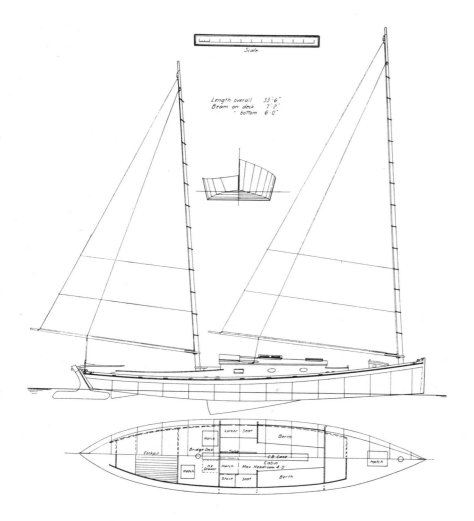

Scale

Length overall   33'6"
Beam on deck   7'2"
    " bottom   6'0"

take the weight of the house. Under the house, this boat has four feet of headroom, the maximum obtainable in a sharpie of this length without spoiling her. To get full headroom, you would have to go to a sharpie forty-five feet long. Chapelle felt the minimum length for a cabin sharpie along these lines would be twenty-eight feet.

When most people look at sharpie plans such as these, they say, "Isn't she beautiful!" Then they promptly start making changes, such as deepening the hull a bit, giving her a little more beam, giving her considerably more freeboard, adding a few inches of height to the house, and making everything a little heavier all around. If such thoughts are put on paper and built into a boat, the resulting craft is never a sharpie and is often a disappointment.

Chapelle wrote: "It should be remembered that most boat types are developed by means of trial and error, over a period of years, hence modification must be made only after considerable study of the type. In the sharpie this is markedly true; seventy years of continuous evolution cannot be disregarded with impunity." It can also be added that nearly all modifications to the sharpie increase her cost.

The third sharpie shown is a 33½-foot double-

ender that Chapelle designed based on Ralph M. Munroe's *Egret*. She would be cheaper to build than a round-stern sharpie, and Chapelle kept her just as simple as possible in every respect. She would, in my opinion, make an admirable coastwise cruising and exploring vessel for the single-hander, for two people, or for a couple with a child.

This sharpie is 33 feet 6 inches long on deck, with a waterline length of 31 feet 3 inches, a beam on deck of 7 feet 2 inches, beam on the bottom 6 feet, and a draft of 10 inches. Her sail area is 434 square feet.

Her hull is sleek, fair, and simple. In fact, she is deceptively simple. The designer of a flat-bottomed craft has few lines to work with, and if the boat is to be handsome and able, sheer and ne must have their perfect double curvature.

like the tandem centerboard idea for sharpies d feel the second board would be worth its tra cost in this boat. Two boards help both balance and steering and are a bit less in the way below. They give the boat such versatility. For example, if she were sailing around her anchor too much in a shifty breeze, dropping the forward board would quiet her down considerably. On this boat, the skeg might be deepened slightly to give the balanced rudder a bit more protection.

On the double-ender, the sprits have given way to booms. But her rig is still very simple, consisting in its entirety of two masts, two booms, two halyards, two topping lifts, and two sheets. I'd add lazy jacks, in the belief that being able to haul the sails right down (using the bitter end of the halyard as a downhaul) with the booms broad off without the sails thrashing around in wind and water would be a blessing in a boat like this and well worth the extra strings. The masts have a strong taper, from 6½ inches to 1½ inches in diameter, to give them that vital flexibility.

A sharpie needs to be sailed fairly free when on the wind. You have to concentrate on footing rather than on pointing. She won't eat up to weather, but she'll fly along and won't take overly long to reach an objective to windward. Off the wind, she can be really fast. Due to her

moderate sail area, she's not a particularly good ghoster, but she's light enough to be rowed in a calm.

The sharpie's foresail can always be kept full off the wind, either with the wind far enough forward to fill it to leeward or, if the wind is too far aft for that, wung out on the windward side. The absence of standing rigging allows the boom to be squared right off so the sail won't jibe.

All her gear can be kept very simple and light, and she is a very easy boat to sail. For instance, her anchors do not need to be very heavy, a feature that might endear her to sailors over, say, the age of eighty.

On deck, the coaming extended forward from the house keeps gear from getting adrift over the side and would also be a nice place to sit and watch her go when she is running off at high speed. For a rainy day at anchor, a tent over the after end of the foreboom might be a good idea: it would allow the main hatch to stay open and provide a place for standing and stretching and looking across the harbor—so your eyes can refocus when you go back to your book on the transom below. This boat also has about four feet of headroom.

The centerboard trunk looks very much in the way, until you remember that the boat is narrow enough so that you can lean across the trunk and simply remove from the shelf whatever you want from the other side of the boat. She has considerable storage space in the forepeak and under the bridge-deck.

In a boat like this sharpie, you cruise with the weather, avoiding long, rough beats and exposed anchorages. You use your wits and get very close to the weather and the water. Just imagine poking her bow up onto a sheltered beach or into the mud bank of a wild salt marsh. Think of the places she could go. With a boat like this in mind, you can pull out a thoroughly familiar chart and find a whole new cruising experience involving shallow water. Why, in this sharpie a man could hide from the revenue boys for months without leaving the eastern shore of Chesapeake Bay—unless, of course, they cheated and went to aerial spotting.

8/ The *Presto*

Length on deck: 41 feet
Length on waterline: 35 feet 6 inches
Beam: 10 feet 6 inches on deck; 9 feet 1 inch at waterline
Draft: 2 feet 6 inches
Sail area: 878 square feet
Designer: Ralph M. Munroe

The double-barreled myth that the coast of Maine consists solely of deep-water harbors and coves, while the Chesapeake Bay contains only shallow creeks and sand flats, is gradually being—um—eroded. There are plenty of deep anchorages in Chesapeake Bay and plenty of gunkholes along the Maine coast where only the shoalest craft can go. It was a Maine tidal cove that reminded me of the shallow *Presto*.

We were cruising in a small schooner drawing six feet and anchored in Winter Harbor, that deep, narrow fjord that cuts straight into the east side of Vinalhaven Island. Part of the crew, returning from a high-tide dinghy reconnoiter, reported the most beautiful hidden cove they had ever seen. We all rowed in through a narrow entrance between high, tree-covered ledges and agreed, when we saw a huge, wild, secluded harbor, that it was indeed a rare and exquisite spot. Someone asked, "Can we bring the schooner in?"

The answer had to be no. We might have squeezed her in then at high water, but life aboard would not have been pleasant six hours later, for the place nearly dries out. I wished we were in a boat like the *Presto*, for then we could have holed up in there perfectly comfortably for as long as we cared to.

"Ah," you may say, "but surely the schooner, with her eminently seaworthy hull, is a better all-around boat for the rough-and-tumble coast of Maine?" Perhaps, but that raises another myth: that all truly shoal-draft boats are unseaworthy.

Commodore Ralph M. Munroe—wanting a boat that could sail in the shallow waters of Biscayne Bay, yet would be seaworthy enough to sail anywhere on the Atlantic coast—decided to design a boat that he thought would be an improvement on the sharpie, a type whose performance had greatly impressed him. He said the sharpie type provided "the greatest accomplishment for least cost."

So in 1885, Commodore Munroe designed the *Presto*, and a comparison of her lines with those of the New Haven sharpie built by Lester Rowe, described in the preceding chapter, will show the changes he made. (The Rowe sharpie was not built until 1899, but she is an excellent example of the basic sharpie type Commodore Munroe knew.) He made the *Presto* a bit wider and gave her considerably more flare in the topsides. He increased the depth of hull somewhat, gave her bottom a little deadrise, and rounded the bilges. Most important, he added considerable inside ballast, 4½ tons of iron. Her dimensions worked out to: length on deck, 41 feet; length on the

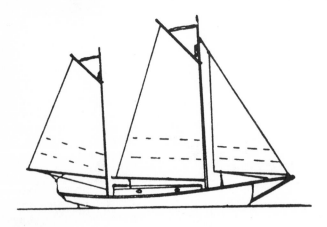

The *Presto*'s sail plan indicates a simple ketch rig with self-tending headsail. She has preventer backstays, but no fixed shrouds. (Reprinted, by permission, from *The Good Little Ship*, by Vincent Gilpin, 3rd ed., 1975; drawn by Capt. Robert P. Beebe, U.S. Navy, Retired)

waterline, 35 feet 6 inches; beam, 10 feet 6 inches on deck and 9 feet 1 inch at the waterline; draft with the board up, 2 feet 6 inches; depth amidships, 4 feet 3 inches. Her centerboard was 11 feet long by 4 feet deep.

That Commodore Munroe was satisfied with the *Presto* is shown by the fact that he designed a number of other similar boats in later years, all with the same basic hull form, though in the later models he did increase the beam slightly to make

the boats foot a little faster when on the wind. Some of the *Presto*'s successors were the *Egret*, the *Wabun*, the *Micco*, and the *Utilis*.

To answer the obvious question and start working on that myth, Commodore Munroe can be quoted: "None of them were ever capsized to my knowledge." In fact, all of these boats performed very well up and down the Atlantic coast for years, including getting caught out in northers in the Gulf Stream.

Commodore Munroe often told his favorite story about the way the *Presto* could sail:

Not long after her trial trip I invited several friends to see another international race. The day came in with a rainy southeaster and, none of my guests appearing, I started in *Presto* under full sail, with a small boy for crew, and worked out across the bar to Gedney's Channel sea buoy, with wind and sea increasing all the time. We had seen the yacht fleet lying in the Horseshoe with no sign of getting under way, and I was about squaring off for home when a large tug with the N.Y.Y.C. burgee headed our way. We hove to and waited, still under full sail and quite comfortable, while the tug was laboring hard, completely disappearing in clouds of spray every few seconds. As she approached I drew away the jib, and passed close aboard. There was no one on deck, but abreast of us a pilot-house window was dropped a bit and someone waved a handkerchief. She soon turned and ran for the Hook, and we followed.

Next morning I had a note from my old friend Louis Bayard, then Secretary of the Seawanhaka-Corinthian Yacht Club, saying: "I waved to you from the *Britannia* yesterday outside the bar. You were apparently enjoying a pleasant sail; it was quite the contrary aboard the tug.

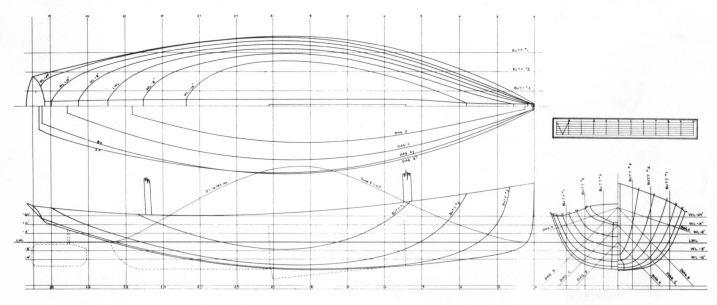

The lines of the *Presto* show a modified sharpie drawing 30″ on a waterline length of 35′6″. (Reprinted, by permission, from *The Good Little Ship*, by Vincent Gilpin, 3rd ed., 1975; drawn by Capt. Robert P. Beebe, U.S. Navy, Retired)

Left: The *Presto* on a nice reach in Great Kills, on the outer shore of Staten Island, N.Y. (*The Commodore's Story* by Ralph Middleton Munroe and Vincent Gilpin)

Right: She goes on by, displaying her fine form for the camera. (*The Commodore's Story* by Ralph Middleton Munroe and Vincent Gilpin)

A. Cary Smith, Phil Ellsworth, and others on board, were much interested in the performance of *Presto*, and Smith laid a wager that I was mistaken in the 30-inch draft and other dimensions I gave him, saying no such craft could possibly carry her sail and make such good weather of it. When can you lay her on the beach and let us measure her?" I made the appointment, they all came, and after a pleasant discussion the bet was paid to Bayard.

So the *Presto* was a great performer. It must be remembered, though, that she was always expertly handled. She would be found wanting in stability at angles of heel greater than ninety degrees. For this reason, I don't believe she could be called the ideal ocean cruiser, but I do feel that in view of her proven performance and the fact that vessels that sail coastwise have every opportunity of avoiding the worst weather, she would make an ideal coastal cruising boat. This is not to make any apologies for her behavior in rough water. Her light displacement would allow her to rise to the seas, nor would she trip on her keel when driven bodily to leeward by a breaking sea. Her flare and weight of inside ballast would give her sufficient initial stability. I should say, though, that if I were to meet that ultimate wave I hope never to meet, I'd rather not be in the *Presto*. (My first choice, actually, would be a deeply submerged, nuclear-powered submarine.)

The *Presto*'s hollow entrance must have been approved by Nathanael G. Herreshoff, that good friend of Commodore Munroe's and great utilizer

of concave waterlines in the bow. While I'm talking about the shape of the bow, I might as

Slipping along in a light air, her yard-and-sprit topsail doing its work (*Yachting*, November, 1926).

Four of the modified sharpies designed by Commodore Munroe photographed by him at Biscayne Bay: the *Egret* is in the foreground getting her bottom scrubbed; anchored off are the *Nethla, Nicketti,* and *Presto,* from left to right. (*Yachting,* June, 1937)

well discuss pounding, that old sharpie nemesis. The man who scorns flat-bottomed boats says you can never get them to stop pounding, while the defender of the flat-bottomed faith will remind you that any boat will pound, given a certain angle of heel and a certain wave shape. (I can verify that even the most beautiful concave flaring bow Nat Herreshoff ever created is capable of hitting a sea just wrong on rare occasions.) Here again, it is instructive to compare the *Presto*'s lines with those of the Lester Rowe New Haven sharpie. See how Commodore Munroe did away with the troublesome flat triangular bottom up forward by rounding back and deepening the forefoot slightly and giving the bow sections considerable deadrise. I doubt pounding was a problem in the *Presto.*

The main advantages of a centerboard in a boat are apparent, but there are ancillary advantages that may not be immediately obvious. In shoal but friendly waters, the centerboard makes an ideal sounding machine. Under similar conditions, it can also be used as a brake or a temporary anchor.

The *Presto*'s balanced rudder certainly made for most sensitive and responsive steering. One wonders, though, if its shoalness might mean some loss of steering control when a big sea ran up under her quarter.

The *Presto*'s ketch rig was a simple one. Vincent Gilpin, Commodore Munroe's great friend and student, quotes his mentor as saying,

"I would cheerfully sit up all night to cut out one superfluous rope from a sail plan." The *Presto* had no permanent shrouds but did have preventer backstays that could be brought aft and set up in a strong breeze.

The *Presto*'s working sail area was 878 square feet, broken down into a mainsail of 412 square feet, a mizzen of 266 square feet, and a jib of 200 square feet. Her topsail (see photo) added an additional 274 square feet up where it would do the most good in a light air. Her mainmast stood 35 feet above the deck, and her mizzen 29 feet 6 inches. The length of the bowsprit outboard was 9 feet.

Her jib and mizzen were loose-footed, yet self-tending. The topsail was set on a club and sprit and was sheeted from the middle of the foot. It could be swung out on the opposite side from the mainsail when running before the wind.

It would be wonderful to see the *Presto* centerboarder rejuvenated. She'd make an admirable cruising boat for any coastline. Just imagine the fun of ghosting her into a totally secluded cove running way up into the middle of some Maine island and knowing that you could lie there in perfect comfort at low tide with your anchor in plain view out ahead. Then you'd watch the tide come back, gradually filling every nook and cranny and sending her afloat again. Yes, there is a place for the sharpie on the coast of Maine, nor would she fail to make a good account of herself on the Chesapeake Bay.

9/ The *Alice*

Length on deck: 51 feet 10 inches
Length on waterline: 43 feet 11 inches
Beam: 13 feet 7 inches
Draft: 4 feet
Sail area: 1,100 square feet
Designer: Ralph M. Munroe

Some cruising men have shallow-draft boats out of necessity: their home waters are shallow, so they have the choice of sailing a shoal-draft boat or wading. Others have shallow cruising vessels out of choice: they want to go gunkholing where most other boats can't follow, or, for some reason, they are simply attracted to the virtues of a shallow-draft boat under sail and are not dissuaded by her drawbacks.

Commodore Ralph M. Munroe got into shoal-draft cruisers through a combination of the two motives. To be sure, the waters of his adopted Biscayne Bay were shoal, but also, he had been impressed with the way the sharpie type of hull could sail, in deep water as well as in shoal. So he designed the *Presto*, described in the preceding chapter, a modified sharpie that was the first of a successful line of shoal-draft cruisers.

In 1920, thirty-five years after the *Presto* had appeared, Henry Howard, an experienced cruising man who had always had deep-draft vessels, had the good fortune to meet Commodore Munroe at Coconut Grove, Florida. Howard was thinking about a boat shoal enough to get up and down the Inland Waterway comfortably, but he didn't want to give up a boat that could also go to sea. Munroe convinced him that the two capabilities were not necessarily incompatible, and Howard asked the Commodore to design him a boat.

Munroe drew a set of lines similar to those of the *Carib*, a boat he had designed that had proved most successful. He also drew a sail plan, giving her a straightforward gaff ketch rig, with a single headsail.

The plans of the ketch were sent to the office of John G. Alden, where Sam Crocker was given the task of giving the lines their final fairing and of drawing up an accommodation plan according to what Howard wanted inside the boat.

The design work was completed in 1923, and the boat was built the following year by A. C. Brown and Sons at Staten Island, New York. She was christened *Alice*, after the owner's wife, Alice Sturtevant Howard.

The Howards, with their son and daughter and three others for crew, took the boat south soon after her launching in the fall of 1924. She performed well in the Inland Waterway and she performed well at sea; the cruise to Miami, the West Indies, and back was most successful.

Henry Howard described the boat and her maiden voyage in a series of articles in *Yachting* magazine from November 1925 to February 1926. These articles evoked so much interest and

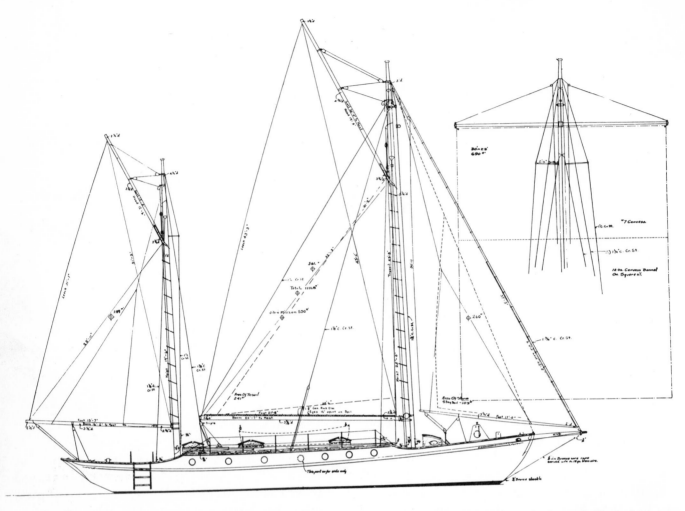

Above: The *Alice* has a roller-reefing mainsail and a big squaresail of nearly 700 square feet, the lower half of which is a removable bonnet. (*The Yacht Alice* by Henry Howard)

Below: For such a shoal boat, she has quite a deep-bodied look to her, for she has moderate deadrise. (*The Yacht Alice* by Henry Howard)

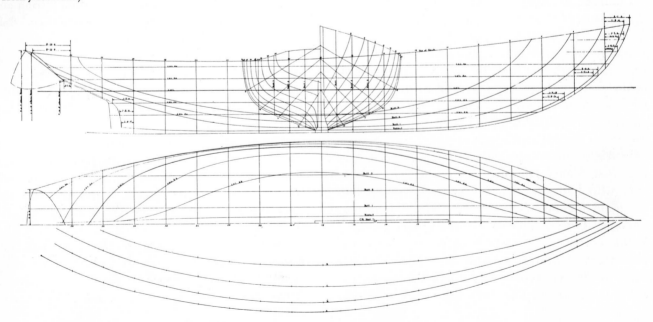

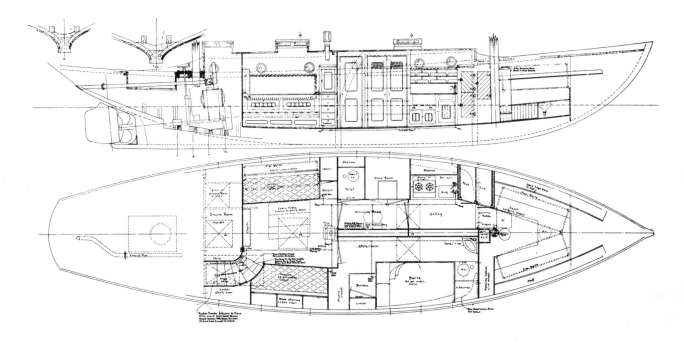

Above: The spacious layout is nicely arranged around her big centerboard trunk. (*The Yacht Alice* by Henry Howard)

Below: Her construction plan hints at the strength obtainable with a raised deck. Note the height of the centerboard trunk. (*The Yacht Alice* by Henry Howard)

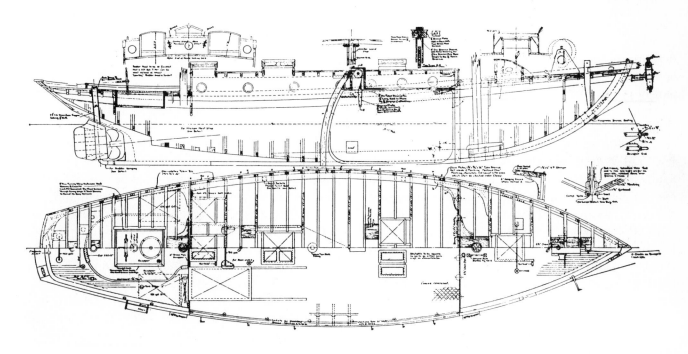

comment—large, centerboard cruisers not being so very popular—that Howard expanded the articles into a book that was published by the Charles E. Lauriat Company of Boston in 1926. The book is unfortunately long out of print. Its title page reads: "The Yacht 'Alice': Planning and Building,

by Henry Howard; A Cruise from New York to Miami through the Inland Waterway, by Alice Sturtevant Howard; A West Indies Cruise, by Katherine Howard." The last-named co-author was, of course, the daughter.

The Yacht "Alice" contains as complete a

The *Alice*'s single-cylinder Bolinder diesel is a remarkable-looking piece of machinery. (*The Yacht Alice* by Henry Howard)

description of the ketch as there is in print of any comparable vessel. Howard was an engineer, and he went into detail.

And, of course, the boat herself is an interesting and successful example of the shoal-draft cruiser. She is, in my opinion, one of the very few raised-deck vessels that manages to look handsome. This is probably because the forward end of her raised deck has been kept low, and the bow, having good sheer, rises a bit above it. Also, there are nice curves in the rail leading up to the raised deck. Perhaps the real secret, though, is that the rail of the raised deck has been given a very slight sheer, rather than merely being a straight line.

The ketch is 51 feet 10 inches long on deck, with a waterline length of 43 feet 11 inches, a beam of 13 feet 7 inches, and a draft of 4 feet. Her sail area is 1,110 square feet, with 561 square feet in the mainsail, 289 in the mizzen, and 260 in the jib. Her squaresail has an area of 690 square feet.

She was built with an oak backbone. Her double, sawn frames are molded from 2⅜ inches to 3¼ inches, sided 1⅞ inches, and spaced sixteen inches apart from center to center. The frames are white oak below the waterline and locust above. Her planking is 1½-inch yellow pine.

Perhaps the element that stands out most in the lines drawing of the *Alice* is the nice, easy run of the shoal-draft boat. Her midsection shows that she would be quite stiff, for her bilges have just a bit of hardness well below the waterline and a bit of flare has been retained in the topsides. There is a slight hollow in the forward end of the load waterline.

Of course the raised deck, which is built integrally with the hull, should perhaps be considered as part of the hull. Certainly it would increase the vessel's buoyancy and stability in a knockdown—provided the side deadlights and deck openings were shut and sealed and didn't carry away.

At any rate, the *Alice*'s hull would be quite easy to drive, and the boat should have an easy motion. And if you find yourself using the word *easy* to describe a cruising vessel, the chances are that she was designed by somebody who has cruised a lot.

The ketch's jib and mizzen are big enough to

The *Alice* close-hauled in light going. (*The Yacht Alice* by Henry Howard)

work her to windward in a breeze of wind, though the mizzen would want a reef tied in to achieve the best balance. The sail plan also shows a main trysail, with essentially the same area that the mainsail would have if scandalized, and a stem-head storm jib, set flying. The *Alice* has a roller-reefing mainsail, for Henry Howard was highly impressed with Claud Worth's development of that gear, and he duplicated Worth's design for his own boat. The yard for the squaresail hoists on a jackstay to keep it reasonably rigid yet allow the spar to come down with the sail.

The running backstays are far enough forward so that they could probably be left set up when short-tacking. The lazy jacks on jib and mizzen would keep those sails under control when lowered; the mainsail, with its roller-reefing gear, could also have lazy jacks, hung from the topping lifts with bights around, but not attached to, the boom.

The engine in the ketch is a Bolinder diesel from Stockholm, Sweden. It is a one-lunger that develops 15 brake horsepower at 450 r.p.m.

The *Alice* has a controllable-pitch propeller, with a diameter of thirty inches. This makes a nice wheel for an auxiliary engine in a sailing vessel. When using the engine while sailing, the pitch can be increased for best efficiency. Then, when punching into a head sea, the pitch can be reduced appropriately. Or, when sailing with the engine shut down, the pitch can be increased to its maximum so the wheel is feathered for minimum drag.

It is interesting to look at a speed/horsepower table calculated by W. Starling Burgess for the *Alice* under power in a flat calm.

Knots	Brake Horsepower
4	3.7
5	6.0
6	10.5
6.65	15.0
7	19.8
8	45.4

She's a fine vessel to be going on board. (*Yachting*, January, 1938)

Thus it can be seen that the 15-h.p. engine gives the *Alice* a speed in a calm of a strong 6½ knots. At this speed, she goes 5¼ miles on one gallon of fuel.

The arrangement plan of the ketch has been worked nicely around the big centerboard trunk: the trunk is used merely as a partition. She has a nice saloon entered by a curving stairway and warmed by an open-tile fireplace. There is ample headroom and working room around the engine, and even a skylight over the engine to let in light if you're working below or to let you see what's going on down there when you're on deck. The large storeroom on the port side just abaft the galley looks lavish today; it would be very useful on a long trip.

With her shoal hull, straightforward rig, and relatively simple engine, the *Alice* is indeed a versatile cruising vessel. Here is a brief account by Henry Howard of one leg of a cruise on an occasion when he didn't want to wait for favorable conditions. With the *Alice*, he had the choice.

Last March I drove her across the Gulf Stream from Havana to Key West in the heaviest norther of the winter, under mainsail and engine, making the distance, about 95 nautical miles from Morro Castle to the wharf at Key West, in 21 hours. The run was almost dead to windward and anyone familiar with the Straits of Florida in a winter norther will agree that it can kick up a rather nasty sea. The boat behaved wonderfully, however—did not pound at all—and we steered her with a tiller with the greatest ease. The most surprising thing was the way she would get on top of the very steep head seas, into which she was being driven by both engine and all the sail she could carry to advantage. No solid water came over the bow or on deck and a number of times, both day and night, I stood forward by the main mast to better enjoy her performance.

10/ A Catboat

Length on deck: 28 feet
Length on waterline: 27 feet
Beam: 11 feet 6 inches
Draft: 3 feet
Sail area: 700 square feet
Designer: Richard O. Davis

When modern sailors defend their high-sided, hog-sheered, reverse-transom boats to their traditionalist friends, they often use the old adage, "Handsome is as handsome does." The boat performs well, so who cares what she looks like, the argument goes. Indeed, the only boat that ever beat my lovely old Herreshoff sloop in a race was about the ugliest craft I ever saw.

What we traditionalists are often tempted to believe, however, is that the converse of the adage must be true: if a boat is handsome, then necessarily she must perform well. Perhaps this theory can be tested a bit on this design for a handsome and curvaceous catboat.

An interesting feature of the construction of this catboat is that the designer, Richard O. Davis, specified that the centerboard trunk be made of bronze and be flanged to the keel. That would be an expensive way to keep it from leaking today. I would suggest, as an alternative, judicious use of sawdust down the slot.

It is true that centerboards and their trunks can give trouble in a boat, of course, but in my view, every problem they can create is small enough payment for the tremendous versatility they give to a boat by allowing her to change her underwater shape and draft at will.

When Horace S. Crosby and others began to develop the Cape Cod catboat as a separate and distinct type of craft in the 1860s, they were working from a heritage of the New York sloop, turned cat, and made gradually more able as she was used farther east, out from behind the protection of Long Island. The boats were developed for fishing in the exposed water around Cape Cod, and they had to be able to sail from harbors that did not allow deep draft. The seaworthiness, stiffness, roominess, and shoal draft that the Cape Cod fishermen needed are qualities that today make for a boat that can serve admirably as a daysailer and coastwise cruiser.

This Davis cat is one of the handsomest I have seen. Her sections and transom are shapely, there is just enough curve in her stem, and her sheer line is just as pretty as can be. The curved bowsprit, nicely proportioned rig, and rounded cabin trunk following the sheer line make her mighty easy to look at.

The sections are worth studying in detail, especially in comparison with those of a powerful twenty-six-foot Cape Cod cat designed by Manley H. Crosby in 1895. It can be seen that the Davis cat has considerably more deadrise than the Crosby. She would thus have less initial stability and sail at a greater angle of heel, though this would be compensated for to some extent by her hard bilges relative to the Crosby cat. But the Davis boat, although the larger of the two, has only fourteen inches of freeboard, compared to the Crosby's eighteen inches.

Would those nicely modeled sections on the Davis boat, coupled with her handsome, deep sheer, mean that her lee rail would go under too easily? Fenwick Williams, a Marblehead, Massachusetts, naval architect who has designed successful catboats, commenting on this design in a letter to me, believes this might well be the case. Much as I'd like to believe that this most handsome catboat would sail better than any other, I tend to agree with Mr. Williams. Some modification of this design, in the way of a bit less deadrise and a bit more freeboard amidships, might well be in order. All of which makes me wonder, and wish I could find out, if a boat has ever been built to this design.

The sail plan of the Davis cat shows a mainsail of 700 square feet. (*Yachting*, September, 1926)

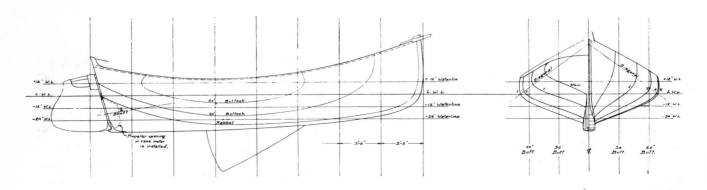

Above: Her lines show lots of deadrise for a catboat and a strong sheer with low freeboard amidships. It's too bad no halfbreadth plan is available to show her waterlines. (*Yachting*, September, 1926)

Below: The inboard profile and accommodation plans show a snug cabin with berthing for three. The transom on the starboard side is 12 feet long. (*Yachting*, September, 1926)

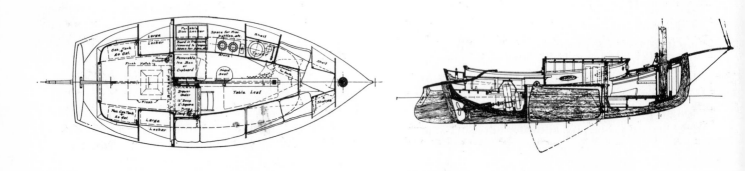

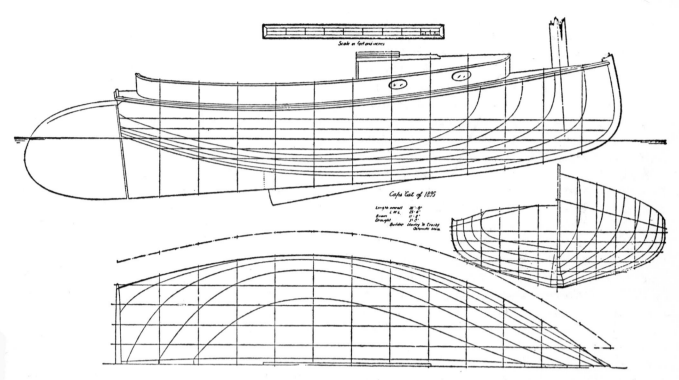

A Cape Cod catboat of 1895 designed by Manley H. Crosby. She is 26' long on deck, with a waterline length of 26'4", a beam of 11'2", and a draft of 3'. The Davis cat has considerably more deadrise than the Crosby, which would make the Davis boat tender by comparison. (*American Sailing Craft* by Howard I. Chapelle, International Marine Publishing Company)

One of the advantages of a low-sided boat to be used for fun on the water is that she will give her crew a greater sense of being afloat than would a boat whose side has to be climbed with a ladder. And for swimming and washing out the fry pan, there's just nothing like low freeboard.

A catboat makes an admirable motorsailer. Her hull is as easily driven as many hulls designed for power alone, and her single spar, with little standing rigging, has a minimum of windage. As a matter of fact, many of the early, small power draggers that were developed in southern New England with the advent of the internal-combustion engine were little more than Cape Cod catboats with a raised deck forward and a tiny, off-center, one-man pilothouse at the after end of the raised deck. Later these draggers gained freeboard and draft and became narrower.

The great advantage of a catboat is that you just have to put up one sail. While it is thus generally realized that the cat is an admirable lazy-man's rig, it is sometimes overlooked that the cat is a fast rig, because the more the sail plan is broken up, the less efficient and weatherly it becomes. Of course, the big mainsail on this boat would have to be reefed often. In a hard breeze, for example, the triple-reefed sail, showing 325 square feet, would be all this easily driven hull could desire. For this reason, this boat is not a good singlehander. Seven hundred square feet of sail is too much for one man in a breeze. A very handy structure on this boat would be a stout gallows frame across her broad stern. Why are schooners allowed this admirable reefing aid, while catboats have to get along without it?

The three clew reefing earings should be kept rove off, but with their cheek blocks abaft the reef cringles, rather than directly below them, as shown on the sail plan. This would allow the earings to be used as outhauls. They could simply be stout lanyards led from one side of the boom through the cringle and down through the cheek blocks on the other side of the boom and inboard to cleats well forward on the boom, so they could be reached even with the boom broad off. Then there could be a three-part tackle all made up on the boom to apply purchase to whichever reef earing was being used. It might be well also to use reefing lacelines instead of reef points on the after two-thirds of the sail. Then the sail could be reefed even when partially set on any point of sailing without having to climb on the boom. She ought to have double topping lifts, one for each side, and they should be quite heavy.

Of course there is an easy, quick way to reduce this 700-square-foot mainsail to one of 275 square feet. It can be scandalized by dropping the peak. Take the weight of the boom on the lifts, and then slack the peak halyard right off. The gaff will sag off harmlessly to leeward, and the whole upper part of the sail will be blanketed by what is left standing, namely, a broad trysail with its head at the throat of the gaff sail. I learned this the easy way one day when a peak halyard, from which I expected one season too many, parted. The mainsail was scandalized just beautifully in two seconds. A good winter rig for this boat might be a triangular sail set on the throat halyard, with the gaff used as a boom.

Whether or not catboats should have bowsprits is an argument that probably will never be settled. I favor the idea, because the bowsprit is such a handy anchor derrick and also because it gives a much better spread to the headstays; and because (heresy of heresies!) I like the idea of setting a jib on a catboat to ease the steering a bit on a broad reach in a breeze o' wind. The jib might also be useful by itself for running off in a squall or for lazing along towing a mackerel jig.

This catboat steers with a tiller, but I would prefer a wheel. It's going to take some power to hold the rudder over with a fresh breeze on the quarter; why not let the steering gear do the work?

The box covering the top of the engine has been shaped to present the minimum obstacle in the cockpit, but it might be handier to square it off for a permanent cockpit table. The companion hatch ought to be double width, so you can go below on either side of the centerboard trunk. And as to the head taking up all that valuable space in the cabin, well I'd prefer the versatile cedar bucket.

11/ The Skipjack*

> Length on deck: 37 feet
> Length on waterline: 34 feet
> Beam: 14 feet 2 inches
> Draft: 2 feet 10 inches
> Sail area: 900 square feet

When the surveyor of the Chesapeake Bay skipjack I was considering buying said she was too fat, I said to myself, "Just you keep jabbing around with that chisel, old man, and never mind the insults." The strength of my reaction should have told me that I had already decided to purchase the vessel.

We kept on, however, with the objective analysis. She had been built to dredge oysters in 1949 and had dredged until 1956, when she had been converted to pleasure use. I was interested in her as a family cruising boat.

The conversion had been carried out well. The small cuddy forward had been enlarged by extending it aft, making a large after cabin. The house had been kept reasonably low, however, and abaft it had been left considerable acreage of flush deck. Beneath this deck was an engine. It happened to be defunct, but then, who needs power in a sailing vessel?

Best of all, her rig had not been altered in any way. Her sails were vertical-cut in the traditional fashion, and they were made of some beautiful, heavy Dacron, a big advantage in the hot, humid Chesapeake climate.

It was true that the surveyor's tool did not always bounce back off hard, springy wood. She appeared to be a bit spongy in a few spots, but all these minor defects were above the waterline. I mentioned this fact to the surveyor to try to cheer him up, but he was unimpressed by the revelation.

There followed several days that should have won me an Oscar. There was a careful weighing of pros and cons; there were calm, dispassionate discussions of the vessel with boat-minded friends; and, of course, there was a reasoning together with wife and children.

The curtain came down on October 14, 1963. She was mine.

Her solidness and weight could not be immediately absorbed. I owned her six years, and every so often during that time, when I stepped aboard and looked around, I couldn't believe she really could be quite so massive.

---

*The Skipjack had a name when I got her; she was named after the previous owner's mother, *Daisy B*. Since I hadn't had the pleasure of knowing Daisy, the name meant nothing to me, but I didn't dare change it for fear of bringing bad luck to the vessel. Her original name had been the *Sister*. We always referred to her simply as "The Skipjack," which was entirely satisfactory.

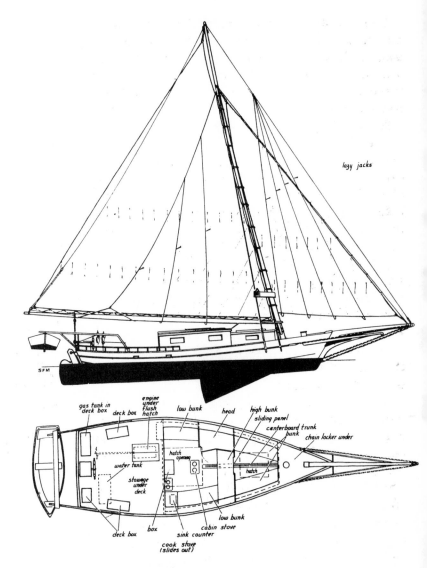

Right: Sam Manning's plan of the skipjack shows her long, straight keel, general flat-iron shape, and big sail area. (Drawn by S.F. Manning)

Below: Slipping along with the skiff in tow and her people spread out around her spacious after deck. (Drawn by S.F. Manning)

She measured 37 feet long on deck. Her waterline length was 34 feet. One day, soon after she had been acquired, I stretched a tape measure across her middle and discovered that her extreme beam was 14 feet 2 inches! Moreover, her beam was carried aft to the extent that her transom was 10½ feet wide! Her draft was 2 feet 10 inches.

Of course she had a big centerboard. One of the great things about this board was that when you wanted to paint it, you just took it out and painted it. You backed off a big nut on the bronze pin that went right through the trunk just above the sole in the fo'c's'le. Then, once a line was made fast to a becket that was worked onto the forward, top corner of the board, you knocked the pin out, plugged the holes, and dropped the board out of the trunk.

You could then reach under the boat with a boathook, bring out a bight of the forward line, and, slacking away forward and on the pendant aft, pull the board out from under and to the surface. As long as you kept the forward line rove up through the trunk, the centerboard went right back in again after painting.

I don't know what that skipjack displaced, but my best guess is a dozen tons. Her bottom and side planking and deck were two-inch yellow pine. Her keel was three four-inch-thick timbers bolted together to form a member a foot broad and probably more than that deep. The deck beams were four-by-four stuff.

With this sort of beam and weight, her initial stability was little short of miraculous. Though her freeboard amidships was only eight inches, helped artificially by another eight inches of bulwarks, when sailing close-hauled under full sail, it took about a fifteen-knot breeze to put her down that eight inches so the water was sloshing in and out of the freeing ports.

Her mast was a bit longer than the usual equal-to-the-length-on-deck formula for skipjacks. It was a heavy, tapered spar stepped with a huge rake and then sprung well forward at the top by the headstays so that the main halyard block, when hung as a plumb bob, came just over the after end of the centerboard trunk, another rule of thumb not to be violated in a proper skipjack. In the course of working on the vessel, I always looked forward most to scraping and slushing down that spar. It was good sailorizing.

The boom was as long as the boat on deck and was kept varnished. It was a handsome spar, not too stiff and heavy enough not to lift too much off the wind in a breeze.

The long bowsprit was beveled on the bottom and square on top, so it was always comfortable to walk or sit on. I liked to work out on the bowsprit, furling the jib or something. There were plenty of things to climb around on out there, what with the longhead rails, bowsprit shrouds, and double chain bobstays.

When I got the skipjack, she had two Danforth anchors, a little one and a big one. The little one, a fifteen-pounder, looked fine to keep on the stern ready to hold her off a dock or up across a small evening breeze on a hot night. I like really substantial ground tackle at the other end of the boat, though, because I don't get on with

A bow view, showing her anchor stowage and head rigging. (Drawn by S.F. Manning)

engines, so I can't depend on them to help solve the nasty lee shore problem.

I traded the thirty-five-pound Danforth for a fifty-pound yachtsman's anchor (less holding power under ideal conditions of scope, bottom, and absence of squalls from unexpected directions, but greater holding power under normal conditions) and I was given an eighty-pound old-fashioned anchor. The latter I wedged between the samson post and bulwarks away forward and lashed to the bowsprit inboard. The former hung from its rode on a bowsprit chock. I ran a line from a cleat forward round the shank of the anchor just above the crown and then parbuckled the anchor up snug against the bobstay. This kept it secure, out of the way, and ready for use simply by letting go one end of this "crown line" and letting go the rode, without having to touch

Watching the races off Annapolis. Who forgot to slack the weather jib sheet? (Photo by Robert de Gast)

the anchor. It looked right, too, slung under the bowsprit that way.

At the stern she had heavy pipe frames running aft above the bulwarks, perhaps three feet off the deck. These formed stern davits ten feet apart, and my sailing skiff fit them perfectly. It was always very satisfactory to come in and anchor, lower away the boat from belaying pins on the davits, unhook the falls and leave them dangling just above the water, and then take the rig—mast and boom, with sail bent, folded together and lashed—from its resting place across the davits and step it in the skiff. Five minutes after anchoring, you could be under sail again in a

perfect miniature "skipjack," complete with little mast hoops on her leg-o'-mutton sail.

There were two other sets of belaying pins farther forward on the pipe rails that formed the davits, one pair for the jib sheets and one pair for the double-ended mainsheet. This arrangement put the sheets up nearly at waist height, where you could really pull on them. There was never any difficulty in getting the sails flattened in in a breeze. She had four parts on the mainsheet and a two-part tackle on the clew of the jib with its hauling part made up to another two-part tackle to produce, in effect, a four-part rig.

Skipjacks are noted for their array of lazy jacks, and I rigged up plenty of them. I had four-legged lazy jacks on both mainsail and jib. Coupled with downhauls, these made a wonderful device, an especially worthwhile one for single-handed work.

For a downhaul on the mainsail, I used to take the bitter end of the main halyard and tie it into the head cringle with a bowline. The jib downhaul was conventionally rigged from the head of the sail down through a block on the end of the bowsprit and in on deck where it was belayed.

To lower and temporarily furl either sail, all you had to do was throw off the halyard and haul her down. Unless you had coiled the halyard with twists in it, there was nothing to stick or jam, and you knew you could get sail off in a twinkling. The great thing was that you could haul down the mainsail with the boom broad off running before it if you wanted to. The lazy jacks held the sail up on the boom and you could forget the sail until you were good and ready to pay attention to it again on your own terms. And when coming in to an anchorage or dock, you could haul down the jib and know it would be neither in the water nor in the way of handling the anchor or bow line.

Furling the mainsail was always a pleasant job. The Dacron was heavy enough to feel like canvas; it was smoother, of course, but not like that terribly slippery stuff you can't hang onto. Because the head of the mainsail on a skipjack goes up four feet or so above the hounds, there is no mast hoop for that distance down from the head of the sail. So when the sail is lowered, the head can come well aft into the furl, and you can really make a neat job of things all the way up to

Well, yes, she is a bit broad. Broad enough to take easily a set of lawn furniture, the chaise longue of which may be detected just to the right of the skiff's stem. Away to leeward under her boom are a Chinese junk and a small aircraft carrier. (Photo by Robert de Gast)

the mast. There is no big, unmanageable bulge.

A tremendous, fully battened awning came with the skipjack. It lashed up under the main boom, which was raised fore and aft (it had jaws, not a gooseneck) to give headroom. The awning covered the whole after deck and most of the house and had let-down screen sides. Sitting under it on a hot day, you felt you had it made.

She had a huge companionway hatch. This let plenty of light and air below and also gave full headroom when open. It was nice to be able to stand working at the galley stove or sink and still be able to supervise harbor activities throughout 360 degrees.

She had a high, thwartships bunk, which I immediately claimed in the well-founded belief that she would never heel much anyway. The advantage was that you could lie in that bunk and see out the companionway and big, rectangular cabin ports. Since I have to see every boat that goes by, this saved a lot of steps.

Just forward of my bunk, a full bulkhead went right across the boat, dividing the after cabin from what we called the fo'c's'le. There was a sliding panel in it just above my bunk with a handle on the after side only. My wife and I turned over the fo'c's'le to the children.

Never having sailed a workboat before, I was most anxious to learn how her sailing qualities would compare with the comments one hears and reads about such vessels. There are places where you can read that a skipjack—or a Friendship sloop, pinky, or Block Island boat, for that matter—is a phenomenally fast type, or incapable of taking solid water on deck, or amazingly weatherly, and so forth.

There are also places where you can read that the fine sailing qualities of these same types have been grossly exaggerated and that, if the truth be known, they really have great difficulty getting out of their own way.

I did not expect my skipjack to be a particularly fast example of the type. Since she was a small boat for dredging oysters, a good deal of attention had to be paid to her carrying capacity. Her beam-to-length ratio was the highest of any skipjack whose dimensions I have seen.

I expected she would fall between the extremes of the predictions of her admirers and her detractors, and of course she did. But if her general ability under sail did not surprise me, some of her particular traits did.

She was surprisingly fast to windward in a light air, surprisingly slow running and reaching in a moderate breeze, and—to my unceasing amazement—would steer herself on any point of sailing in any strength of wind I had her out in, provided the wind was reasonably steady and the seas were reasonably regular.

In a really light air, when everybody had bare steerageway, I found that to windward she would hold her own with most yachts her size. I think this was due to her large sail area (900 square feet), the fact that her very drafty sails were well suited to that particular condition, and the fact that her tremendous hull resistance (large wetted surface of rough cross-planking and big, solid, three-bladed wheel) didn't matter too much at very low speed.

Reaching and running in a moderate breeze, she should have been reasonably fast, but her hull resistance, increased by considerable weather helm, evidently held her back.

She didn't come alive and start to go and feel right until it was blowing over twenty knots. This is not true of most skipjacks, of course. I recall running in about a fifteen-knot breeze in the *Robert L. Webster*, a sixty-footer, and being amazed at how fast she went.

The self-steering business fascinated me. With her long boom and great tendency to round up when heeled (her shallow, vee shape meant a small change in heel caused a relatively large change in the balance of the immersed hull), she carried plenty of weather helm. Off the wind, her long boom gave her plenty of turning moment and, if really pressed in a breeze, she balanced with the helm nearly hard over. But she balanced!

It was the oddest feeling to sail along with no one at the helm, the wheel nearly hard over, and the outboard rudder damming up a huge pile of water under the lee quarter to cancel out the forces trying to round her up. As long as conditions of wind and wave held steady, that skipjack held steady.

She balanced, too, on the wind, of course. She also would steer herself under power, with a bit of left rudder put on to compensate for the port-side wheel.

I puzzled over her extreme steadiness, being reluctant to lay it all to the straight line of thirty-six feet from her forefoot to the after end of the rudder. Then I realized that the skipjack, by coincidence, had the same dimensions as Joshua Slocum's *Spray*, except that the *Spray* was a bit deeper. The vast beam was there in both boats, and both boats had the extremely broad transom. The wide bearing the hull carried all the way to the stern evidently resists yawing.

At any rate, my credulity for Slocum's self-steering tales increased greatly.

Perhaps three events from the log of my skipjack are worth mentioning.

After the first spring haul-out for painting, I decided reluctantly that the practical thing to do would be to take out the defunct engine and put in one that might run. I had located a Gray 4-162 that a waterman was retiring from his tonger—nobody seemed to know how old this engine was, but it hadn't rusted out yet—and since the same model machine would be coming off the beds, the hook-up would be straightforward.

Thus the morning of April 23, 1964, found me preparing to get underway from Arcady Semenoff's Yard in Warehouse Creek on the South River, Annapolis, where she had been hauled and painted, to sail around to the East-port Marina on Back Creek, where the "new" engine would be installed, a distance of all of ten miles. I was sailing her alone and expected to make the run in a couple or three hours.

To quote from the log:

23 April. Went aboard at 0900. Bent jib, rigging jib halyard and jib lazy jacks halyard aloft, man from the yard hoisting me up. Underway at 1300 under "tow" of yard man rowing in skiff. When clear in the creek, set mainsail and jib. Cast off skiff. Beat out of the creek in baffling light airs. Had to drop the anchor which I had rigged on the bowsprit to keep off the bank when a puff prevented her tacking. Finally got clear and commenced beating down the South River into a gentle SSE breeze. Hit the centerboard off Poplar Point and in clearing it, carried away the lanyard, leaving the board full down, but apparently none the worse for wear. Later discovered the lanyard had parted right at the edge of the board; rigged a line right under the hull using a splitting wedge for sinker and could use it to raise and lower the board. Off Mayo Point, wind fell light. Lost steerage way and anchored on flats (depth six feet) about two miles west of Thomas Point Light at 1700. Left sails standing. Faint air struck in from SE at 1900. Got underway, made about one-half mile, getting into deeper water, and was becalmed again. Anchored and dropped sails at 1930. Turned in. Turned out at 2130, gentle breeze from SE. Got underway on mainsail. Pleasant going, "conning" from the main hatch, boat steering herself, full moon throwing a lot of light through a thin layer of clouds. Cut inside Thomas Point Light and ran down to Tolly Point buoy. Then jibed over and steered for Greenbury Point. Breeze increased, then fell light at Greenbury Point and died off Back Creek. Anchored and dropped the sail at 2330.

24 April. Underway on mainsail at 0530. Gentle NE breeze sprang up. Ran into Back Creek and tied up at the Eastport Marina. While warping into a berth clomped around on a motor boat's decks with my lines thinking she was uninhabited. Up comes the captain in his undershirt and gives me, "What the hell are you doing?" I told him and said I was sorry I'd woken him up at 0600. He ended up putting on his jacket and coming out into a

light rain that was just starting, to help me tie her up. Berthed right beside my "new" engine sitting on the dock ready to come aboard.

In the summer of 1966, I finally became sufficiently worried about the few rotten places in the vessel to want to take serious action. Not that I had a yachtsman's philosophy about the boat. I had come to recognize the great good sense of the Bay watermen, who, when thinking about the condition of their skipjacks, concentrate their attention on the good wood. The boats are heavily built, and a little rot won't weaken them.

But there does come that point at which things can't be allowed to go on. So on July 18, I took her round to Fishing Creek, picked my way through its shallow, unfamiliar entrance with considerable help from a wildly gesticulating powerboat man who was kindly concerned over the fact I was about to run her into six inches of water, and dropped the heavy anchor off the small, neat wharf of Walter Tyler. Walter is a waterman who had agreed to pull up some soft deck, replace the four-by-four beams beneath, and lay new deck. There was also a new piece to go into the house forward on the port side, and the top plank of the transom had to be renewed on the starboard side.

I was to help Walter when I could and scrape and slush down the mast while she was there. Thus began three weeks of some of the best days I had with the boat.

Working with Walter was an education. He pushed himself hard, and the day I started scraping the mast at seven, he gave me to understand he'd be a bit disappointed in me if it turned out to take me more than one day. So we stuck at it, me going up the mast foot by foot in the boatswain's chair, scraping as I went, and Walter down on deck prying large quantities of rotten wood out of the boat.

As soon as I got up a little way, the shavings started blowing back all over the boat on the light morning land breeze that was stirring. Although Walter's efforts promised to make a mess of her anyway, I lamented to him about having to litter the deck with my mast shavings.

He said, "When we scrape the mast, we anchor off the stern."

The wisdom of this simple expedient was plain, so I let myself back down to the deck to help him take the anchor rode aft. For the rest of the day, only the heaviest, orneriest shavings were able to keep themselves from being blown over the bow, from which they made a thin trail straight down the creek.

Walter got about a ton of spongy stuff out of her, and he was mighty clever about the way he sneaked the waterway plank out from under the bulwarks—"waists," he called them—without disturbing things. He simply cut off the lags that went down through everything.

"We'll put new ones in after," he said.

He got a lot done that day, and I could hardly quit and disappoint him, so I scraped the whole mast in twelve hours, a job I usually stretched over at least two full weekends.

Yet for all the work Walter did, he missed nothing that occurred during the day within his sight or hearing. He was always stopping halfway through a saw cut and looking around, like a teacher writing at the blackboard who stops in mid-word and spins around, hoping to catch mischief red-handed. Thus would Walter pace himself, while at the same time keeping up on all the affairs of his world.

When the long day's work was done, Walter

The skipjack as she appeared in about 1953 going out to dredge oysters.

paddled me ashore in his skiff, standing in the bow and working his oar on one side of the boat only, as if he were stalking a crab. The boat went straight, without much effort, and not too slowly, either.

Ashore, he invited me to sit with him a bit, till dark, on a rough bench that had a thick tree-trunk for a backrest. Then he started telling about the old days on the Bay, and I wished I had a built-in tape recorder.

The third item from the log is perhaps worth sharing simply because it may give sailors some measure of the complete satisfaction it gave me. On July 26, 1967, five of us "young men" started out about 1830 for an evening sail to see what she would do with a fresh southeaster. With a reefed mainsail and full jib, we beat down the South River and out into the Bay. Well pleased with the way she handled the big chop, we turned to run back up the river at dusk.

Off Harness Creek, we were hailed by a power-boat, lying to. We rounded up and luffed along-side to learn that the fellow was broken down—"I think it's the fuel pump." He asked if we had an engine and could tow him up the river to his dock.

We answered both questions in the affirmative, passed him a line, and paid her off to start the tow. I guess he expected us to start the engine, but with a fresh breeze, towing a twenty-five-foot powerboat was easy work for a skipjack. We proceeded at a majestic four knots, and I enjoyed every foot of the two miles.

Always did want to bring in a disabled power-boat under sail.

When we were moving to Maine, it came time to sell the skipjack. We advertised her in the *National Fisherman* and received a lot of inquiries. One fellow, a producer of television shows from Ipswich, Massachusetts, came to see her early in the game. He really appreciated her and said she was his kind of boat. Beyond that, he was noncommittal.

The two young couples from Washington, D.C., who threatened to form a syndicate to buy her and went for a trial sail with me, fell in love with her, and were amazed at how easily she handled. But then they went and bought another boat.

The doctor from Connecticut wanted her very badly and his son coveted that skiff. But they already had quite a fleet and finally decided she was just too much to add to it.

The retired Army colonel and his wife thought she'd be an ideal retirement home in Florida. I was dubious about that, but took them for a trial sail anyway. We beat down the river into a moderate breeze. Mrs. Colonel complained that her proposed retirement home didn't tip enough when sailing. My offers to take tire-kickers sailing declined sharply.

Then the TV fellow came back. He arrived at noon on the day we were to leave at five. You might say he had me over a barrel, but, being a gentleman, he didn't press his advantage too hard. He did ask a lot of questions about her condition and what had to be done to maintain her.

I dutifully pointed out the few soft spots in her that I knew about. We discussed various ways of replacing this or that member, when and if the need should arise.

Over a late sandwich, with the clock moving in-exorably toward the hour of our departure, we discussed the possibility of his buying the skip-jack. The casual conversation came around to how he would get her to Ipswich, just supposing he should end up in possession of the vessel.

"I think the thing to do would be to put up a couple of A-frames on deck, get Bobby Orme to lift the stick out and lay it across them so she'd go under the low bridges, and run her up inside under power."

"You wouldn't sail her up outside?"

I hesitated. "Well, you know these boats were really developed for the Bay here, not for the ocean," I said gently.

His reaction was quick. "You really don't think it would be safe to sail that skipjack up outside?" he said, his voice rising. His look of anguish told me I must have said something wrong, something that offended him. No, worse; I had said something he thought was against the boat.

It was then I realized she was no longer mine.

12/ The *Roaring Bessie*

Length on deck: 34 feet
Length on waterline: 30 feet
Beam: 12 feet on deck; 10 feet at waterline
Draft: 5 feet

Block Island lies ten miles straight out from the long sand beach that stretches from Point Judith to Watch Hill Point, Rhode Island. It is a place where the sou'wester seems to grow to nearly gale proportions every summer afternoon and where the northwest and northeast gales of winter howl across open water. Island boat-builders always had to bring out their timber from the mainland; the trees on Block Island don't grow very tall.

In the old days, there was no harbor at Block Island. A bight with a shelving beach on the east side of the island was used as a landing place. It provided a lee in southwesterly or northwesterly weather, but if the wind went into the east and blew at all, any boats moored bow and stern to stakes off the landing place had to be brought in and hauled up the beach with oxen, no matter the hour of day or night.

Around 1870, breakwaters were built to fence off a small area of the landing place and make it into a snug harbor. Some years later, a cut was dredged through into Great Salt Pond on the northwest side of the island, transforming the

pond into a large, deep, landlocked harbor, one of the best on the coast.

But when the Block Islanders were building boats in which they could fish ever farther from the island, and in which they could carry people and goods back and forth to the mainland, one of the requirements was that the boats be suitable for landing on and launching from the beach.

The boat that the islanders developed was a stout, beamy double-ender with Scandinavian heritage. The boats had great flare, very low free-board amidships, and such a strong sheer and such high ends that they earned the nickname "cowhorns." They ran from sixteen feet to forty feet long on deck and were always built lap-strake.

The rig of the Block Island boat was strictly Dutch, being a cat schooner, with overlapping lug foresail, loose-footed mainsail, and short gaffs hoisted on a single halyard.

The immediate American ancestor of the Block Island boat was the Chebacco boat, an open double-ender used for fishing along the northern

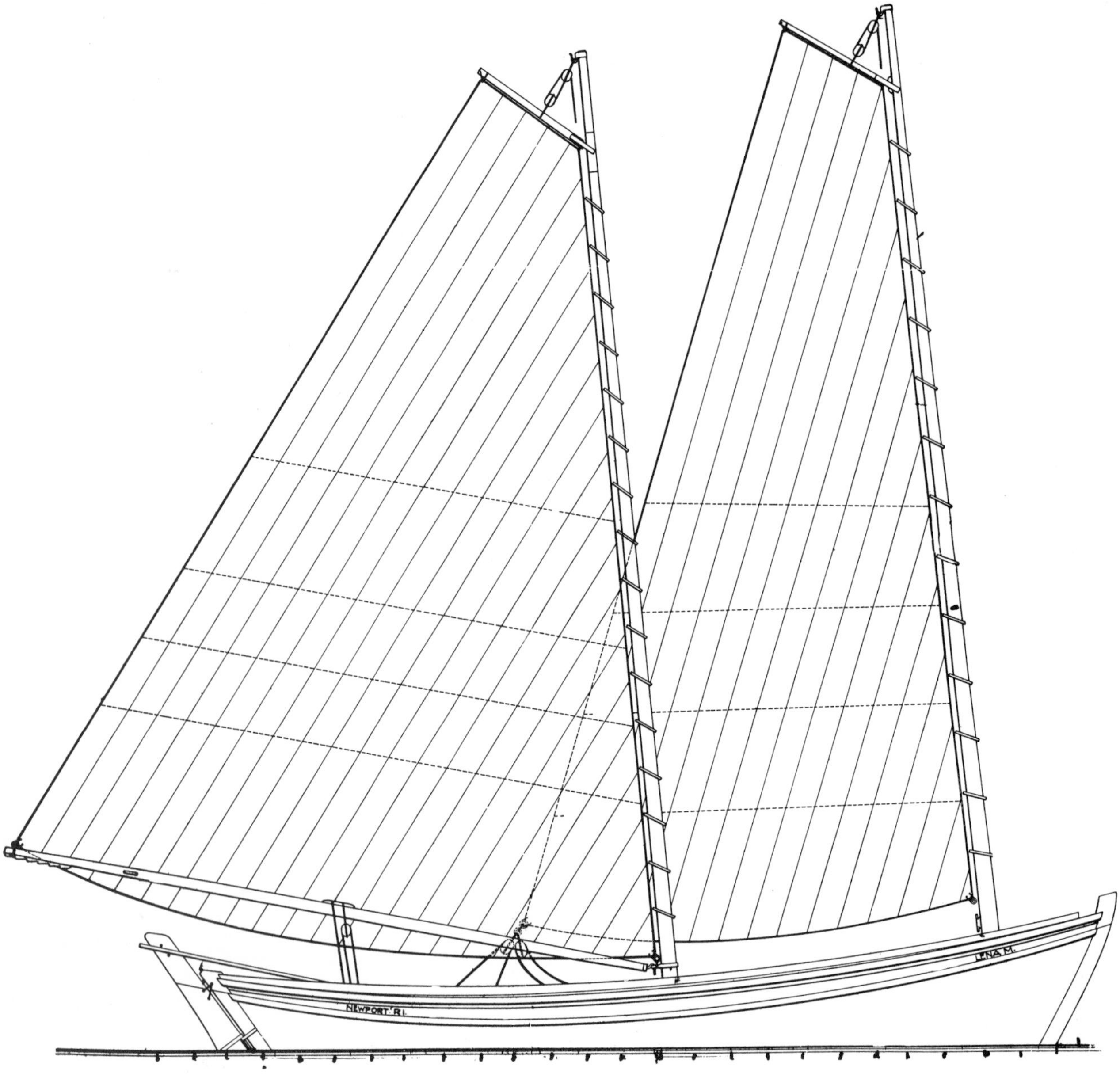

The sail plan of the *Lena M.*, and hence of her replica, the *Roaring Bessie*, is pure Holland. Her many reefs were used often, for this was a boat that loved to tiptoe through a big seaway, but hated to be driven. (*Rudder* Magazine, © April, 1912, Fawcett Publications, Inc.)

New England coast and so named because many were built at Chebacco, later Essex, Massachusetts.

In the heyday of the Block Island boat, around 1875, some sixty of the craft were in use at the island. They earned a great reputation for seakindliness and downright ability in a big breeze and rough water.

The example shown here is the *Lena M.*, easily the handsomest of the handful of the type whose lines have been taken off and preserved. She was 34 feet long on deck, 30 feet on the waterline, with a beam of 12 feet on deck and 10 feet at the waterline, and a draft of 5 feet.

The lines show the hull of a wonderfully balanced sea boat of great buoyancy. Block Island boats had a very lively motion, but they seldom took solid water on deck. The Block Island boats were ballasted with beach stones, as shown in the construction plan. This kept the

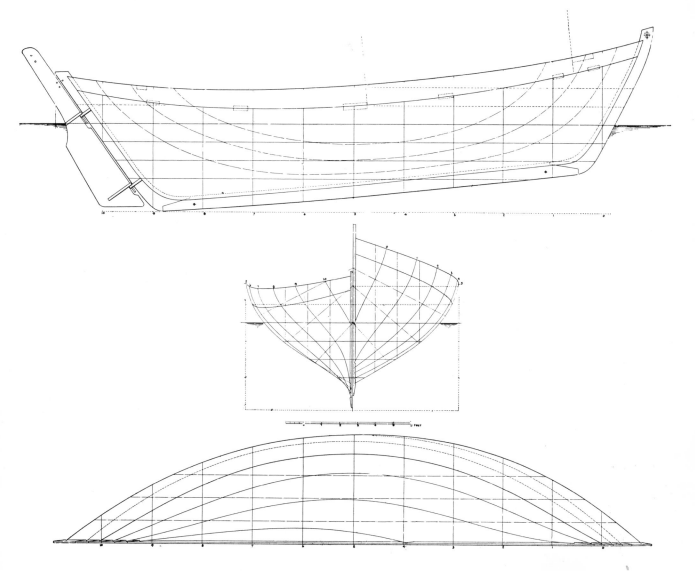

The lines of the *Lena M.* show a well-balanced, seakindly hull of Scandinavian lineage. (*Rudder* Magazine, © April, 1912, Fawcett Publications, Inc.)

motion from being violent, and the ballast was clean, easily swapped for fish or cargo, and cheaply replaced.

With their well-balanced ends and long, straight keels, the boats had considerable self-steering ability. A tiller comb shows in the deck plan. The tiller could be set between pegs on the comb and left unattended while the skipper, often sailing shorthanded, went forward to attend to some little thing. Or, when tacking, the tiller could be held hard alee in the comb so she would sail around onto the other tack while the helmsman helped shift the big foresail over.

While the *Lena M.* was decked over, the smaller and earlier Block Island boats were open except for a very short deck at each end. With such low freeboard, water would slosh in over the lee rail when sailing to windward in a seaway, and temporary washboards were usually fitted, held by pegs in the gunwale. The low freeboard made the boats handy for fishing and for rowing, for long oars were used in a calm.

Typical construction for a Block Island boat of the *Lena M.*'s size was keel and frames of oak or larch, the frames being two inches square and spaced on thirteen-inch centers. Some builders bent their frames; others sawed them out. The planking was typically ⅞-inch cedar. The boats

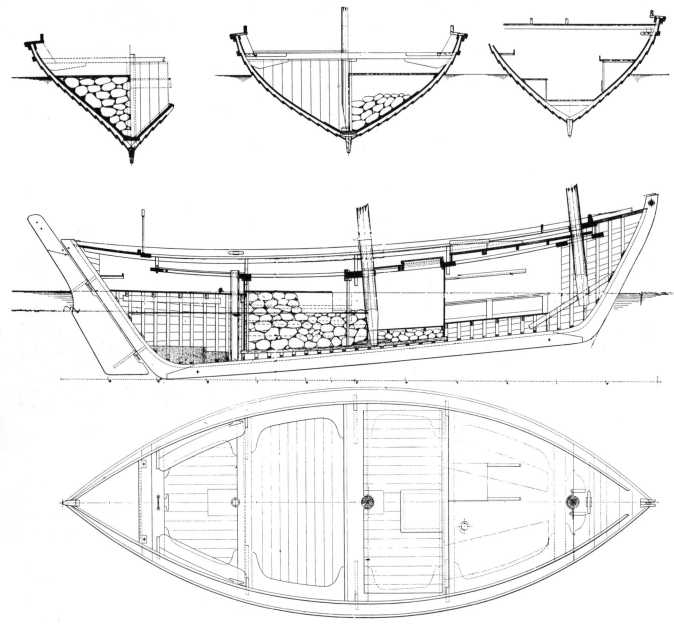

The *Lena M.*'s construction plan indicates the great space she has on deck, her cramped quarters below, and the arrangement of her beach-stone ballast. (*Rudder* Magazine, © April, 1912, Fawcett Publications, Inc.)

were usually painted with dark green topsides set off by the gunwale and perhaps the rubbing strake picked out in black or white.

The Dutch rig seems appropriate to the Block Island boat, since the island is named for Adriaen Block, the Dutch explorer who rediscovered it in 1614. The boats carried no standing rigging whatsoever. The masts had a straight taper and were thin enough near the top to be quite springy. They were generally made of spruce. The mainmast was set almost exactly amidships.

In the smaller, open version of these boats, the mast partners were hinged iron collars so that the masts could be unstepped handily when the boats were hauled out on the beach.

The Block Island boats were not big sail carriers. They had to be reefed down early as it breezed on, but then they drove along easily under reduced sail. The boats had to be used for livelihood and basic transportation in most any weather, so what was needed and achieved was a craft that would handle easily and safely in heavy

The *Roaring Bessie* living up to her name on a beam reach. (*Rudder* Magazine, © April, 1912, Fawcett Publications, Inc.)

The *Bessie* showing off her broad beam. (*Rudder* Magazine, © April, 1912, Fawcett Publications, Inc.)

going. There was no thought of driving these boats through heavy seas. The idea was to ease the boat along, giving with the biggest seas and heaviest gusts and taking from the smooths and lulls.

The *Lena M.*'s sail plan shows four reefs in each sail. Most of the Block Island boats had a fifth reef in the foresail. The *Lena M.* had 400 square feet in the mainsail and 300 square feet in the foresail. Each sail, quadruple reefed, would show 120 square feet.

The foresail must have been a brute to handle. It would seem logical to use a come-along tackle on the hauling part of the two-part foresail sheet. It would be a temptation—but a great mistake—to shorten the foot of the foresail and give it a boom to make it self-tending. The boat just wouldn't sail well without that overlapping foresail.

It would also seem logical to get one part of the mainsheet farther aft on the boom. One solution was to put an oval traveler through the top of the sternpost, making a wide enough circle

In 1936, the *Bessie* got a leg-o'-mutton sloop rig. (*Yachting*, January, 1937)

up around the tiller to allow it plenty of freedom. This traveler could then take another mainsheet block working with a block farther aft on the boom so as to get a better purchase on that spar for trimming the big mainsail.

It would be good to carry a pole to boom out the foresail when chasing away before the wind.

The Block Island boat is a fascinating craft, and more complete descriptions of the type can be found in Charles G. Davis' *Ships of the Past* and E. P. Morris' *The Fore and Aft Rig in America.*

Martin C. Erismann was a yachtsman of means with a strong interest in the small working craft indigenous to the East Coast. He bought the *Lena M.* at Block Island in 1910 and sailed her home to Marblehead. His intention was to rejuvenate her, but when the yard began picking out her soft insides, the picking went on and on and on. It was clear that a rebuilding job would really result in more of a replica than in a repaired *Lena M.* Accordingly, Erismann decided to let the *Lena M.* go and to build a replica from scratch.

The great Lawley yard at Neponset, Massachusetts, built for Erismann an exact replica of the *Lena M.*, except that the boat was carvel-planked instead of being lapstrake. When she was launched in 1911, she was christened the *Roaring Bessie.* Erismann sailed her as a yacht for several seasons. She was most successful and created quite a stir wherever she went.

Her only drawback was the rather cramped accommodation. The uncrowned forward deck of the Block Island boats had, of course, been reproduced exactly in the *Roaring Bessie*, with the result that the cuddy forward had four feet of headroom, and the galley just abaft it had but three feet. The latter situation was improved by a large hatch and a stool on casters. (I wonder what the top speed of the stool was in a seaway.)

One day fifteen years ago, when I was "supervising" harbor activities along the Annapolis waterfront, I looked up to see a most ablelooking double-ended sloop turning into the harbor from the Severn River. Her rig and house were conventional, but her hull certainly was not. In fact, she looked astonishingly like a Block Island boat between the waterline and the rail. The reason became clear when she passed close enough for me to read her name on the quarter: *Roaring Bessie.*

So the old girl was alive and well and living in nearby Whitehall Creek. And with a leg-o'-mutton sloop rig! I wondered what Martin Erismann or the old-timers on Block Island would have thought of that. I didn't think much of it at first, but further observation of *Bessie* led me to realize that her conversion had been done in a practical and intelligent way.

There was the time we were about to start a race from Annapolis to Newport in an ancient and wonderful Herreshoff sloop when we discovered minutes before the start that there was not a drop of fuel on board for the stove. Since we didn't relish the idea of waiting three days for the next hot meal, we looked around for someone from whom we might beg some kerosene. The *Roaring Bessie* was jogging along nearby, out watching the start of the race. We went close aboard, and her owner, Bob Bates, kindly tossed over a couple of cans of the wanted liquid. *Bessie*, with her rich heritage and long experience, seemed to take in these shenanigans with a knowing smile. She probably only allowed her skipper to give away some of her stove fuel because the thoroughbred that came ranging alongside was six years her senior.

Above: Sailing on the Chesapeake Bay in 1975 with her present sloop rig. (Photo by David Q. Scott)

Right: David Scott, the *Bessie*'s owner, can see her on her mooring from his front porch. (Photo by David Q. Scott)

One pleasant spring afternoon when Bob Bates was dressing *Bessie* up for the summer, I had the pleasure of going over the boat with him. It was then that I noticed how snug and practical the sloop rig was. The center of effort had been kept quite low; the rig was a modest one.

It turns out there were two rig changes made to the *Bessie* between her original Block Island boat rig and her present sloop rig. In 1924, John Alden designed a normal schooner rig for her, and in 1936, V. Mindeleff, Jr., took her to the lower Potomac River and put in a double-head leg-o'-mutton sloop rig with an overhanging boom. The *Bessie*'s present rig has a single headsail and short boom with permanent backstay.

The cabin house had been added sometime in the Thirties. It certainly increased the usefulness of the boat for cruising. Aft is a comfortable saloon with transoms port and starboard, each with a folding berth above. Next forward are a head to starboard and lockers to port. The galley is all the way forward. There is full headroom throughout! It seems an admirable rig for extensive cruising for two people. I might have made the house a bit shorter to allow somewhat more generous deck space aft.

The *Roaring Bessie* is now owned, I am happy to say, by my good friend David Q. Scott. David keeps her tied up right in front of his house on Mill Creek (the next one to Whitehall, near Annapolis) and takes good care of the great old girl between cruises.

In one of the Scott family's recent Christmas cards, David sketched her on a wintry spin on Mill Creek. (Drawn by David Q. Scott)

13/ The *West Island*

Length on deck: 30 feet 10 inches
Length on waterline: 30 feet 1 inch
Beam: 11 feet 6 inches on deck; 10 feet 3 inches at waterline
Draft: 3 feet 4 inches
Designer: Christopher Briggs

The centerboard double-ender *West Island* was built at Westport, Massachusetts, by Christopher Briggs about 1892 for use as a tender for a "fishing camp" on tiny West Island, just off Sakonnet Point, Rhode Island. Briggs built the boat from a model he had carved. His inspiration was the Block Island boat, but he had to make his double-ender with less draft than these craft, for she had to be able to tuck in close to West Island in shoal water. In the process, he took the rake out of the stem and sternpost by comparison with the Block Island boat, and the West Island was said to have a "catboat bow" and a "Norwegian stern." But with the shoaler draft model, he really just needed to straighten up the bow and stern to increase the lateral resistance of the forefoot and deadwood areas.

But if the *West Island*'s profile ended up looking quite different from that of a Block Island boat, her sections show clearly the Block Island influence. She has a very similar hull form to that of the Block Island boat, but with the draft, freeboard, and flare all reduced somewhat.

The *West Island* is 30 feet 10 inches long on deck, 30 feet 1 inch long on the waterline, with a beam on deck of 11 feet 6 inches, a beam at the waterline of 10 feet 3 inches, and a draft of 3 feet 4 inches with the board up. Her freeboard is 3 feet 7 inches at the bow, 2 feet 5 inches aft, and she has a minimum freeboard of 1 foot 10 inches. The ballast is 2½ tons, all inside.

She is planked with cedar on oak frames with galvanized fastenings. Her masts are Oregon pine.

It is interesting to compare the lines of the *West Island* with those of the *Lena M.* in the preceding chapter. Like the *Lena*, the *West Island* would depend on her ample beam, considerable weight of inside ballast and flare in the topsides for stability.

Some well-known sailors owned this boat when she had done tending her fishing camp. Sam Wetherill said that under her cat ketch rig (shown in the photo of her at anchor), she had quite a strong weather helm. He also said it was hard to shorten sail and still keep the boat balanced. It would have taken considerable reefing to achieve this, to be sure.

Hank Meneely added a bowsprit and a jib about 1922, and he told me this change greatly improved her performance to windward.

Bill Dyer gave her the Marconi ketch rig of 514 square feet shown in the photo, taken in about

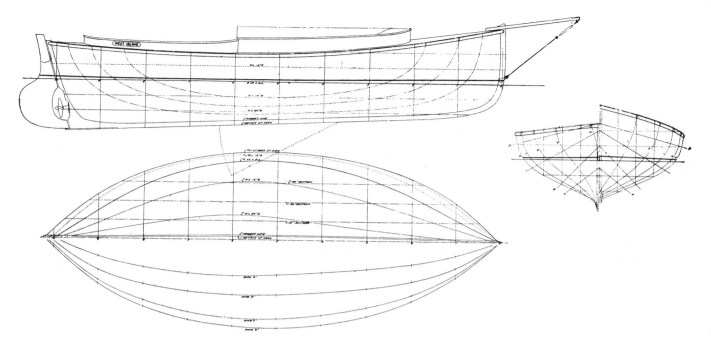

The lines of the *West Island*, a centerboard double-ender inspired by the Block Island boat. The lines were taken off the boat by W.F. McNary of John G. Alden's office. (*Yachting*, May, 1927)

1926. He said she would sail well under jib and mizzen, or under the mainsail alone, but I'd expect her to carry weather helm with jib and mizzen unless the mizzen were reefed.

Meneely's sail plan was probably the best one; it's often a mistake to put tall sails on a wide, shoal hull to try to make her weatherly. A hull like that of the *West Island* seems to go best to windward by cracking off a little and footing fast, so that if the rig is an especially close-winded one, that particular capability is rather wasted.

Wetherill said the *West Island* was an excellent rough-water boat, that she went to windward well, and that she had the easiest motion of any boat her size he ever was in. He also praised her for sailing on her bottom and for her self-steering capabilities.

Dyer was even more lavish in his praise of the boat's ability to sail herself. He said she'd steer

Left: The *West Island* at anchor with her original rig. (*Yachting*, May, 1927)

Right: Bill Dyer put a modern, jib-headed ketch rig in her. (*Yachting*, May, 1927)

herself dead before it, wing and wing, until the sea ran in from the quarter to throw her off. The counterbalancing characteristic to this extreme steadiness on the helm was that she was rather slow in stays.

When Sam Wetherill had the *West Island*, a two-cylinder, two-cycle, 16-h.p. Lathrop was installed under a box in the cockpit. It swung a big three-bladed wheel. Hank Meneely took out the engine, removed the wheel, and closed up the aperture.

Bill Dyer put in a Ford engine turning a two-bladed, twenty-inch wheel with a twelve-inch pitch. This combination was reported to have driven her at 7½ m.p.h.

There is no accommodation plan available for the *West Island*, but I can quote Bill Dyer's excellent description of her arrangement:

To starboard of the centerboard as one enters the cabin are hooks for wet oilskins against a clothes press where one can hang (on hangers) six suits of clothes and keep them dry. Next comes a cushioned berth with lockers above for everything but the kitchen stove (and that's to port). Next forward, a real spring built-in berth, thirty inches wide and six feet eight inches long with a reading light overhead and a shelf alongside for "junk." Curtained off over the foot of these forward berths is a shelf running the width of the boat for stowing suitcases, light sails and "duffle." Abaft the port berth, which duplicates that just described, is a cushioned seat with a coal locker under. The medicine locker acts as a back rest, container and shelf. The Shipmate takes up the after end of this section and has a wood locker under. Let me say here that charcoal briquettes and a coal stove are a hard combination to beat for real service on a boat. Next comes the sink with plenty of space underneath for pots and pans. A cover fits over the sink, making a good sized dresser, and running water is supplied by gravity from a 20-gallon copper tank strapped to the under side of the deck in the chain locker and filled from the deck. Abaft this is the toilet, which may be curtained off from the remainder of the cabin. Last but not least is a real "he-man" refrigerator with room for everything from soup to nuts. The port hatch over the toilet compartment allows ice to be placed in the box directly from the deck.

On the after end of the centerboard box is constructed a built-in radio that can get Chile on cold nights and Newark on hot ones. The aerial consists of one wire from main mast to mizzen above the spring stay, thence down the mizzen into the cabin. Taking her by and large, she's very comfortable.

14/ The *Tidal Wave*

> Length on deck: 32 feet 4 inches
> Length on waterline: 31 feet
> Beam: 11 feet on deck; 10 feet on waterline
> Draft: 5 feet
> Sail area: 659 square feet
> Displacement: 10½ tons
> Designer: Philip L. Rhodes

What is it that's so intriguing about a double-ended boat? It may be the thought of her seaworthiness, for the sharp stern seems well able to cope with a following sea, and, with little turbulence in the wake, such a sea is less likely to be disturbed into breaking. It may be the symmetry of line that many double-enders have, often with attendant self-steering qualities. Or it may simply be the notion of that pointed stern slipping easily through the water, leaving scarcely a trace of its passage.

Whatever the factors, the intrigue has been experienced by boatmen through the ages. It was evidently experienced by Samuel Wetherill, one of the owners of the shoal-draft double-ender *West Island*, which was described in the preceding chapter.

Wetherill, who thought the *West Island* was about the best boat around, decided he wanted a keel version of her. He commissioned Philip L. Rhodes to make the modification to the *West Island*'s design.

The new boat, the *Tidal Wave*, was made about one foot longer on the waterline than the *West Island*, just to get a little more room inside. At the same time, Rhodes reduced the beam by six

inches to keep the bulk of the boat down, since she would be deeper. Besides adding the keel, he increased the depth of the hull by two inches, so the new boat had more deadrise than the old. He increased the freeboard by three inches to gain headroom in the cabin. Freeboard was still moderate, for the *West Island* was quite a low-sided boat.

When Rhodes looked at his lines, after these basic changes to the *West Island*'s design had been made, he was less than happy with what he saw. The boat had a strange, pinched appearance.

Rhodes opined to Wetherill that it might not be possible to take one set of fair lines, make basic, even though not drastic, changes to the dimensions, and end up with a new fair set of lines. Wetherill was smart enough to catch the implication. He told the designer to go ahead and make the *Tidal Wave* a Rhodes boat.

Given a free hand, Phil Rhodes went to work. He raised the stern a bit, swelled out the deck line a little both fore and aft, and then fussed and faired until she looked just right. The *Tidal Wave* is certainly a close cousin of the *West Island*, but she is also unquestionably a Phil Rhodes design.

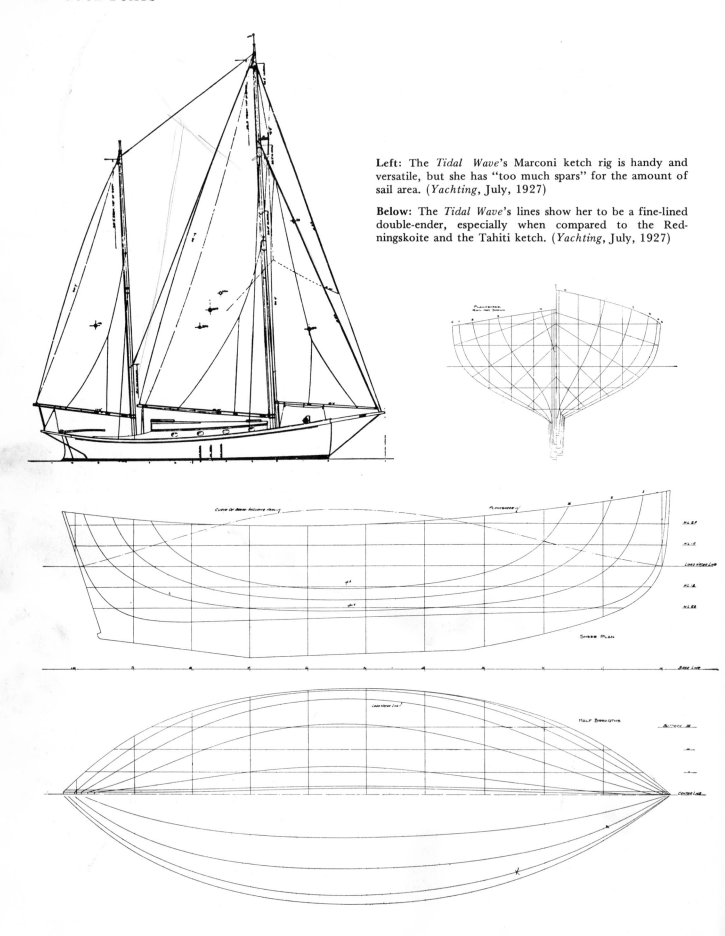

Left: The *Tidal Wave*'s Marconi ketch rig is handy and versatile, but she has "too much spars" for the amount of sail area. (*Yachting*, July, 1927)

Below: The *Tidal Wave*'s lines show her to be a fine-lined double-ender, especially when compared to the Redningskoite and the Tahiti ketch. (*Yachting*, July, 1927)

This boat has an admirable hull form for ocean cruising, as well as for coastwise work, in my opinion. It is interesting to compare her lines against those of two similar, but more famous, ocean cruising types, the Redningskoïte, or Norwegian sailing lifeboat, designed by Colin Archer, and the Tahiti ketch, designed by John G. Hanna.

A comparison of the waterlines of these three double-enders is revealing. The rotundity of waterline seen in the Redningskoïte and Tahiti ketch is not to be found in the *Tidal Wave.* By comparison with her pleasingly plump, popular sisters, poor *Tidal Wave* is "all ends."

Poor *Tidal Wave*? With hope that my lightning rods are in good working order, I dare to say that the *Tidal Wave* would sail rings round both these great designs of Archer and Hanna. The *Tidal Wave* must, of course, sacrifice something to the Redningskoïte and the Tahiti ketch in return for her speed. I think the sacrifice would be in carrying capacity (which can certainly be important on a long cruise), but I doubt there is any sacrifice in seaworthiness.

Ah, you say, but of what use is speed when crossing an ocean under sail? Well, I have to admit that since the days of competitive carrying of fish to market, harbor piloting, and tea hauling under sail, speed at sea in a sailing craft has more spiritual than practical value. But just why is it we want to sail across an ocean in a traditional boat of ancient heritage? Certainly there are more practical ways to cross today.

All back full! This book is supposed to be about boats, not anthropology. (But if you happen to be interested in both small boats and what they mean to men, you might go to the library and take out J. R. L. Anderson's *The Ulysses Factor*, as well as T. C. Lethbridge's *Boats and Boatmen*.)

It is interesting also to compare the performance of the *Tidal Wave* with that of her predecessor, the *West Island*. Bill Dyer, who had owned the *West Island* and who sailed with Wetherill in the *Tidal Wave*, had this to say:

"*Tidal Wave*, in comparison with *West Island*, is far closer-winded, stiffer, and seems to carry headway better through a short, steep sea when on the wind. Off the wind, *West Island* may be a bit faster, and makes less fuss forward. On every other point, *Wave* is *West Island*'s superior."

Wetherill admitted that the *Tidal Wave* didn't steer herself quite as well as had the *West Island*. This was probably because the deadwood had been cut away a bit to make her a bit handier in stays.

The *Tidal Wave* was built during the winter of 1929-30 at the Minneford Yacht Yard, City Island, New York. She must have been a relatively easy shape to build.

The boat's dimensions are: length on deck, 32 feet 4 inches; length on the waterline, 31 feet; beam on deck, 11 feet; beam at the waterline, 10 feet; draft, 5 feet; displacement, 10½ tons; and sail area, 659 square feet, not counting the jib topsail. She has 6,000 pounds of ballast on the keel, and another 1,500 pounds inside.

The *Tidal Wave*'s backbone and frames are all of oak. Her knees are hackmatack. She has 1⅛-inch yellow pine planking and canvas-covered, 1⅛-inch pine decks. She is fastened with galvanized nails.

The Marconi ketch rig has always impressed me as being a lot of mast for the amount of sail you get. The rig was a favorite of L. Francis Herreshoff, but most of his ketches were moderate-displacement craft that were exceptionally easily driven and so didn't need a large sail plan. He could keep his mast heights quite reasonable. On the *Tidal Wave*, I'd prefer to see a gaff mainsail.

The *Tidal Wave*'s rig certainly looks handy, though. For one thing, she could balance very well under mainsail alone, which is an exceedingly useful characteristic in a boat if you're going to do a lot of knocking around the coast.

After the boat was sailed, running backstays were added to both masts, but these were only set up as preventers in a lumpy sea or unusually hard breeze. There are no sheets to tend when tacking, once the jib topsail is taken in, and all the working sails have lazy jacks.

Wetherill's mainsheet lead is worth noting. This is a rig borrowed from working craft, where the ability to put a man's weight on the sheet is appreciated. Rigged this way, the sheet can also be swayed in with a turn on the cleat, much as one often sets up a halyard.

Wetherill's "Mule," as he called the sprit topsail he set between the *Tidal Wave*'s masts, is also worth looking at. He may have borrowed the sail from Ralph M. Munroe, who may have borrowed it from local workboats he saw sailing around

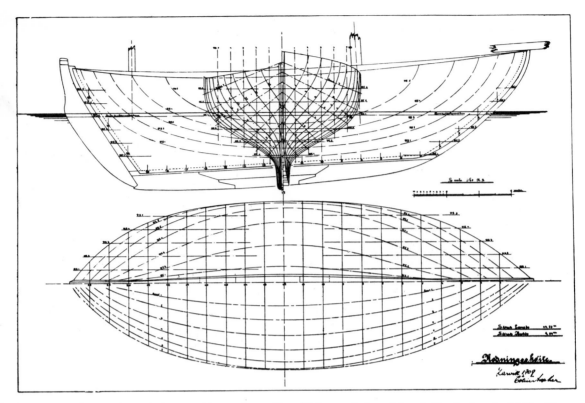

Above: The lines of a Redningskoite, or Norwegian sailing lifeboat, designed by Colin Archer in 1909. (*Fore and Aft Craft and Their Story* by E. Keble Chatterton)

Below: The lines of a Tahiti ketch designed by John G. Hanna in 1923. (*How to Build Tahiti* by Steve Doherty, Seven Seas Press)

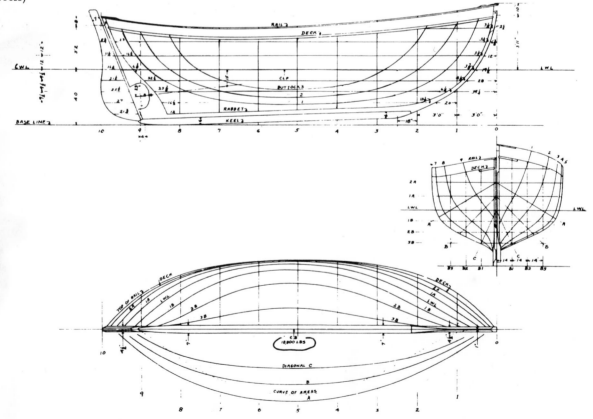

southern islands. The sail sets to windward of the mainsail. It must be taken in and reset when the vessel changes tacks. Its area is up high, where a light sail should be.

The *Tidal Wave*'s auxiliary engine was placed farther aft than is shown in the arrangement plan, both to make better use of the space in her deep-sectioned stern and to enable the mizzenmast to be stepped on the keel. The engine is a Gray 4-30. There is a twenty-five-gallon gas tank strapped up under the deck in the after peak. She has a feathering 17-inch-by-9-inch wheel.

The arrangement shows a reversal of the most common layout used in craft of this size, with the galley being moved forward and the two bunks coming aft. The advantages of this arrangement are that it gives the cook a place of his own to work in and it probably makes the best possible use of the space back in the quarters of the boat. The disadvantage is that there is more

motion in the galley, which has a way of lending a certain complication to the preparation of food when it's rough.

Another advantage to this layout is that you end up with a forepeak that can really be used for storage. If the two bunks are forward, they inevitably seem to contain both people and sails. Many folks get along just fine with sails, of course, especially if they happen to be dry.

The headroom in the *Tidal Wave* is 6 feet under the carlings aft, 5 feet 9 inches at the forward end of the house, and 4 feet 5 inches in the forepeak.

Her water supply is carried in two forty-gallon tanks, one under each midship transom.

I think the *Tidal Wave* is a design worthy of consideration for the person who wants an able, comfortable, and handy cruising boat that has a good turn of speed and is fully capable of going offshore.

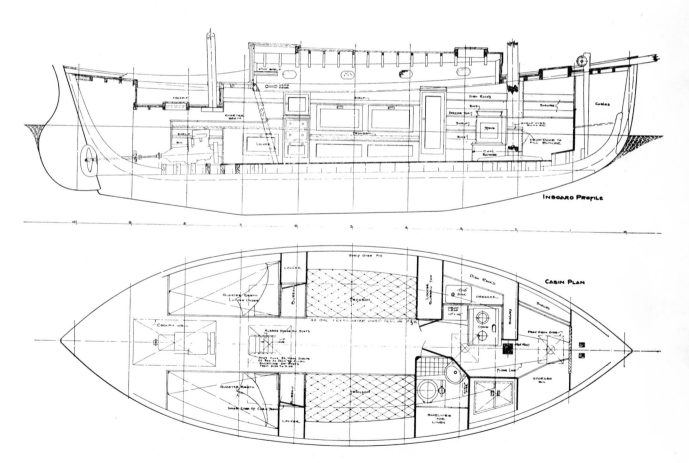

With her galley forward and her two bunks aft, the arrangement of the *Tidal Wave* looks "backwards" to many, but it is, like much else in boat design, merely a compromise. (*Yachting*, November, 1930)

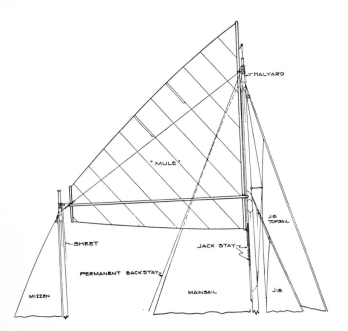

Her sprit topsail was dubbed the "Mule," more for its ability to haul than for its stubbornness. (*Yachting*, March, 1931)

The *Tidal Wave* slipping along close-hauled, making, as usual, more fuss forward than aft. (*Yachting*, January, 1931)

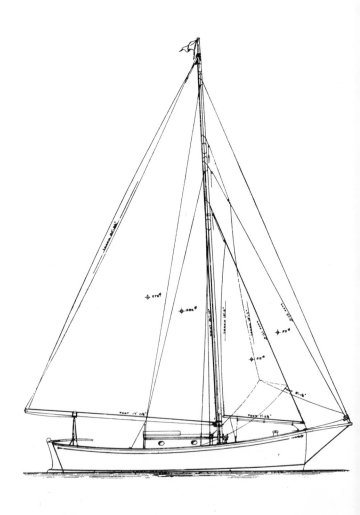

A 23-foot, sloop-rigged version of the *Tidal Wave.* Her sail area is 382 square feet. (*Yachting*, October, 1928)

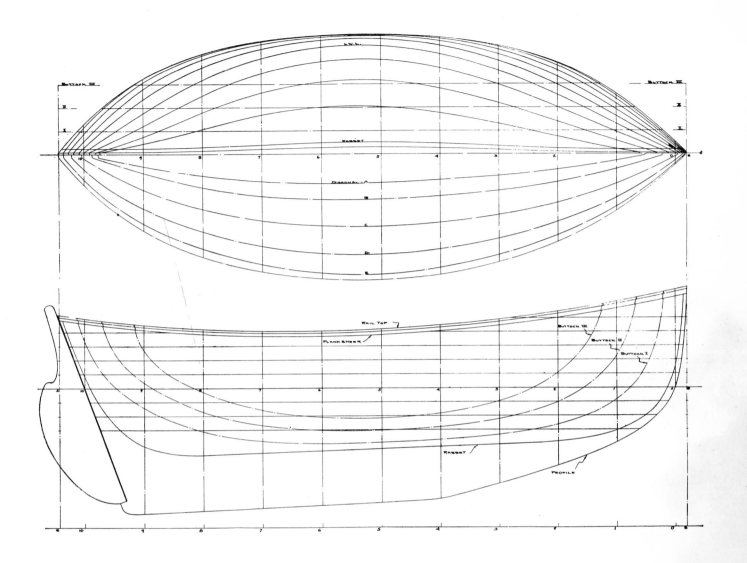

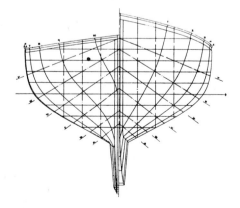

The little sloop is 23′ long on deck, 22′3″ on the waterline, with a beam of 8′6″ and a draft of 4′6″. (*Yachting*, October, 1928)

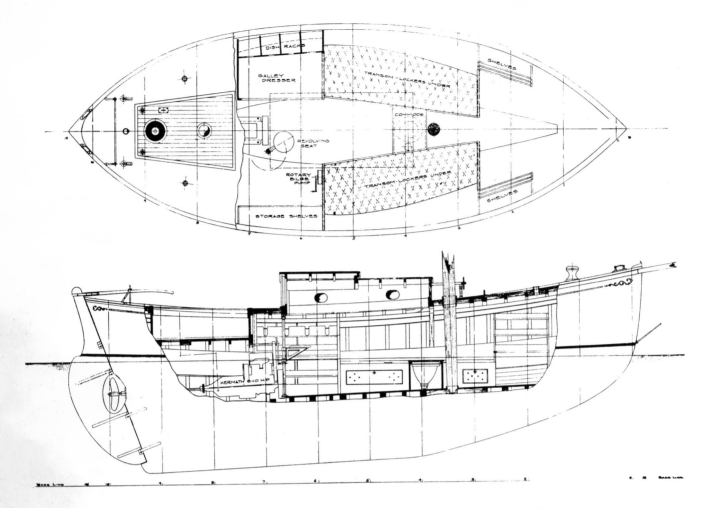

The 23-footer is laid out for two people. (*Yachting*, October, 1928)

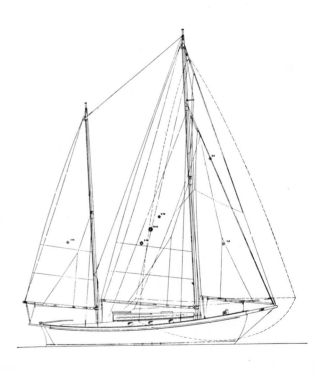

The *Dog Star* is a small edition of the *Tidal Wave*, being about four feet shorter on the waterline. Her sail area is 545 square feet. (*Yachting*, February, 1932)

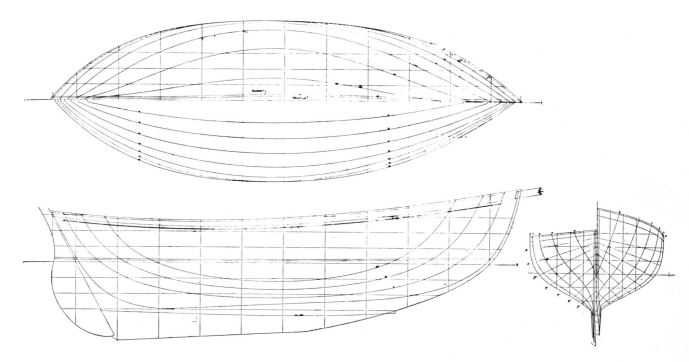

Above: The *Dog Star* is 30′8″ long on deck, with a waterline length of 27′1″ a beam of 10′2″, and a draft of 5′. (*Yachting*, February, 1932)

Below: The *Dog Star*'s arrangement is similar to that of the *Tidal Wave*, except that the quarterberths have been moved up forward. (*Yachting*, February, 1932)

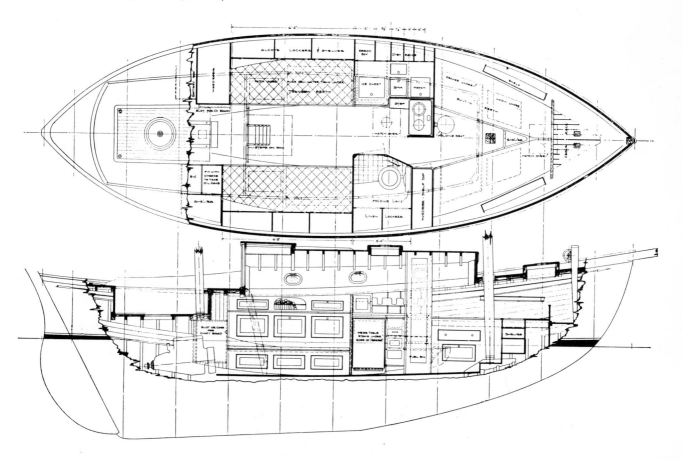

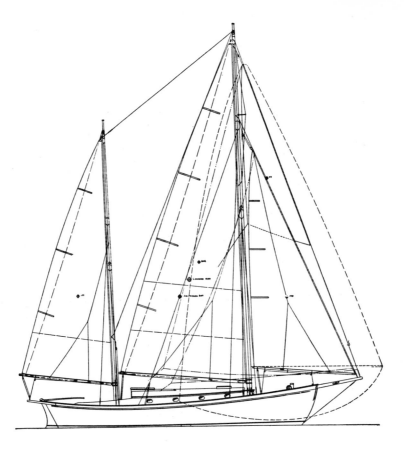

Above: The *Yojo* is a successor to the *Tidal Wave*. She has a bit more sail area, with 689 square feet. (*Yachting*, August, 1931)

Below: The *Yojo*'s ends are lengthened out by 2′7″, and her deadwood is not cut away. With the exception of her length on deck of 34′11″, her hull dimensions are identical with those of the *Tidal Wave*. (*Yachting*, August, 1931)

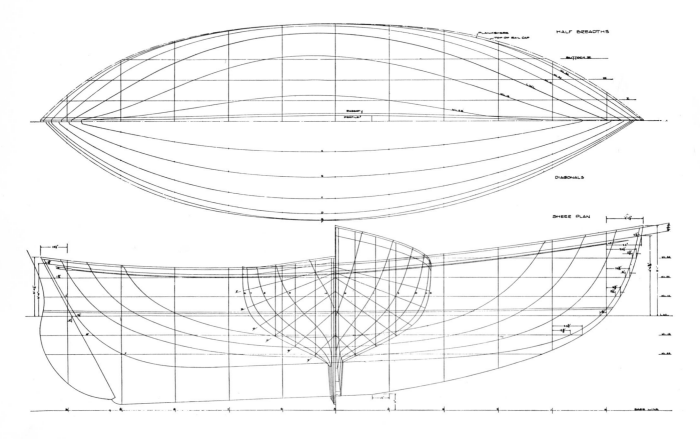

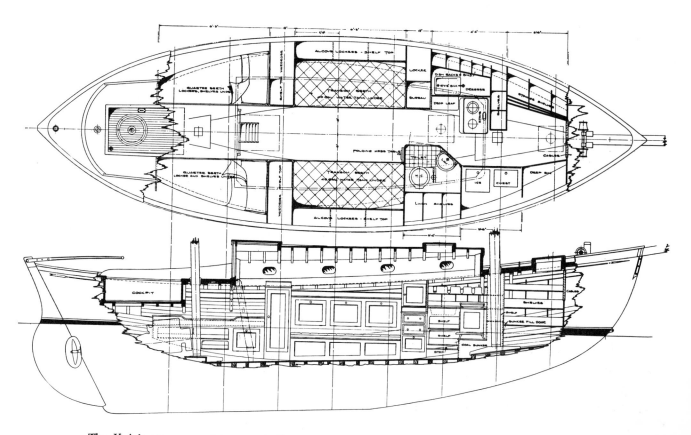

The *Yojo*'s arrangement is very similar to the *Tidal Wave*'s layout. (*Yachting*, August, 1931)

The *Narwhal* is a cutter-rigged version of this design, with the ends even more drawn out. Her sail area is 864 square feet. (*Yachting*, May, 1931)

Left: The *Narwhal* working to windward under jib and mainsail. (*Yachting*, November, 1931)

Center: The *Narwhal* has a canoe stern with inboard rudder. She is 39'11" long on deck, and has other hull dimensions identical with the *Tidal Wave*, her waterline length being 31', her beam, 11', and her draft, 5'. (*Yachting*, May, 1931)

Bottom: The *Narwhal* has a single quarterberth, berths outboard of transoms in the saloon, and two berths forward. (*Yachting*, May, 1931)

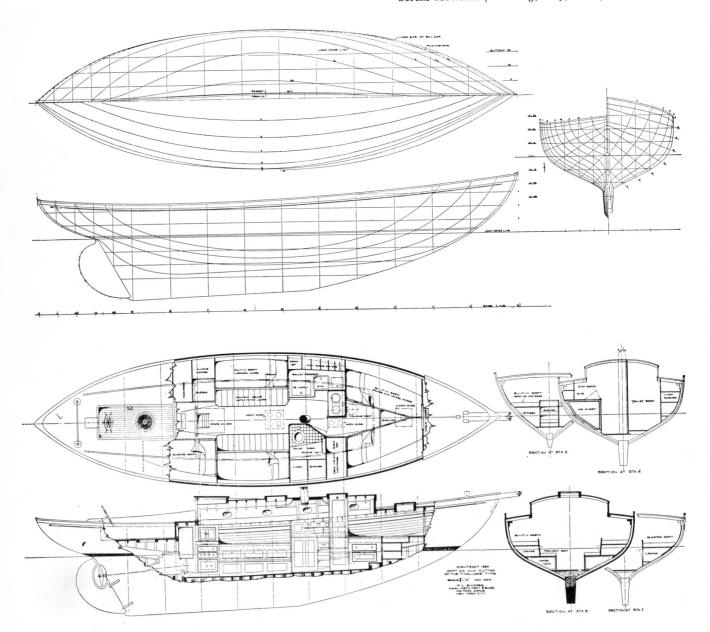

Right: The *Saona* is a shoal-draft, canoe-stern version of the *Tidal Wave.* Her sail area is 730 square feet. (*Yachting*, March, 1932)

Center: The *Saona* is 39′ long on deck, with a waterline length of 32′, a beam of 11′6″, and a draft, with the centerboard up, of 3′9″. (*Yachting*, March, 1932)

Bottom: The *Saona* is arranged with a separate fo'c's'le forward. (*Yachting*, March, 1932)

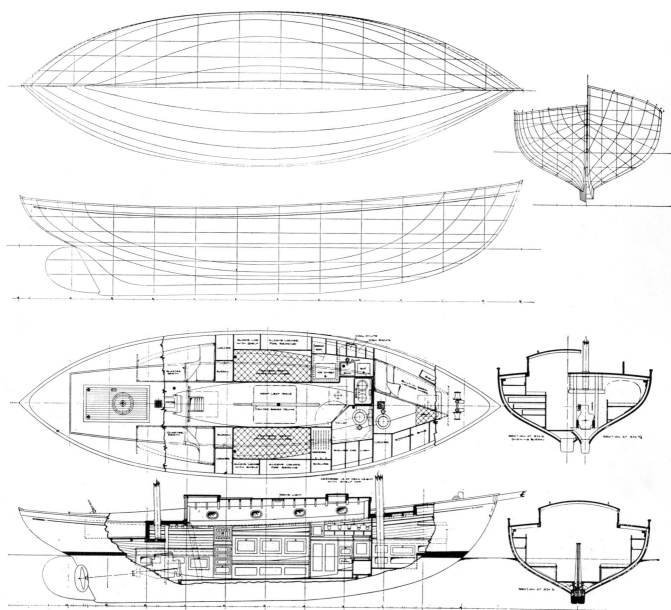

15/ The *Wild Duck*

```
Length on deck: 26 feet
Length on waterline: 23 feet 2 inches
Beam: 9 feet 2 inches
Draft: 4 feet
Sail area: 350 square feet
Designer: Murray G. Peterson
```

One of the first boats I noticed in the harbor upon moving to Camden, Maine, was a pretty and able-looking little double-ended ketch. She looked a sweet boat to sail, yet I never saw her off the mooring. She was sold away, and I later was glad to learn that her new owner, Frank D. Browning, of North Stonington, Connecticut, has her underway a lot.

The ketch is named the *Wild Duck*, and she was designed twenty years ago by Murray G. Peterson. The design was inspired by the Block Island boat, as can be seen readily from her lines. But Murray Peterson made some changes, since it was not intended that the little boat should fish and carry year round, as did her ancestors. He rounded the stem profile slightly, gave the boat a bit less deadrise, and hollowed out her garboards, at the same time giving her a bit less extreme flare in the topsides. He drew finer waterlines forward and fuller waterlines aft, by comparison with the typical Block Island cowhorn, and also gave the boat a less extreme sheer than the cowhorn had.

He ended up with a most seakindly and able little vessel, and one less burdensome and probably a bit faster on her feet than the Block Island boats. Mr. Browning says she "has a particularly nice motion under all conditions."

She is quite full on deck at the bow and stern (this shows up more clearly, somehow, in the close-up, deck-view photographs than it does in the lines), but is quite fine-ended at the waterline. This hull shape gives considerable deck space and makes her dry, yet keeps her sharp enough to sail well.

The *Wild Duck* was built at Camden, Maine, in 1957 by Malcolm Brewer. It would come as no surprise to anyone who has seen a boat take shape in Mr. Brewer's boatshop to learn that the ketch was beautifully built. Her decks are teak, and all exposed wood below is varnished cherry. As can be somewhat appreciated from the photos, the boat is like a nice piece of furniture.

She is 26 feet long on deck, 23 feet 2 inches on the waterline, with a beam of 9 feet 2 inches, and a draft of 4 feet. Her sail area is 350 square feet, with 180 in the mainsail, 96 in the mizzen, and 74 in the jib. Her overlapping jib has 112 square feet.

Her short gaffs, reminiscent of those on the

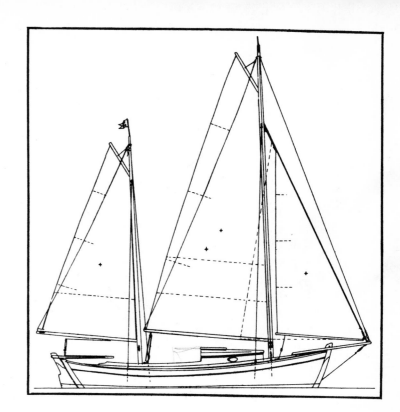

Right: The *Wild Duck* has the short gaffs of her cowhorn forebears, but their big cat schooner rig with the overlapping foresail has been replaced by a handy ketch rig. (Frank D. Browning)

Below: The Block Island boat heritage of handsome ability is evident in her lines. (Frank D. Browning)

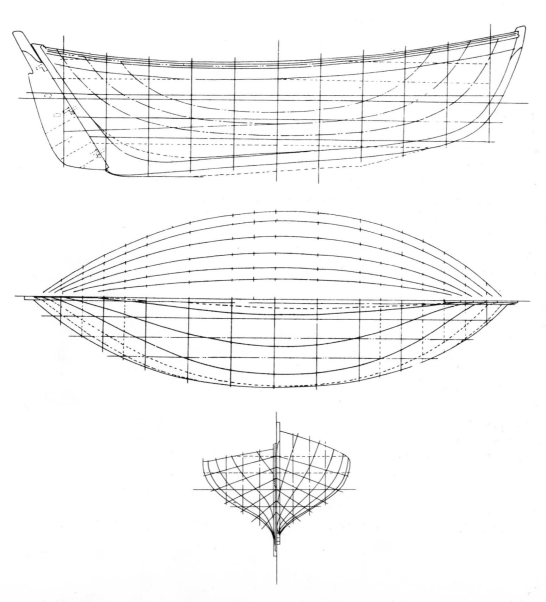

The *Wild Duck* stepping along close-hauled. (Frank D. Browning)

And on her mooring in the Mystic River, Noank, Connecticut. (Frank D. Browning)

Block Island boats, give a fairly tall, narrow sail, yet one that is more versatile than the jib-headed sail, for you can adjust the shape somewhat by the amount you peak up the gaff. The idea is to peak up the sail as much as possible without quite getting wrinkles from peak to tack when the sail is full. There will be some such wrinkles when the sail is first hoisted, but these will disappear when she fills away. The stronger the breeze, the more peaking up the sail will take without wrinkling when full. This kind of trimming can produce considerable variation in the set of the sail, but there are limits, and no amount of setting up or slacking off the peak halyards will make a poorly cut gaff sail set well. Judging by the look of the mainsail and mizzen in the photo of the *Wild Duck* under sail, these limits have been exceeded with those particular sails. They look full near the head, just where they should be flat, and flat near the tack, just where they should be full. And of course the throat halyard should be set up rather hard to eliminate those wrinkles along the luff.

The *Wild Duck* has no winches, as they are unnecessary in a boat of her type, and Mr. Browning reports that the overlapping jib can be flattened in quite easily. Of course in a cruising boat, one never minds giving her a little luff to make such work easy. The working jib, setting on a club, is self-tending when tacking. Such a rig is always appreciated when beating home up a narrow harbor on a late afternoon in the early

winter with the temperature dropping every minute. That's when fingers rebel against being ordered out of warm pockets to take hold of cold, stiff jib sheets.

In a boat with several sail combinations that balance well, there is often a temptation not to reef, and in the *Wild Duck*, it seldom would be absolutely necessary to reef. It's fun, though, to sail a boat at her best in a hard breeze by giving her just the right amount of sail, and in a boat of this size, that usually means reefing. For example, if sailing the *Wild Duck* to windward in a moderate breeze that begins to increase, it might be well first to reef the mizzen, then to single-reef, and finally double-reef the mainsail as it continued to breeze on. With jib, double-reefed main, and reefed mizzen, she would stand some real breeze and go far better than, say, under jib and mainsail, or jib and mizzen. It might be well to put a third reef in the mainsail and have a storm jib that set up off the deck a couple of feet. The boat has an able hull for rough water, so it would be a shame to be limited by an inability to shorten her right down if you wanted to get her to windward in a hard chance. Off the wind, the combination of sails to produce a short rig is, of course, far less critical. She could, for example, be run off nicely under jib alone.

The ketch's stem that extends up through a slot in her plank bowsprit is a nice detail. The inboard end of the bowsprit is left raised off the deck a bit to form a horn, which, together with a

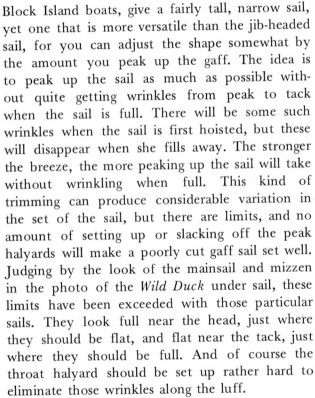

These deck views show her practical, double-cockpit arrangement and give some hint as to the excellence of her construction. (Frank D. Browning)

heavy wooden pin driven through the spar athwartships, forms the perfect arrangement for securing the mooring pennant, anchor rode, or bow line.

The *Wild Duck*'s power is a 22-h.p. Palmer. Her engine controls are out of sight (and the weather) under the cover formed by the bridge deck.

The boat's double-cockpit arrangement has the effect of keeping the weight of her people nearly amidships instead of farther aft, as is the case in many boats. The *Wild Duck* can take a sizable party on board without going down by the stern, nor will her helmsman feel the surge of the crowd against his tiller. The forward cockpit is self-bailing; the after steering well is not. For normal, prudent, coastwise sailing, there is no reason why she should take any great amount of water into the well. This well makes a fine steering station. Mr. Browning writes that the "helmsman can stand and lean waist high against the coaming all day comfortably or stand or sit on the seats (which fold up)." All sheets are within his reach; the *Wild Duck* would make an admirable singlehander.

Mr. Browning says of his boat's accommodations: "The cabin is that rare design which has comfortable space for two. It is very simply and sensibly planned, with two good, wide, comfortable berths, a head, water tap (no sink), and a Shipmate stove. To me this stove is a far more desirable luxury than wall-to-wall carpeting and a pair of matched poodles, which today seem to be necessary adjuncts to cruising for most people."

I say a fair breeze and a following sea to the *Wild Duck*, and may her masts never attract pairs of matched cruising poodles!

16/ The *Itatae*

> **Length on deck: 27 feet**
> **Length on waterline: 25 feet 4 inches**
> **Beam: 9 feet 8 inches**
> **Draft: 4 feet**
> **Sail area: 421 square feet**
> **Designer: William Garden**

A few years ago, in the spring, I was exploring Gloucester Harbor in a boat and looking over all the interesting craft, when suddenly there was a fine little double-ender right under my nose, lying quietly at anchor. Her name was *Itatae*, and I determined to track down her origin and plans if possible.

It turned out she was designed by Bill Garden, and he kindly provided me with drawings and a photo of the boat. It also turned out her name is pronounced Ee-Tah-Tee and that she was named after the pilot boat in James N. Hall's book, *Far Lands*, a story of South Sea migrations. The boat was built by Paul Luke in East Boothbay, Maine, in 1954, for Edward Dane. Mr. Dane obviously appreciated good boat design. For eighteen years, he had owned the *Bounty*, a fifty-seven-foot ketch designed by L. Francis Herreshoff, a small edition of the *Ticonderoga*.

The *Itatae* is 27 feet long on deck, with a waterline length of 25 feet 4 inches, a beam of 9 feet 8 inches, and a draft of 4 feet. She has 2,500 pounds of outside ballast. Her sail area is 421 square feet, with 230 in the foresail and 191 in the mainsail. Her power is a Universal Utility 4 with a direct drive.

The lines of this boat are sweet and symmetrical. She has a fine underbody and considerable flare in the topsides, not only in the ends, but also in her midsection. There's a slight hollow in the load waterline both forward and aft. She has a strong and pleasing sheer. She should be a good sea boat, lively and dry.

The hull is easily driven, so the rig need not be large. She wouldn't need to be reefed often, as she would carry her sail well, with her outside ballast and the stability gained from immersing her flared topsides.

Note that she has no shrouds, Block Island boat style. Her masts are seven inches in diameter at the deck and well tapered. The absence of main shrouds would be particularly helpful in trimming the foresail. The jumper strut near the head of the foremast takes the thrust of the fore gaff and gives the forestay a better angle of pull.

Her sails and the foresail gaff are set on tracks. These apparently gave a bit of trouble during the

Opposite: The *Itatae*'s rig is a snug version of the sail plan for a Block Island boat. She has plenty of cockpit space and a snug cabin for two. (William Garden)

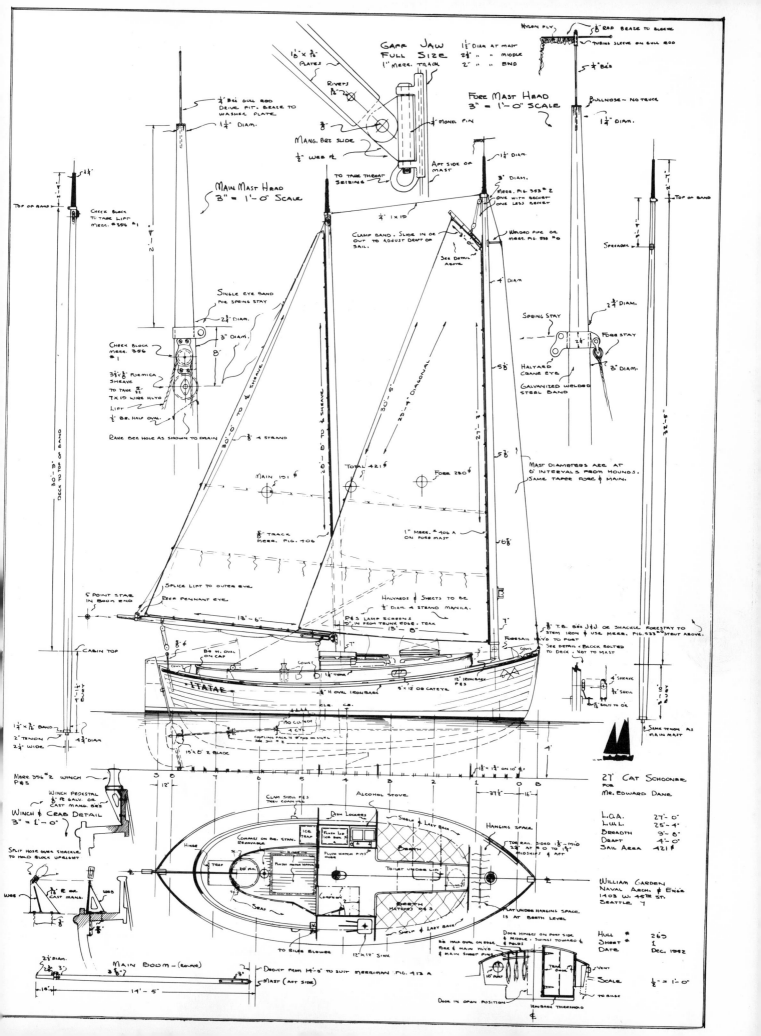

GAFF JAW
FULL SIZE

FORE MAST HEAD
3" = 1'-0" SCALE

MAIN MAST HEAD
3" = 1'-0" SCALE

"ITATAE"

WINCH & CRAB DETAIL
3" = 1'-0"

MAIN BOOM — (ROUND)

27' CAT SCHOONER
FOR
Mr. EDWARD DANE

L.O.A. .... 27'-0"
L.W.L. .... 25'-4"
BREADTH ...... 9'-8"
DRAFT .... 4'-0"
SAIL AREA .... 421#

WILLIAM GARDEN
NAVAL ARCH. & ENG'R
1403 W. 45TH ST.
SEATTLE 7

HULL #	265
SHEET	1
DATE	DEC. 1952
SCALE	½" = 1'-0"

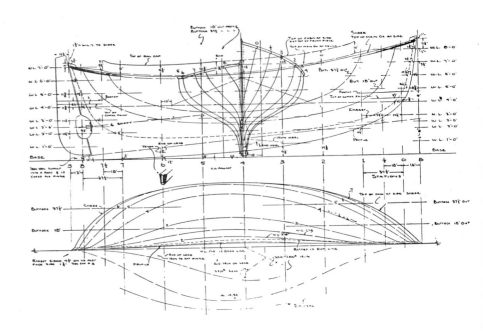

Right: The lines of the cat schooner show a sweet, wineglass-sectioned hull that should keep coming up smiling in a seaway. (*Rudder* Magazine, © August, 1953, Fawcett Publications, Inc.)

Below: The construction plan shows her engine and shaft layout. She has plenty of backbone. (*Rudder* Magazine, © August, 1953, Fawcett Publications, Inc.)

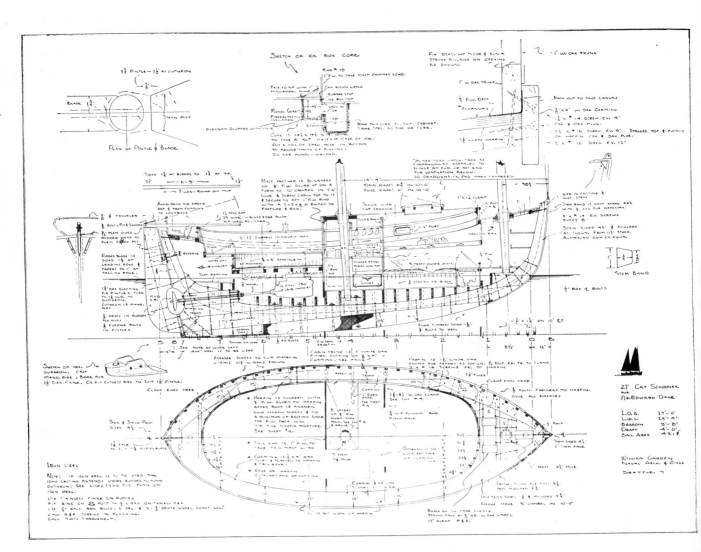

The cockpit is where the action is. That on the *Itatae* is big, deep, and comfortable, with its high, curved staving all around. (William Garden)

boat's first season, until the track was modified somewhat. I'd prefer mast hoops on a boat of this type, in any case, even though there would be a slight loss in the aerodynamic efficiency of the luffs of the sails. I'd gladly trade such loss in a cruising boat for the sure knowledge that a mast hoop won't jam when you want it to come down in a hurry. Not to mention the hoops' usefulness as a ladder if you want to go up the mast. And besides, along about the middle of February, it's mighty nice to have a set of mast hoops or two to get out and sand and varnish and place, carefully spaced, along a tightly stretched cod line to dry. That's almost as good a winter uplift as oiling down a pair of oars.

As with any catboat, I'd be tempted to put a bowsprit on the *Itatae*. With her small foredeck, it would be as handy as could be for anchor handling. And you could set a good big balloon jib, flying, to the end of it when reaching and running in light weather. When running, such a sail would have to be poled out, of course. That would mean you'd probably want two long, light poles aboard, for one would be useful to hold the

clew of the foresail out when before the wind. A long, light pole is mighty handy around a boat, anyway, for a number of things, not the least of which is taking quick, accurate soundings.

Bill Garden gave careful thought to trimming the loose-footed foresail, for there are well-designed pedestals aft on each rail to take the sheet blocks, and the single-part sheets lead forward from these blocks to winches mounted on the cockpit coaming. While winches are generally not needed on a boat this size, they would certainly be handy for getting in the last few inches of foresail sheet when tacking in a breeze. There are times, too, when it's handy to be able to lead an anchor rode back to a winch, as, for instance, when there's not enough wind to sail out a recalcitrant hook.

The oval shape of the trunk cabin and cockpit coaming gives a pleasant unity to the deck layout of the little schooner. Her general arrangement makes plenty of sense, with its large cockpit and cabin with enough sheltered living space for two people to cruise comfortably. The only change Mr. Dane made to Bill Garden's design when he had the *Itatae* built was to move the sink right aft in the cabin so the dish washer could stand up to his work in the companionway. With just about five feet of headroom in the cabin, it would be logical to give the cook a seat, perhaps hinged from the port side of the mainmast.

As to her performance, she evidently could do some sailing in a breeze of wind. Mr. Dane, in writing to Mr. Garden after the boat's first season, stated, "In sailing from Marblehead to Boothbay Harbor, Maine, overnight with a friend during a good northwest wind ranging from 25 to 35 miles an hour, we averaged slightly better than 6½ knots for the 100-odd miles."

It could have been her beautiful wineglass sections that made her go so well that night. It must have been quite a sail—the kind when, after you get in, you want to drink a toast to the vessel.

17/ The No Man's Land Boat

Length on deck: 18 feet
Length on waterline: 15 feet 6 inches
Beam: 6 feet 6 inches
Draft: 1 foot 4 inches
Sail area: 122 square feet

No Man's Land has always fascinated me. What is it about a small, uninhabited island that makes you want to go and see it?

In the case of No Man's Land, one of its attractions to us boys, as we began to feel our oats and make short cruises along the coast to places we considered far from home, was that if you sailed around No Man's Land, you would have sailed in the Atlantic Ocean. We took our boats into what we called the ocean all the time, but always when we looked offshore we knew that there was some island or other between us and Portugal. But if you could sail out to No Man's Land and go round the island, then you would really be out in the Atlantic Ocean with no land at all outside you. That was something worth doing.

So on one cruise in my old, mostly open, Herreshoff sloop, we came out of Menemsha Pond on Martha's Vineyard, worked round Gay Head, and beat offshore against a slowly rising southerly. Pretty soon we raised the low-lying, rather nondescript island that was our goal, for it is less than six miles south of Gay Head and a bit under three miles southwest of Squibnocket Point, the nearest land on Martha's Vineyard. In the haze and scud of the rising onshore breeze that day, it seemed farther.

We reached No Man's, and sailed round as close to its gravelly, boulder-strewn shoreline as we dared. We got our thrill of a few minutes of open-ocean sailing, and of course experienced that moment of doubt as we reached fast right along the southern lee shore of the island—doubt about getting too close in, hitting an uncharted (or even charted) rock, and quickly joining the cobblestones rolling noisily up and down the beach in the surf. It seemed a truly lonely place, and we were glad enough to lay the boat off the wind for Cuttyhunk.

No Man's Land is a little less than a mile and a half long, and the island has an average width of about half a mile. In the second half of the nineteenth century, families from the Vineyard used to spend the summer on the island so the men would be closer to the fishing grounds around it, and probably also as a sort of summer holiday from the civilized humdrum of their big home island. They set up light housekeeping in cabins along the north shore of No Man's.

The island has no cove, much less a harbor. The fishing was longline trawling, day trips. The fish had to be taken in to market, and there was a certain amount of gear and supplies that had to be fetched and carried to the island. A distinctive, small, double-ended beach boat was developed to meet these particular requirements. The type is generally called the No Man's Land double-ender, though the boats also were used on Martha's Vineyard, Nantucket, and the south shore of Cape Cod.

The type was in use as early as 1856, according to Howard I. Chapelle. The boats were originally shoal-draft keel craft, but centerboards began to appear by 1886. At first, the double-enders were seventeen or eighteen feet long; in later years, some as long as twenty-four feet were built. The boats were built in some quantity at New Bedford, Fairhaven, and Providence, as well as by their owners at home.

Weight is critical in a beach boat, and the No Man's Land boats were lightly built. They were planked with cedar over oak frames and were nearly all lapstrake, though a few were carvel planked. They were copper fastened. An iron strap protected the bottom of the keel.

The boats carried a two-masted rig, nearly always with a spritsail on each mast. We would probably call the rig a cat ketch today, for there was no headsail, and the foresail was about twice as big as the mainsail. The word *mizzen* was never applied to these craft. About 1890, when the boats grew in size and were not always hauled up the beach, some of them carried gaff foresails or were gaff-rigged on both sails.

There was an athwartships hole through the stem at the waterline. When the boat was to be hauled up the beach, a peg was tapped into the hole so the hauling tackle could be hooked onto the boat nice and low. Some accounts say men

Above: The sail plan of the Huntington No Man's Land boat shows a gaff-rigged foresail and sprit mainsail. Most of the boats were sprit-rigged on both masts. (*Yachting*, April, 1932)

Below: Huntington took off the lines of this No Man's Land boat in 1932 after the boat had been abandoned on Martha's Vineyard. (*Yachting*, April, 1932)

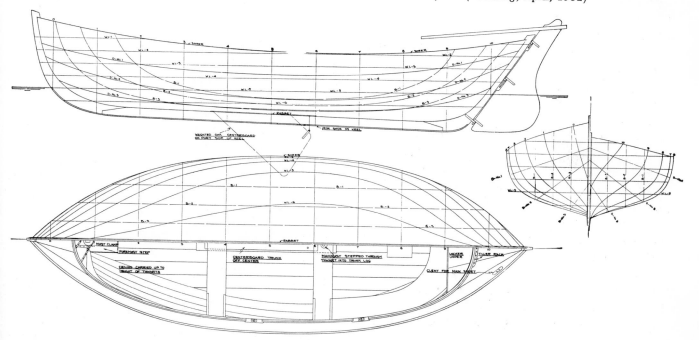

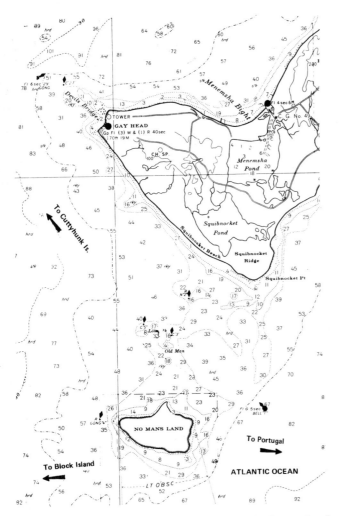

No Man's Land, the lonely sentinel off the end of Martha's Vineyard, is a well-named island.

did the hauling; others state that oxen were used, in one account the beasts being referred to as "stunted oxen." If one of these boats were to carry an ox out to the island, it might be as well if it were "stunted." The boats were hauled up on long wooden "ladders," hooked together in sections. The "rungs" were wooden rollers.

It is interesting to compare the No Man's Land double-enders with the Block Island boats, larger, deeper craft developed for similar uses.

Frederick R. Huntington took the lines off a No Man's Land double-ender beached to die on Martha's Vineyard. He figures the boat had been built in the early 1890s. Mr. Huntington's plans are reproduced here; this boat has a sweeter, fairer model, in my opinion, than any No Man's Land double-ender whose lines have been published. She's a handsome, able, roomy boat, and

if anyone wants to adopt a workboat for pleasure use, this craft, I think, would make an admirable choice.

She is 18 feet long on deck, with a waterline length of 15 feet 6 inches, a beam of 6 feet 6 inches, and a draft of 1 foot 4 inches with the board up. Her least freeboard is 1 foot 5 inches, and she has 2 feet 6 inches freeboard at the bow and 2 feet at the stern. The sail area is 122 square feet, with 80 square feet in the foresail and 42 in the mainsail. The foremast is 15 feet long, the mainmast 10 feet long, the fore gaff 8 feet long, and the main sprit 11 feet.

The No Man's Land boat has a rather high, full stern for launching off the beach stern-first. This gives her quite good bearing aft for a double-ender.

The accounts of these boats emphasized their weatherliness rather than their speed. I don't think the chroniclers meant these double-enders were close-winded, for doubtless they would not be; what they meant, I believe, is that for a small boat they were able to work to weather in a very strong breeze and rough sea. Moreover, there is no reason why this boat shouldn't have a good turn of speed off the wind, for she has a nice, flat run.

The No Man's Land boats were often rowed long distances when the breeze failed. This boat could certainly be shoved along nicely in a calm with lengthy, well-balanced oars. There is plenty of room in the boat to move around and vary the rowing position on a long pull. With three or more people aboard, she could be rowed nicely with two pairs of oars, with passengers and oarsmen swapping off now and then.

The Huntington boat's off-center centerboard is typical of the type; this construction avoids cutting a slot in the keel and prevents jamming the board with gravel on beaching. On many of the boats, the weighted centerboard was rigged so it could be lifted right out of the trunk. This handy operation was made possible by the use of one or another type of "patent hanger." On the forward edge of the board, a lifting rod that looked like a pump handle was attached at the lower corner to a cross pin through the board that rested on a hanger on each side of the well.

The No Man's Land boats used sandbags for ballast. This form of movable weight has many advantages in a small boat that is used in water

Above: A 20-foot No Man's Land boat ending her days in the Martha's Vineyard beach grass. (*Yachting*, March, 1932)

Right: This nicely built replica of a No Man's Land double-ender makes a fine-looking little vessel. (*The National Watercraft Collection* by Howard I. Chapelle, International Marine Publishing Company)

that washes at least a few sandy beaches. The stuff is cheap, clean, heavy, and easily disposable. The bags won't dent wood, even when accidentally dropped by a small boy when the boat lurches, and they will conform to the shape of whatever corner is assigned them. Beachcombers can use them to replace ballast with treasure.

The gaff foresail shown on the Huntington boat supposedly would be more "efficient" than a spritsail, because the curve of the sail wouldn't be interrupted on one tack by the sprit. But the sprit rig in a boat of this type has the great advantage of portability. You can take the lower end of the sprit out of its snotter, bring it back to the clew of the sail, roll the sail up on it against the mast, wrap halyard or rope forestay round and round everything, and then lift out the mast with its sail and all its gear in one fell swoop. Of course, with the gaff rig, the sail could be furled and tied up under the gaff and then the gaff peaked right up alongside the mast to achieve something of the same effect, but it's not as neat an arrangement.

The two-masted rig with big foresail and small mainsail is extremely versatile. The foresail can be reefed down as it breezes up, or the boat can be sailed with foresail alone. With a spare mast step in the forward thwart, the boat can be sailed as a catboat with either mast stepped in the spare hole. With just the little mainsail stepped in the forward thwart, the rig becomes very snug indeed.

A spare sprit might be a handy thing to carry and could be used to pole out the foresail when running. The Huntington boat shows cleats on the quarters for the mainsheet, but many of the No Man's Land boats had travelers over the tiller.

The No Man's Land boats carried quite a short rig, for a large spread of sail and long spars were neither needed nor wanted in their work. If this boat were to be used as a yacht, it might be fun to experiment with a large, light-weather jib, tacked down to the spare sprit run out as a bowsprit. If you wanted to get fancy, you could even rig a bobstay to the hauling-out hole in the stem.

Another thought would be to use the rig shown for spring and fall sailing and give the boat a larger summer rig by using the foremast as the mainmast of a gunter-rigged sloop, stepping the mast in the forward thwart. She could then carry a big jib tacked down to the stem head. Such a rig would be far less handy than the two-masted sprit rig, but it would get her along appreciably faster in a light breeze.

With sprits for ridgepoles and sails for a tent, the little double-ender could be converted into a nicely protected floating camp at the end of the day's run. The boat has plenty of room and carrying capacity for taking along ample quantities of the necessities of life.

A small boat like this Huntington No Man's Land double-ender has plenty of fun and little frustration wrapped up in her. Her owner commits only a reasonable amount of time and resources to his vessel, yet he has a boat that is handy to use on many occasions for many purposes. He also has a boat that can go out in any reasonable weather, as the boats proved, working for many years in the rough-and-tumble waters around the sentinel island of No Man's Land. If anybody builds one, he should by all means sail her out to the little island off Martha's Vineyard. It's worth the trip.

18/ The *Glad Tidings*

> Length on deck: 39 feet
> Length on waterline: 31 feet
> Beam: 9 feet 6 inches
> Draft: 5 feet
> Designer: Howard I. Chapelle

To conjure up a picture of the epitome of sea-worthiness, imagine a pinky hove to under double-reefed foresail in a gale well offshore. She holds her head up, has a reasonably easy motion in the wild, confused seaway, and takes little heavy water on deck. These full-bodied, well-balanced, American double-enders were every bit the fine rough-water vessels they looked to be.

The pinky took her name from a general type of northern European trading vessel of various rigs known as the pink. These were sizable craft with a sharp stern and a false overhang. The smaller double-enders American fishermen developed along the New England coast in the nineteenth century evidently were reminiscent of the bigger trading vessels with the similar distinctive stern configuration.

The pinkies, like the Block Island boats, were descended from Chebacco boats. The Chebacco boats averaged forty feet long on deck, whereas the later pinkies were typically fifty feet long. The pinky added a bowsprit and headsail to the cat schooner rig of the Chebacco boat. This development and the use of the term *pinky* for the new type occurred about 1816, according to Howard I. Chapelle, writing about pinkies in his book *American Sailing Craft* (originally published in 1936 and reprinted by International Marine in 1975).*

The Essex pinky developed a great reputation for ability in heavy weather. Chapelle records that two pinkies were among the few vessels that were able to beat out of Chaleur Bay in a great gale, in October 1851, that sank many Gloucester fishing schooners.

The Essex pinkies were very heavily built of the best oak. They had closely spaced, double, sawn frames. Their topsides were usually painted dark green, with a black wale and bulwarks, all set off with a stripe of red, yellow, or white.

Most of the pinkies built in Maine and the Maritime Provinces were more full-bodied than the Essex pinkies and had less sheer. But perhaps the finest development of the type was the Eastport pinky, which was finer than either the Essex or other Down East pinkies. The Eastport pinkies were built to work closer to shore than the other types in the herring fishery of the 1850s and 1860s, and they were faster than the other pinkies. They were no less able, however, giving

---

*It's shameful how easily free advertising can be inserted in a book when author and publisher are but one person.

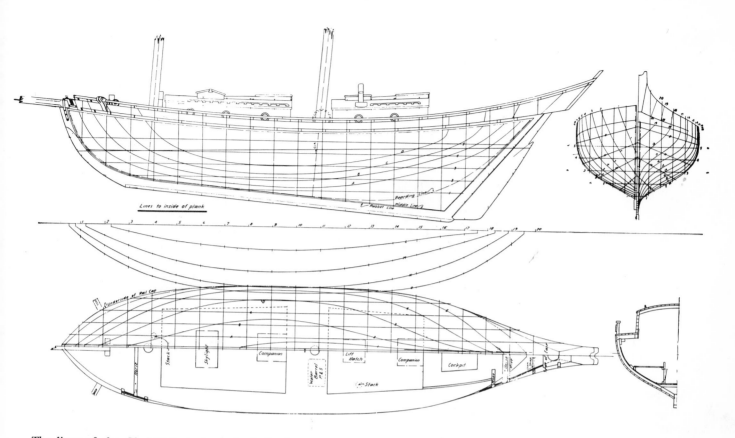

The lines of the *Glad Tidings* show the hull of an able vessel that could come in from sea after a gale with no bad news. (*Yachting*, February, 1938)

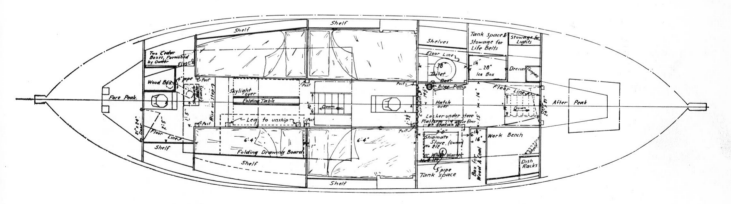

She is well laid out for four people, and her midships berths between the houses are out of the way for the off-watch. (*Yachting*, February, 1938)

up carrying capacity, not seaworthiness, for their speed.

Of course the pink stern is the famous part of this craft. It has its own good looks, but it was developed instead for its practical value. The high, open, overhanging bulwarks joined right aft by the tombstone protect the rudder and helmsman, support the horse for the main sheet, and can act as a boom crutch. The structure is useful

for drying nets or anything else, and it forms what is obviously the best seat in the boat. If the pinky's crew can maintain sufficient dignity of demeanor, she has no need of a head.

The gist of the chapter Chapelle wrote on pinkies in *American Sailing Craft* was that Americans seeking wholesome cruising boats and recognizing the admirable sea-keeping qualities of the double-ender should stop importing foreign

The *Glad Tidings* heeled over "just so" in even a light breeze, but there she hung, refusing to go much farther, breeze on though it might. (*Yachting*, February, 1938)

double-enders designed for foreign conditions; they should start looking to American double-enders, such as the pinky, developed to sail in their own home waters. In 1937, wanting to build an able cruising boat to take him and his family between Cape Cod and Nova Scotia in summer and fall, he decided to take a dose of his own medicine and have a pinky built for his own use.

Chapelle selected a small, lean, builders' half model and drew her lines, stretching the boat out from an on-deck length of 34 feet to 39 feet. Her waterline came out at 31 feet, her beam 9 feet 6 inches, and her draft is 5 feet. All her ballast is inside. The boat was built in the traditional manner for the type, the only changes being that she has two good-sized deckhouses and full cruising accommodations instead of the usual short, raised deck and small cuddy forward and fish hold aft. Her backbone and skeleton are of oak, the planking is white cedar, and her deck, houses, and interior are pine. This is all native Maine stuff.

She was built in the winter and spring of 1937 by Roger I. Sawyer at Milbridge, Maine. She was launched on July 12th of that year, having been christened the *Glad Tidings*.

Chapelle cruised in her extensively that summer. The reputation of the pinky for ease of motion in a rough sea was substantiated. As to stability, he found that she went over quite easily and then hung with the deck edge seven or eight inches out of water. Even in a fresh breeze, the deck wouldn't go all the way down. He found that the *Glad Tidings* balanced well under short sail in a strong breeze, sailing well with either jib and mainsail or under foresail alone. She steered easily and would steer herself when close to the wind.

Chapelle said she was surprisingly fast for a boat of her displacement and sail area. Of course, one cannot expect real speed from such a combination. The pinky is above all an able vessel, and among extremely able craft, she is no slowpoke. If a good pinky, a good Norwegian pilot cutter, and a good Tahiti ketch were to race across the Atlantic some autumn, I'd bet on the pinky. Chapelle said that in a moderate breeze, the *Glad Tidings* would average something over four knots through the water close-hauled, and would do over six on a reach under the same conditions without making much fuss.

The boat was originally rigged with a lug foresail, but for the sake of handling ease, the sail was cut down and given a boom. This accounts for the less-than-ideal shape of the sail as it appears in the photograph.

The jib is rigged with a bonnet in the traditional way. Chapelle said unlacing the bonnet and taking it off was a faster way to reduce sail than reefing, but lacing it back on and resetting the jib took more time than shaking out a reef. The old-timers knew what they were about; you're always in more of a hurry to take sail off than put it back on.

The hull of the *Glad Tidings* looks wholesome and able, in keeping with her type. Her sheer is particularly pleasing.

She has no engine, though the design was planned so that a powerplant could go in abaft the after companionway with an off-center wheel. With no power, it would be logical to add sail to the rig by sending up a main topmast, so that a main topsail and fisherman staysail could be carried. This was the normal rig of the later pinkies. They never carried fore topmasts.

A good sail on this boat would be a balloon jib to use reaching in light weather or to pole out when running. Then the foresail could be taken in. Few things are more frustrating in life than a schooner's foresail when running. It's nice to think of running for miles wing-and-wing, but all too often the thing slats and bangs all night instead of pulling.

Chapelle made all his berths in the *Glad Tidings* 6 feet 4 inches long, not only because he approached that height himself, but also to enable a smaller man to keep his sea bag at the foot of his berth. She has a coal-or-wood-burning heating stove forward, as well as a coal-burning galley range aft. With no plumbing in the boat to freeze up, she is ideal for cold-weather cruising. Her drinking water is kept in fifteen-gallon wooden barrels on deck in way of the mainmast. You'd think they'd freeze in very cold weather, but Pete Culler says not—that is, if you remember to put a dry salt cod over the dipping hole and cover the cask with a heavy piece of tarpaulin. The *Glad Tidings* is *that* kind of boat.

I never heard Howard Chapelle lay claim to being a great environmentalist, but he did have a chemical toilet in this boat in 1937. Maybe it was just that the tombstone was a little cold to the touch down in Nova Scotia in November.

Full-and-by, with a nice peapod astern.
(*Yachting*, February, 1938)

19/ The *Mocking Bird*

> Length on deck: 31 feet 6 inches
> Length on waterline: 24 feet
> Beam: 8 feet
> Draft: 4 feet 6 inches
> Sail area: 400 square feet
> Designer: Ralph Wiley

Ernest A. Bell, a college student, was leaving Nova Scotia, where he had been on summer vacation, to return to school. The first stage of his reluctant journey took him by small coasting steamer down the shore to Halifax. Bell wrote:

It was blowing half a gale from the south of east, and "t'ick-a-fog," and the skipper had shut her down to see if he could not catch a sight or sound of Pennant Whistler. Through the fog, to starboard, came the sound of a mouth horn, or conch shell. A greasy and perspiring individual, leaning out of the half-door of the engine room, "opined" that the sound emanated from a fishing boat.

Shortly, through the fog, appeared brown sails and a white hull, between forty and fifty feet long. The boat seemed to approach slowly, to hesitate a moment, and then to leap past in the manner of boats passing at sea—a phenomenon on which Conrad remarks in *Chance*. But there was time to observe two or three men in yellow oilskins, the helmsman standing with the end of the great ten-foot tiller behind his back, lifted slightly from the comb, and the load of barrels and boxes partly covered by a tarpaulin or, more likely, by the brown staysail (it was not set) in her waist.

The man with the shell waved his hand to my friend, who acknowledged the salute graciously. They were then close aboard. The tiller was swung a trifle to weather; the loose-footed overlapping foresail filled with an audible snap, and away she went, at eight or nine knots, her lee rail occasionally awash, and with a smoothness and lack of fuss in that broken water which, somehow, no other boat has ever seemed to me quite able to attain—and I have known some good ones!

My friend of the lubrication and perspiration remarked, 'ere he disappeared below, possibly in answer to a jangle of bells, "The three Baker boys! Damn good boats, them Tancook whalers!"

The Tancook whaler thus dramatically sighted by Ernest Bell carried off with her into the fog the heart of a schoolward-bound boy. Bell later sailed in a Tancook whaler and made up his mind to assist in any way he could in preserving the lines and details of the type for future generations.

The Tancook whaler originated at Tancook Island in Mahone Bay as an inshore fishing boat. The type was developed by local families of builders—the Stevenses, the Masons, and the Langilles being prominent among them. The introduction of this distinctive type—perhaps based on the New England or Hampton boat, and perhaps with some additional influence from the whaleboat, as the name implies—began about 1860. Early examples of the type were from twenty-four to twenty-eight feet long, and were planked lapstrake. By 1900, the whalers had reached lengths approaching fifty feet and were

The sail plan of the Tancook whaler shows a rig that is moderate, well proportioned, and, indeed, quite snug once the staysail is taken in. (*Yachting*, February, 1933)

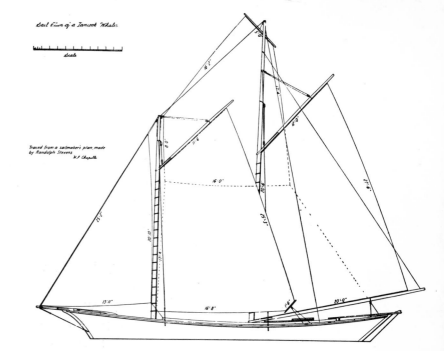

Sail Plan of a Tancook Whaler.

Traced from a sailmaker's plan made by Randolph Stevens. H.I. Chapelle.

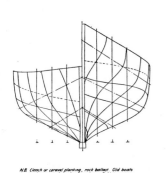

N.B. Clench or carvel planking, rock ballast. Old boats had plank keels, wider than shown. Rabbet on stem often straight instead of flaring as shown. Some boats have no centerboard.

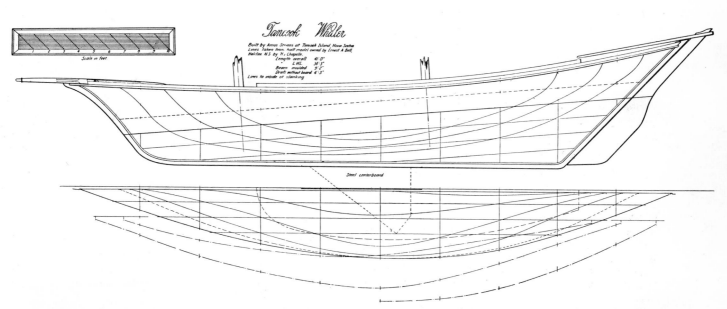

Tancook Whaler

Built by Amos Stevens at Tancook Island, Nova Scotia
Lines taken from half model owned by Ernest A Bell.
Halifax N S by H. Chapelle.
Length overall   41'0"
L W L   34'3"
Beam moulded   9'2"
Draft without board 4'3"
Lines to inside of planking

Steel centerboard

Scale in feet.

The lines of Ernest Bell's model of a Tancook whaler made by Amos Stevens of Tancook Island, Nova Scotia. Pretty and dainty, she looks able to charm her way through rough water. (*Yachting*, February, 1933)

carvel planked. Before World War I, a forty-six-foot Tancook whaler, with sails and two dories and fitted out for fishing, cost $450.

The whalers carried stone ballast, had steel boilerplate centerboards, and had large, open cockpits, either abaft a small forward cuddy or between the masts, in which case the cuddy would be abaft the mainmast.

The anchorage at Tancook Island is not well protected, and one of the requirements of the type was that she lie well to a mooring in a gale and heavy sea. The boats were normally fitted with a heavy iron ring around the foremast to which the mooring pennant was made fast. It was led through a chock on the bowsprit, where it was lashed in place with a lanyard rove through a hole in the bowsprit.

The Tancook whalers had a great reputation for speed, and it was said they were exceptionally fast once the sheets were started. Additional de-

Right: Ralph Wiley's *Mocking Bird* has a handsome profile, with her high, curved bow, her clean, flush deck, and her straightforward rig. (*Yachting*, June, 1943)

Below: The *Mocking Bird*'s lines retain the main qualities of the Tancook whaler while gaining stability and buoyancy. Yet the low-sided sheerline that is a practical necessity for fishing gives the working craft a grace that can never be equaled in the yacht that will indulge in more freeboard. (*Yachting*, June, 1943)

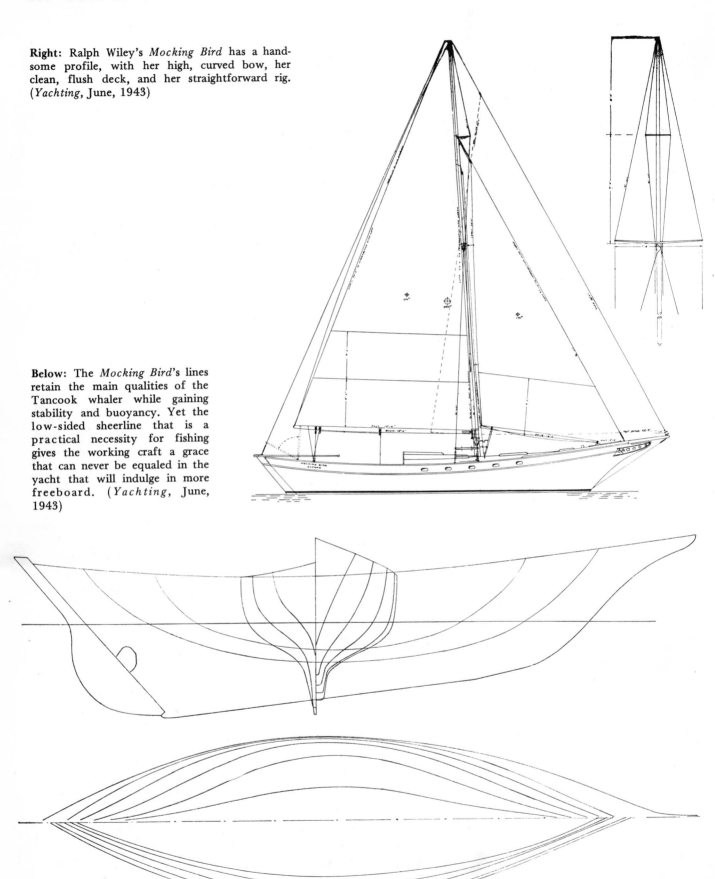

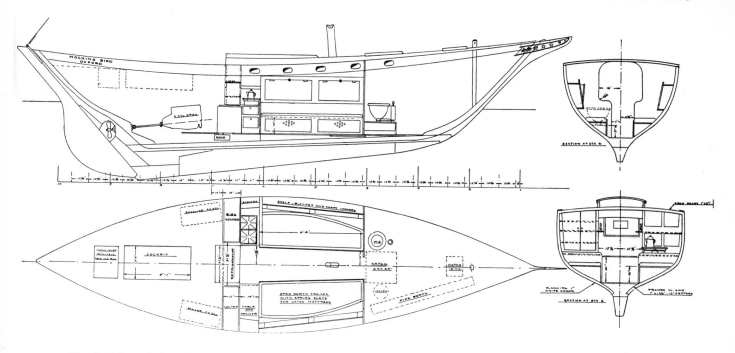

The double-ender's cabin was laid out for two, but there is a spare berth forward. (*Yachting*, June, 1943)

tails on these fascinating craft may be found in Howard I. Chapelle's *American Small Sailing Craft.*

At the time when Ernest Bell set about making a record of the Tancook whalers, one of the last Tancook Islanders who had intimate personal knowledge of the building and handling of these craft was Amos Stevens. Bell asked Stevens to make a model of a typical Tancook whaler as he had known them, and Stevens produced the little gem whose lines are shown here, the drawings having been made from the model by Howard Chapelle.

The schooner, as modeled by Stevens, would be 41 feet long on deck, 34 feet 3 inches on the waterline, with a beam of 9 feet 2 inches and a draft of 4 feet 3 inches with the board up.

The sail plan for the model was drawn by Randolph Stevens and traced by Chapelle. It shows a mainsail of 350 square feet, a foresail of 300 square feet, and a jib of 150 square feet, for a working sail area of 800 square feet. For light weather, there was a 260-square-foot staysail set from the mastheads.

The lines show a boat that is as pretty as can be. Although she looks delicate almost to the point of frailty, one can visualize her slipping through rough water with an agility that might be the envy of more rugged and able-looking vessels.

Her narrow hull, with its fine, hollow ends, appears quite tender, but there is a hardness to her bilge below the waterline that would give her a certain amount of power to carry sail. With her moderate draft and inside ballast, she should have a very easy motion.

No great sail carrier, she would be very easily driven and should be sailed under a short rig in a breeze of wind. The rig is ample, but it is rather low once the staysail is handed. In hard weather, she would go well under jib and reefed mainsail, or just with the reefed foresail alone.

The big, overlapping foresail would be well worth its trouble, and a come-along clapped onto the sheet might well be handy to strap it down in a breeze.

If this vessel were left with her big, open cockpit between the masts, she would be a most versatile craft indeed, from a daysailer extraordinary to a cargo carrier or longliner.

Ernest Bell wrote about the Tancook whalers and published the plans of his model in an article in the February, 1933, issue of *Yachting*. The beautiful little schooner captured the hearts of many readers, among them a boat designer and builder in Oxford, Maryland, named Ralph Wiley. At about the same time as he was admiring Bell's little dream ship, Wiley happened to be introduced to a real Tancook whaler. He was on the

No disturber of the peace, the *Mocking Bird* slips along without doing much violence to the water. (*Yachting*, April, 1941)

New York Yacht Club cruise, a guest on a fifty-foot schooner reaching along in Vineyard Sound, racing with all light sails set and everybody constantly tending sheets. "Out of Robinson's Hole appeared a tiny, thirty-foot double-end schooner, a Tancook whaler," Wiley wrote. "Her course converged with ours. When abeam, her skipper, puffing contentedly on a corncob pipe and wearing a derby hat at a jaunty angle, stepped forward, 'wung' out the foresail, and proceeded to leave us behind. By the time we reached harbor, the derby-crowned skipper had anchored, furled his sails, and gone ashore."

One of Wiley's boatyard customers bought the little vessel, and Wiley had her in his yard to study for the next couple of years. Between Bell's article and plans and the Tancook whaler in the flesh in his yard, Wiley had sufficient inspiration to design and build five modern sloops based closely on the Tancook whaler model.

The biggest modification Wiley made was putting all of the ballast outside and deepening the keel, eliminating the centerboard. He also increased the freeboard. The result was an increase in stability and buoyancy, but he still had a narrow, moderate-draft, light-displacement boat with moderate sail area. The modern rig was doubtless a bit closer winded and easier to handle. But he had retained the essential characteristics of the type.

Wiley appears to have achieved something that is most difficult: the intelligent modification of a working craft into a yacht. Some of us might still prefer to sail the original Tancook whaler, but the choice here is really a matter of taste, not a question of selecting good over bad.

The preceding plans are those of Wiley's *Mocking Bird*. She is 31 feet 6 inches long on deck, with a waterline length of 24 feet, a beam of 8 feet, and a draft of 4 feet 6 inches. Her working sail area is just under 400 square feet.

Wiley said she balanced very well, always steering easily and often holding her own course. He once sailed her fifty miles close-hauled in rough water in nine hours.

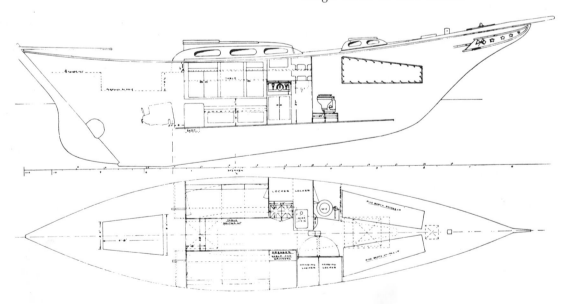

The layout of the *Fox*, Ralph Wiley's 38-foot version of the type.

The *Mocking Bird* has a number of interesting wrinkles, such as her folding boom crutch, out of the way yet ready for instant use; her sliding staysail club to adjust the curvature of the foot of the sail exactly to the skipper's taste; and her backstay running through a hole in the tiller to the exact pivot point of the rudder. Her roller Genoa jib is handy in light and moderate weather.

The *Mocking Bird*'s flush deck is good looking, strong, and roomy both on deck and below. Wiley wisely made no attempt to get full headroom in this boat.

Another typical Wiley innovation that can be seen in the cabin plan is the two companionway ladders, one on each side of the hatchway, with the treads running fore and aft instead of athwartships. You always use the lee ladder, which becomes easier and easier to climb the more the boat heels, rather than the reverse. And in port, you can put a plank across between the ladders for comfortable companionway sitting for the purpose of supervising harbor activities.

Redwood Wright, of Woods Hole, Massachusetts, the *Mocking Bird*'s owner, wrote me as follows about the boat:

The *Fox* working to windward. She has proven a highly successful cruising and racing boat. (Ralph H. Wiley)

Ralph Wiley sailed the *Mocking Bird* in the Chesapeake for fifteen years and then sold her in 1956 to Olcott Gates, who took her to Maine. Before the sale, Wiley had modified the rig somewhat, removing the headstay and jumpers, running the forestay to the masthead, and eliminating the jib club.

Ollie, his wife Jane, and their five children sailed the *Bird* for five summers from a base in Cutler, Maine, and left her in the winter at Hal Vaughan's yard in Harborside. Ollie is a geologist, and he had the idyllic assignment of surveying the coastal islands of Maine, working of course from the *Mocking Bird*.

We bought the boat in 1961 after a trip to Vaughan's in March to look her over. She has been in the water every summer since then, and most winters too, comfortably weathering the ice in the landlocked Eel Pond in Woods Hole. She appears to be good for many years to come. Our only regret is that we don't have the time to sail her as much as we would like—but that is offset partially by the fact that, unlike most boat owners, I see the *Mocking Bird* nearly every day as I go to and from work in a building overlooking the Eel Pond.

We are as proud of her sailing ability as of her appearance. She slips along easily in light airs; when it freshens, she heels until her rail is not quite buried and works her way through the Buzzards Bay chop with a minimum of fuss and spray.

She is getting older, however. This summer she has been leaking more than usual, and some leaks and dry rot have developed in the deck—which is Masonite set in rubber compound over pine planks, and was tight for thirty-two years, a pretty good record for any deck construction. Incidentally, she is planked in one-inch white cedar, copper-riveted to white oak frames.

We have discussed the headroom problem off and on for years and have concluded, each time, that even a graceful cabin house would detract from her fine lines and cut down the truly glorious expanse of deck, which provides an unobstructed view forward, a fine play area for the kids, and opulent sunbathing. Most of the things you want to do below decks can be done sitting or lying down, anyway, and besides, we have a large sliding companion hatch which, as the ads say, provides unlimited headroom.

In sum, after twelve years with the *Mocking Bird*, we find her an extraordinarily able, comfortable, and handsome little vessel, and we look forward to many more seasons with her.

It is little wonder that the *Mocking Bird* has performed so well over the years; her design is soundly based on one of the greatest boat types ever developed.

20/ The *Three Brothers*

> **Length on deck:** 44 feet
> **Length on waterline:** 38 feet 11 inches
> **Beam:** 13 feet
> **Draft:** 5 feet
> **Sail area:** 1,102 square feet
> **Designer:** Frederic A. Fenger

Doubtless every naval architect worth his salt has at one time or another thrown convention, tradition, and well-proven formulas to the winds and designed a boat based on a pure abstraction that he couldn't get out of his head. And chances are he later discovered boats built according to the principles he thought he was putting on the drafting board for the first time. This is what happened to Frederic A. Fenger when he set about creating a sailing vessel that would be so well balanced she would steer herself.

Frits Fenger discovered that his sailing canoes, with rather deeply rockered bottoms, were good self-steerers. He reasoned that the chief cause was that "the hull was more symmetrical than usual with the outline of the sail plan." The planes of the sails seemed to be balanced by corresponding planes of lateral resistance in the underbody profile. So, when Fenger had designed a ketch rig for his self-steering cruising boat, he began to draw in the lines of a hull whose underwater profile was like a foreshortened reflection of the sail plan.

Since the mainsail was taller than the mizzen, she drew more water forward than aft. Fenger moved the center of buoyancy forward to a point exactly midway between the ends of the water-line, and he also moved the center of lateral resistance forward from what might be considered its normal position. He was trying to bring the center of lateral resistance, the center of buoyancy, and the center of effort of the sail plan very close together and allow them little movement fore and aft when the hull heeled.

Fenger realized the theoretical danger in a hull that drew more forward than aft of wanting to broach in a following sea, but he counteracted this by lengthening out the stern to give extra lateral resistance aft. His notion was that the long, fine stern would tend to follow the pivotal point of the hull, which was well forward.

Fenger later decided to give his craft the modified ketch rig that he had been working on, a rig designed to fill in with sails all of the space between the masts. This rig, which Fenger had first sketched in the early spring of 1924, featured an upside-down main trysail sheeting to the mizzen masthead and set above a mizzen staysail. Fenger's resulting design for a self-steering sailing craft is shown in the accompanying lines and miniature sail plan and was first published in the February, 1927, issue of *Yachting*.

After he had created this vessel, Fenger realized

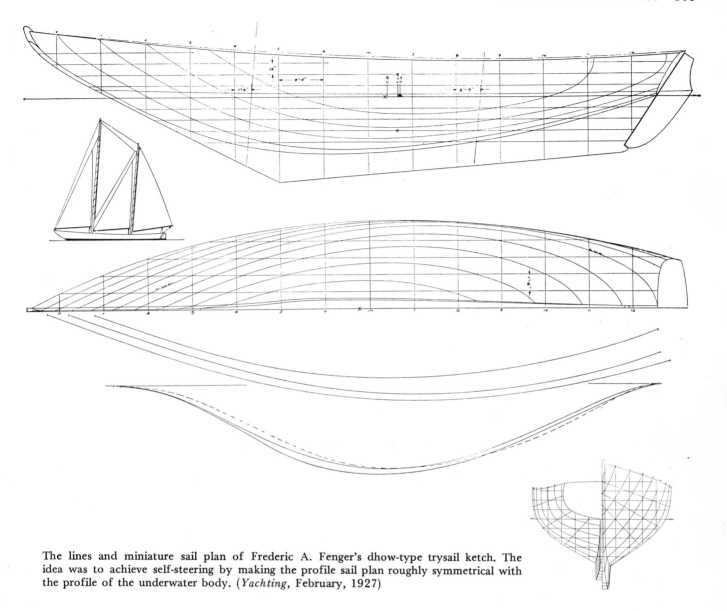

The lines and miniature sail plan of Frederic A. Fenger's dhow-type trysail ketch. The idea was to achieve self-steering by making the profile sail plan roughly symmetrical with the profile of the underwater body. (*Yachting*, February, 1927)

she was indeed not the first craft to draw more water forward than she did aft, for he remembered the open surfboats called cobles used on the northeast coast of England. These craft, as may be seen in the accompanying plan, have a deep forefoot and draw almost nothing aft, except for a deep rudder to achieve balance.

British fishermen who developed the coble over the years, however, had no thought of self-steering. They wanted a boat that could be handled with her stern to the beach and her bow to the breakers both when putting to sea and landing. For ease of beaching stern-first (with the rudder shipped), they developed a boat with reverse drag.

Authorities such as Edgar J. March, E. Keble Chatterton, William Maxwell Blake, John W. Bayes, and Tom Hutchinson all agree, however, that the cobles, though seaworthy craft in the hands of those accustomed to them, were dangerous when running off in a strong breeze and rough sea, in that they tended to gripe and broach to. A following sea could lift the stern, the deep forefoot could dig in, and she'd slew right around. Of course the Fenger vessel is less extreme in this regard, for she does have lateral resistance aft and doesn't have to depend entirely on her rudder to keep her running before it in a following sea.

Then Fenger came upon the photograph that

The lines and sail plan of another craft that draws more forward than she does aft—the coble. The English fishing craft worked off open beaches and always kept her bow to the breakers. (*Yachting*, February, 1931)

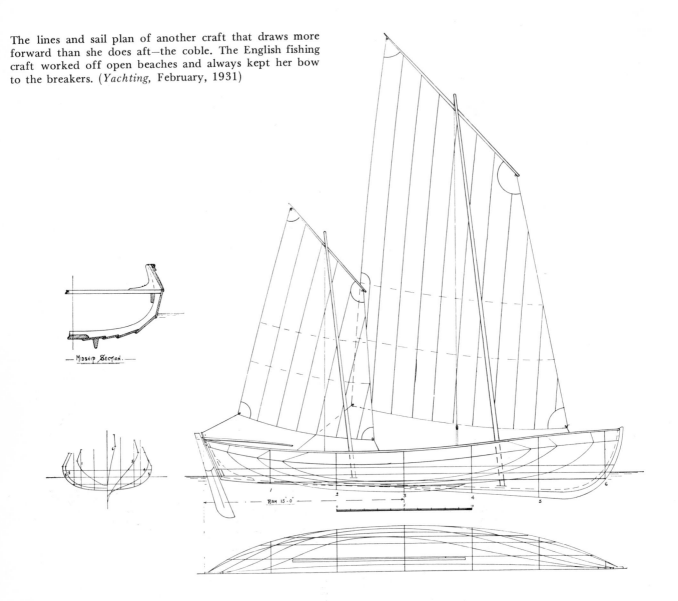

— MIDSHIP SECTION. —

follows of a model of an Arab-dhow-type yacht. Here was a craft that far more closely resembled his own creation. From that moment, he began to consider and call his boat a dhow. And the innovator, probably with a mingling of disappointment and satisfaction, realized that he had been following one of the most ancient of boatbuilding traditions.

It will perhaps be instructive to examine some of the qualities of Fenger's innovative, yet ancient, dhow.

The dhow hull seems admirably suited for working to windward. The deep forefoot would hang on so her head wouldn't be thrown off when working up into a seaway. For the same reason, she ought to keep her head up well when

hove to. Nor should she pitch heavily in a head sea. Her motion should be more like that of an elevator than a hobby horse.

There might be a tendency to gripe and broach when hard pressed in a quartering sea. Any boat needs all the help she can get in this situation, and the dhow would probably need more than most. Fenger thought of adding a modest centerboard dropping out of the deadwood, but then he abandoned the idea. I think it was an excellent notion.

Fenger loved the rigs on the Chesapeake Bay bugeyes, leg-o'-mutton ketches with well-raked masts. The only disadvantage was lack of sail area, and on a cruising boat Fenger was reluctant to add sail by simply making the masts taller. As

The model of a dhow-yacht in the Science Museum, London, that confirmed to Fenger that he was on the right track and inspired him to term his reverse-drag, trysail-ketch design a dhow. (British Crown Copyright. Science Museum, London)

a solution, his fertile mind produced the trysail ketch rig, which increases the sail area by some forty-five percent over that of a leg-o'-mutton ketch with the same spars. He sometimes referred to the rig as a schooner-ketch, because the masts were positioned like a schooner's, yet the rig was clearly ketch.

Of course the great problem with this rig is what to do with the main trysail when running. It has to be boomed out somehow. Fenger saw no immediate solution to this and said she'd

probably have to set a squaresail on the mainmast or twin spinnakers when running. Initially, he left the main trysail boomless and sheeted it to a traveler on a crosstree at the mizzen masthead. He ran stays from the ends of the crosstree to the head of the mainmast so that the crosstree, with the pull of the trysail sheet on its end, wouldn't wring the mizzen masthead. On later dhows, Fenger used the "wishbone" boom, which is like a short sprit running from the mainmast to the clew of the trysail, except that instead of

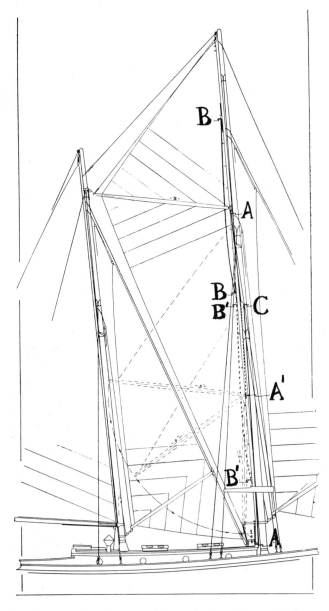

A diagram showing how the main trysail, or wishbone sail, works. (*The Wishbone Rig* by John Morwood)

a way of taking charge just when you don't want it to, especially on the big trysail ketches where wishbone booms are fixed aloft so that the clew of the sail is free to thrash as it is set or taken in. I recall seeing the famous trysail ketch *Vamarie* having trysail trouble at the start of the 1946 Bermuda Race. (The *Vamarie* came out in 1932, though her designer, Jasper Morgan, had put a wishbone ketch rig in an existing boat, the *Prindah*, in 1927.) There was a fresh breeze and building sea off Newport, Rhode Island, that day, and when the lads on the *Vamarie* went to put the trysail on her, it took charge, and she had to go off in a corner and fuss with it for an hour or so while her conventionally rigged competitors used the breeze to go smoking offshore toward Bermuda.

There is a need to get the trysail off when it starts to blow, because its area is high. In the Fenger trysail ketches, much smaller than the *Vamarie*, the trysail was made relatively docile by rigging the wishbone boom to go up and down with the sail, so that it kept the clew stretched out while taking in the sail or setting it. The best description I have found of the way Fenger's main trysail worked is the description he sent John Morwood of the Amateur Yacht Research Society in England. I quote it from *The Wishbone Rig*, AYRS Publication No. 11, in which Mr. Morwood edited and published it:

The main-trysail lies between the arms of the sprit and has a clew lashing to the after end. The clew is adjustable for different amounts of flow in the sail when the sprit is lowered but not when it is aloft. The weight of the after end of the sprit is taken by a lift running to the topmost slide and the halliard so that it goes up and down with the sail. The weight of the forward end is taken by the bolt rope of the luff, through a thimble let into it.

The sheet of the sprit passes through a block on the mizzen-mast and passes downwards and aftwards to the forward end of the cockpit. Up to a main-trysail area of 270 square feet, this sheet is a single part, and, when it becomes hard to get in, it is time to hand the sail.

One important line, the "Trip line" A and A' in the accompanying drawing passes from the sliding sprit jaw through a cheek block C in the drawing on the mast half way to the hoisted position of the sprit jaw and down to a belaying pin at the forward end of the coach roof. This line holds the forward end of the sprit up while the after end is falling into the vertical position on lowering and then allows the sprit end to drop into its "Manger" under perfect control. The "Manger" is an open box at the foot of the mast which holds the after end of the sprit firmly when it is lowered.

being a straight pole, it had two outward-curving sections with the sail between them. That way, the spar didn't interfere with the curvature of the sail on either tack. The wishbone boom was a great improvement, for it stretched aft the clew of the sail, thus taking much strain off the sheet, and thus off the mizzen masthead.

This trysail certainly fills the space between the masts nicely, but in my opinion, a cruising man should think carefully before sheeting a sizable sail to the masthead. A lot of things can go wrong with an arrangement like that. The sail has

Hoisting The Main-Trysail

1. The sail is freed from its stops, which go to the mast.

2. The wishbone spar is hoisted out of the "Manger" by the halliard, a matter of 10 inches. As the head of the sail goes on up the track, the wire running from the top slide to the clew end of the sprit hauls this out into its almost horizontal position and both sail and spar are hoisted right up.

3. When the halliard has been belayed, the trip line is also belayed with a bit of slack so that the sprit may be stopped again in the right position when lowered to be homed in the "Manger."

Lowering The Main-Trysail

1. The sheet is cast off, but the end is belayed to prevent it from running out.

2. The trip line already has been belayed for its pre-determined length.

3. The halliard is then eased away and the sail lowered till the after end of the sprit is hanging downwards over the "Manger," its forward end being held up by the trip line.

4. The trip line is then eased away and the clew end of the sprit is aimed at the "Manger" and the spar is housed vertically by dropping it into the "Manger."

5. The sheet is then belayed so that the slack will clear the mizzen stay and the sail is put in stops. Frits now uses stops of shock cord with hooks and eyes on either side of the mainmast. He also uses this kind of stop for the mizzen, but with that sail they, of course, go round the boom.

Sometimes, when the track becomes sticky through neglect, the upper triangle of the sail may not collapse readily to allow the clew end of the sprit to swing down. For this contingency, a down-haul (B and B' in the drawing) is worked into the luff of the sail at about half way from the peak to the mitre, and it passes inside the sprit arms to be again worked into the luff lower down. When the sail hangs, this line can be reached from the deck, and a light pull on it will collapse the sail and allow the sprit to swing down.

It is a matter of common sense to avoid fouling or rubbing against the mizzen stay when hoisting or lowering the main-trysail. When hoisting to sail away from an anchor or mooring, one can decide upon which tack one will go. The mizzen is then hoisted and, with a short tackle, is held to one side, for example, to starboard for a port tack. The vessel will then be held with her stern slightly to weather and the main-trysail will clear the mizzen stay on hoisting. At sea, under the three lowers, the vessel will maintain her course on her own when close-hauled or with the sheets started, and the sail will go up or come down without interference.

In order to afford more room for hoisting and lowering the main-trysail, the mizzen stay is brought a bit aft of the mainmast to an athwartships traveler or "Bear Trap" at its lower end, which allows it to slide to one or the other side to get it out of the way. However, this movement of the mizzen stay and the staysail on it permits the sail to be more effective and enhances the efficiency of the mizzen. It stands to leeward of the midline when close-hauled and to weather when the wind is free.

William A. Robinson came up with a slightly different way of handling the main trysail during his own independent experiments with the rig in 1932. Recently he wrote me the following interesting comments on his version of the wishbone ketch rig:

We have to go back to the years 1928-1931, when I was sailing around the world with *Svaap*, a conventional, Alden-designed, jib-headed ketch, 27 feet 6 inches on the waterline. During the first half of our circumnavigation, which began in June, 1928, I experimented with ways of improving our performance in down-wind sailing, using various types of squaresails and raffees. With these we made excellent passages in the trades, but eventually I realized that, for a variety of reasons, squaresails did not belong on so small a craft.

As the voyage progressed, I perfected a system of permanently rigged twin spinnakers that were simple to handle, allowed great flexibility, and were efficient even with winds well forward of the beam. They seemed to get the maximum out of *Svaap* in fair winds.

Somewhere along the way I began to think seriously about improving *Svaap*'s performance going to windward. Often, at the wheel, my eyes would keep going back to that big empty triangle between mainmast and mizzen head. I made various experiments that were not very successful, but by the end of the voyage in November, 1931, I had developed on paper a sail plan for something I described in my book as "... an unconventional trysail ketch." I don't remember how I came to use the term *trysail* for the principal sail between the masts, but whatever its name, it seemed to be the solution to the waste space up there that had nagged me during the voyage. At the same time, it seemed to be an ideal type of sail on which to experiment with the principles of aerodynamics.

One crisp day next spring, *Svaap* headed out into Long Island Sound from Port Washington, where she had wintered. She carried an experimental do-it-yourself version of my aerodynamic trysail idea. The sailplan consisted of the old jib and mizzen, the twin spinnakers, and a conventional mizzen staysail. Over the latter was a spectacular three-cornered sail whose luff extended the entire length of the mainmast. It sheeted to the mizzen head, filling quite neatly the empty space between the masts that had long bothered me. The most startling feature of this new sail was that it was extended by a strange divided spar that butted against the mainmast about two-thirds of the way up.

I gazed at my brain-child with some alarm, for it worked rather loosely in its makeshift fittings. It was roughly made of ash, steam bent. My efforts had produced something that looked like an oversize squeezed-in wishbone. The trysail passed inside its two arms, to be adjusted during use to the perfect aerodynamic curve I had read about.

The trysail itself was also homemade, of unbleached muslin sewn by my mother on an ordinary foot-pedal Singer sewing machine.

Out there on the Sound, the breeze freshened. *Svaap* sailed faster than she had ever sailed before, and closer to the wind. She had, however, a strong weather helm. In my enthusiasm, I had forgotten that the new trysail would shift the center of effort of the sails. Later, a longer bowsprit and an outer jib balanced things up nicely, and *Svaap* sailed still faster. She had the feel of a racer.

Delighted with the performance of my makeshift rig, I took the boat to the Nevins yard at City Island, where a competent designer drew proper plans for a finished version of my strange spar and its fittings. Nevins craftsmen took over. The new spar was laminated and was beautifully finished. Its twin arms were sufficiently curved to allow the sail to assume the desired aerodynamic form without chafe. Just down the road from Nevins, Ratsey designed and built the trysail itself, a beautiful example of the sailmaker's art that set without a wrinkle.

We familiarized ourselves with *Svaap*'s new rig on Long Island Sound, and later in the sheltered waters of the Inland Waterway on the way to Florida. In July, 1933, we took off for the Bahamas, Caribbean, Panama, and eventually Galápagos, where *Svaap* was to come to a sad end after being confiscated by the Ecuadorean army.

We faced all kinds of weather on the voyage. The new sail plan was well tested. I had been dubious about the behavior of that strange concoction up aloft once we left sheltered waters. As our experiences grew, I gradually stopped worrying. The spar and its Nevins-built fittings, all the first of their kind, worked perfectly. The trysail could be set or taken down smoothly in less than a minute with two people on deck. Halyard, outhaul, and the sheet to the mizzen head each passed over a single sheave aloft and led down to the foot of the mainmast, where they were handled by one man. A pair of vangs were the responsibility of whoever was at the wheel. They were kept meticulously tended at all times to keep the wishbone under control. Once on course, with everything drawing nicely, the tension on the trysail outhaul was adjusted to give the desired aerodynamic form. This varied, depending on wind force and the angle of the sail to the wind. It was surprising how much a slight alteration in the curve could affect the performance of the sail.

In normal conditions, the wishbone remained aloft, even when not in use. Sheet and vangs kept it from slatting. If it looked as if we were in for a spell of bad weather, it could be swung down parallel to the mast and clamped securely in place.

In conclusion, we found the wishbone rig extremely effective, adding greatly to the performance of the yacht. After all these years I am still intrigued. There are admittedly drawbacks. The rig would be unsuitable for the singlehander. It becomes impractical beyond a certain size. It requires impeccable maintenance to avoid failure of any of its elements. I hate to think what might happen if the sheet or a vang were to let go in a bad roll if the spar were aloft without the trysail to help steady it. [This is precisely what happened to the *Wishbone*, designed by Uffa Fox, the great English architect, builder, and sailor. The vessel was totally dismasted, but one should not be too hard on the design of the rig in this case, for the *Wishbone*'s dismasting was caused by three major gear failures and two major crew errors, perhaps enough trouble to bring down many rigs.] It could be dangerous under almost any conditions with an inexperienced, poorly trained crew.

On the other hand, the trysail in combination with a wishbone must come as near to being 100 percent efficient as any sail ever designed. It automatically assumes a desirable aerodynamic form. Carefully adjusted by the outhaul to suit changing conditions, it becomes very nearly perfect.

Our experience, added to the obvious theoretical possibilities involved, would seem to justify further experimenting with this unique rig, both in the design of new yachts intended for competition, and in improving the performance of older conventionally rigged ketches.

William A. Robinson's Alden ketch, the *Svaap*, sailing under her wishbone rig in Panama Bay in 1933. (*Voyage to Galápagos* by William A. Robinson)

A view of the *Svaap*'s main trysail. (William A. Robinson)

The first of the dhows built to Fenger's design was the *Three Brothers*, a shoal-draft version with harder bilges, a broader transom, and less reverse drag than shown in the original concept of the type. The *Three Brothers* is 44 feet long on deck, 38 feet 11 inches on the waterline, with a beam of 13 feet and a draft of 5 feet. Her sail area is 1,102 square feet. Her power is a 32-40 b.h.p. Buda diesel with 2:1 reduction gear. She was built in 1935 by Oscar Blumquist at Blue Island, Illinois, for Ralph G. Hutchins. She is planked with 1⅝-inch Douglas fir on bent oak frames, 2½ inches by 3 inches, on 12-inch centers. Her keel is molded 14 inches.

Another change Fenger introduced in the *Three Brothers* was to make the waterline slightly hollow forward. He gave her a bowsprit and moved her masts closer together to reduce the size of the trysail and increase the size of jib and mizzen. Not only did she carry a wishbone boom on the trysail, but one also appeared on each staysail.

A moderate-draft dhow, more closely resembling the *Three Brothers* than the original design, is Dr. Alexander Forbes' *Stormsvala*. Her name is Danish for stormy petrel, for she was built in Copenhagen in 1938. Her home mooring was at Hadley Harbor, Naushon Island, Massachusetts. Her dimensions are: length on deck, 48 feet 6 inches; length on waterline, 39 feet 6 inches; beam, 11 feet 6 inches; and draft, 6 feet 3 inches.

Forbes was well satisfied with his dhow. He said she was fast and weatherly and handled well in heavy weather. He wrote: "With all working sails and a fairly strong wind on the quarter, she has logged 8.8 knots. On another occasion, crossing Penobscot Bay with a moderately fresh wind on the beam, with working sails and genoa jib, she logged 8.5 knots."

In a letter written to Fenger on December 26, 1945, Forbes told the designer of sailing the *Stormsvala* on Chesapeake Bay: ". . . we were hit by a 55-mile-an-hour squall, actually measured.

The sail plan of the *Three Brothers*, the first of the
Fenger dhows. The main trysail has been kept small by
pushing the masts together and giving her a big mizzen.
(*Little Ships and Shoal Waters* by Maurice Griffiths,
Conway Maritime Press)

Below: The lines of the *Three Brothers*. Her
draft is very moderate. (*Little Ships and Shoal
Waters* by Maurice Griffiths, Conway Maritime
Press)

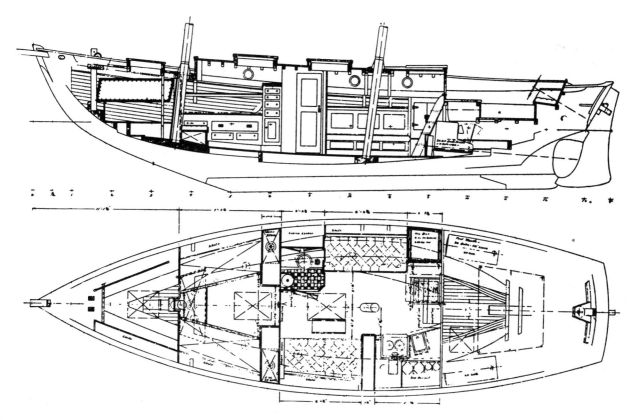

The arrangement plan of the *Three Brothers*. The head and transom on the starboard side cry out to change places. (*Little Ships and Shoal Waters* by Maurice Griffiths, Conway Maritime Press)

We got down the trysail before it struck, and she carried the three lowers beautifully, coming about easily at the height of the squall when I had to tack to dodge a fish weir."

A smaller dhow that Fenger designed for his own use was the *Diablesse*, now owned by Martin R. Haase, proprietor of the Bluenose Boatyard in Chester, Nova Scotia. Mr. Haase wrote me at some length about the *Diablesse*, for he had a close association with Frits Fenger and is an avid student of the trysail ketch rig. Here are some of his remarks:

I bought Frits Fenger's own *Diablesse* in 1949 and have cruised extensively in her along the Atlantic coast, ranging from Nova Scotia to the Bahamas.

Diablesse is 38 feet overall, 33 feet 4 inches on the waterline, 11 feet beam, and draws 5 feet 6 inches. She displaces 26,000 pounds, and her sail area of 829 square feet is divided among four sails: forestaysail, 186; main trysail, 263; mizzen staysail, 110; and mizzen, 270. Note that the mizzen is the largest sail, and as the mizzenmast is stepped in the position of the mainmast in a schooner, the main trysail ketch has been dubbed by some a "schooner-ketch." It is also sometimes called a "wishbone ketch."

I have never considered changing any aspect of the rig, because *Diablesse* sails so well and handles so excellently. Frits Fenger not only conceived the unorthodox rig, but through many years of design work, model testing, and practical experience, he designed every detail so well that every fitting does its job perfectly.

The main trysail ketch was designed as a singlehander, and the four working sails provide seven different balanced sail combinations. There is no provision for reefing any sail, as sail area reduction is achieved by furling a sail. Except in very light air, the end sails are used to get underway and to anchor. The spritted forestaysail can be easily backed, and thus the boat can be steered from forward when handling the anchor. By backing both forestaysail and mizzen, *Diablesse* can be turned in her own length in a crowded harbor.

Once clear of the anchorage, the mizzen staysail can be set anytime; the main trysail is set when sailing close-hauled. (The one disadvantage of this sail is that it must be set and lowered with the boat close-hauled on either tack, but it is an advantage that the boat can be sailing herself comfortably and does not have to be luffing when this sail is set or taken in.) Because of the wishbone sprit on the main trysail, there is very little pull on the head of the mizzenmast, to which the sheet leads. In fact, the sheet is only a single-part line, and when the

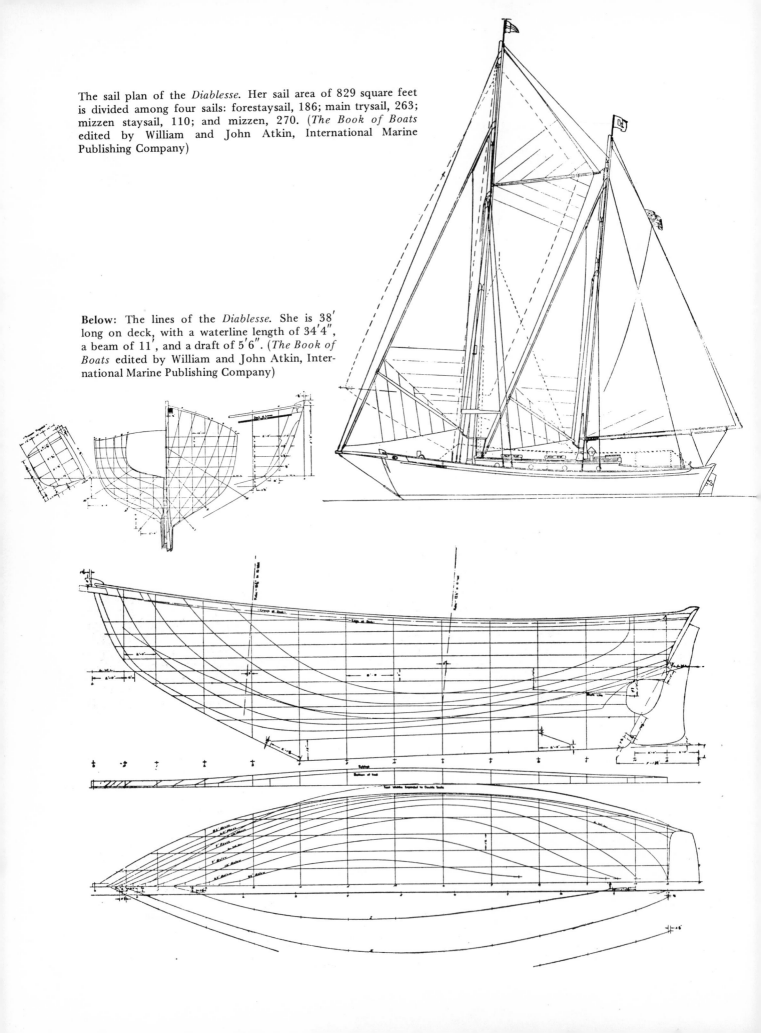

The sail plan of the *Diablesse*. Her sail area of 829 square feet is divided among four sails: forestaysail, 186; main trysail, 263; mizzen staysail, 110; and mizzen, 270. (*The Book of Boats* edited by William and John Atkin, International Marine Publishing Company)

Below: The lines of the *Diablesse*. She is 38′ long on deck, with a waterline length of 34′4″, a beam of 11′, and a draft of 5′6″. (*The Book of Boats* edited by William and John Atkin, International Marine Publishing Company)

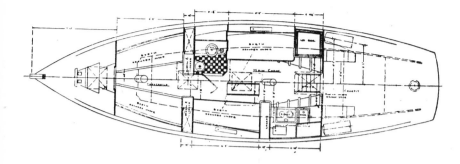

The accommodation of the *Diablesse* is arranged similarly to that of the *Three Brothers*. (*The Book of Boats* edited by William and John Atkin, International Marine Publishing Company)

The *Diablesse* reaching fast up under the shore. (Photo by Martin R. Haase)

pulling becomes hard, it is high time to hand the sail anyway.

When the main trysail is furled, the ketch becomes effectively an under-rigged staysail schooner under her three lowers, and this is a very snug rig when it breezes up. The next reduction is to the end sails, and when the boat cannot take this combination, a gale is blowing. Then, under mizzen staysail alone, one can run, reach, or heave to.

Diablesse is not a slow boat, even though her sail area per pound of displacement is quite low—only about 70 percent of that of normal, heavy-displacement cruising yachts. The main trysail is especially effective to windward in light air, as it gathers in the breeze from high up, which frequently is stronger than that close to the water. I once sailed right by Carleton Mitchell's *Caribee* in the Chesapeake, much to his chagrin. Years later, when he

owned *Finisterre*, he saw *Diablesse* sailing by his home, and he quickly got underway from his wharf and chased us under sail and power. When astern, he cut his engine and eventually overtook *Diablesse*. This achieved, he took off sail and powered home. I'm glad that Mitchell was satisfied that his new boat was better than his old one. But actually, under the same light-air conditions of the earlier meeting, and sailing on a close reach, I think *Diablesse* would outpace the multiple-Bermuda-race-winner, too.

The dhow hull is well suited for the trysail ketch rig, which has its center of effort farther forward than a conventional rig, and I have never found that *Diablesse* had any more tendency to want to broach to in big following seas than the many other boats I have cruised in. An incidental advantage of a deeper forward draft is that if one runs aground, the stern can still be maneuvered to free the boat, while a boat with a drag by the stern wedges on solidly.

Diablesse will steer herself off the wind with the use of a weather twin spinnaker, or, of course, down wind with twin spinnakers. Frits did pioneer work in this regard. The thing I like best about Frits' arrangement is that the poles are set high on the mast and stow vertically while attached along the forward sides of the mast. They top automatically when the sail is hoisted. Also, the twin spinnakers are the same size and shape as the forestaysail so they can be used in either position. I use a weather twin extensively in broad reaching and running while cruising coastwise. If I were to make a long passage down wind, then I'd use twin spinnakers.

Diablesse was built by Roger Sawyer in Milbridge, Maine, in 1937. She is cedar-planked and iron-fastened. She is still in fine condition and has had very little work done on her except for maintenance. One reason for her good state of preservation is that she has been liberally salted continuously and has spent almost all of her thirty-six winters afloat, mostly in northern waters. She spent seventeen winters at the excellent basin at Stonington, Maine, and recently she has been stored afloat at Chester, Nova Scotia, under the care of Bluenose Boatyard. Masts are always removed, and the good, one-piece cover (with ventilation fore and aft) made by Clarence Hale of Sargentville, Maine, ten years ago is still in service, keeping out fresh water.

All *Diablesse*'s original equipment (except for sails and rigging) is still in service, including the reliable 8 h.p. Lathrop 2-cycle, 2-cylinder engine, which is started by hand. About fifteen years ago, the Lathrop people offered me a new modern engine free in exchange for my "antique," which they wanted for their museum, but I decided to keep the old engine, which is virtually indestructible and starts on the first try on compression after months of idleness. The engine turns a 20-inch-by-18-inch wheel at 500 r.p.m., and this gives the type of power that makes it possible for eight horsepower to move a thirteen-ton boat at 5½ knots and do almost as well in a fresh head wind.

There are no rigging winches on *Diablesse*, and all the original Merriman blocks are serving faithfully, as is her excellent Edson steering gear.

After sailing *Diablesse* for twenty-five years, I heartily concur with Frits Fenger's own appraisal of his creation written for William and John Atkin's admirable *First Book of Boats* in 1947:

"Of her much disputed rig, at which many have gawked but few have comprehended, let me say that under its conservative area she is decidedly smart for a cruising vessel of honest pretensions, while there is the added comfort in ease of handling these small sail units. When sailing alone or 'short handed' with well-meaning but inexperienced duffers who best are battened below in a hard chance, one has not that ever-lurking apprehension of being caught with a main sail to reef or hand. Sail reduction has become a matter of subtraction while she tends herself, closehauled, and a stow or furl that calls for no great haste. Most important, she has that windward ability—weatherliness in its true sense—which is as necessary in a cruising vessel as it is desirable in her racing sister.

"For an ex-schooner man of gaff-headed days who thought he would never be content in any craft under fifty feet on deck, the much smaller and far more modern thirty-eight-foot *Diablesse* has proven the worth of the 'little ship'... Well salted and ventilated, she was designed and built to last!"

And she has, and I look forward to many more years of cruising, and even daysailing, in this comfortable and responsive yacht.

The Fenger dhow is an interesting and instructive type and may again find its proponents similar to the forward-looking English chap who is the hero of that great limerick printed in *Punch* for August 5, 1936, which I quote from Maurice Griffiths' *Little Ships and Shoal Waters*:

"A sporting old buffer from Chowes
Was commanding his craft from the bhows.
Asked, "Is it a yacht?"
He replied, "No it's nacht.
I've always been partial to dhows."

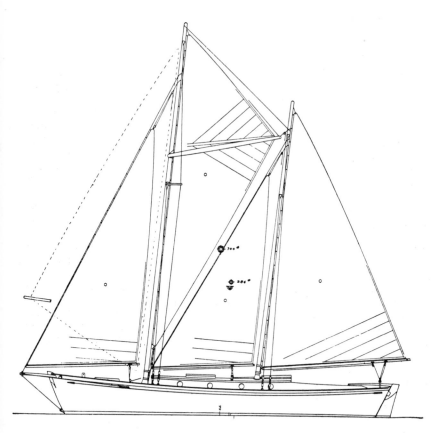

The sail area of this 38-footer is 700 square feet. This version is 34'6" on the waterline, with a beam of 10'6" and a draft of 4'9". (*Yachting*, May, 1933)

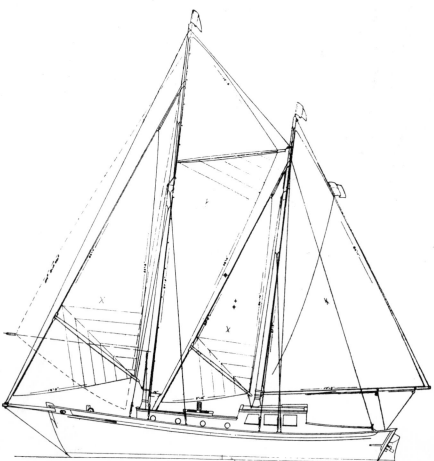

Another variation on the theme is this 38-foot "motorsailer." Her sail area is 723 square feet. She has the same dimensions as the *Diablesse* except for her draft, which has been reduced to 5 feet. (*Yachting*, March, 1936)

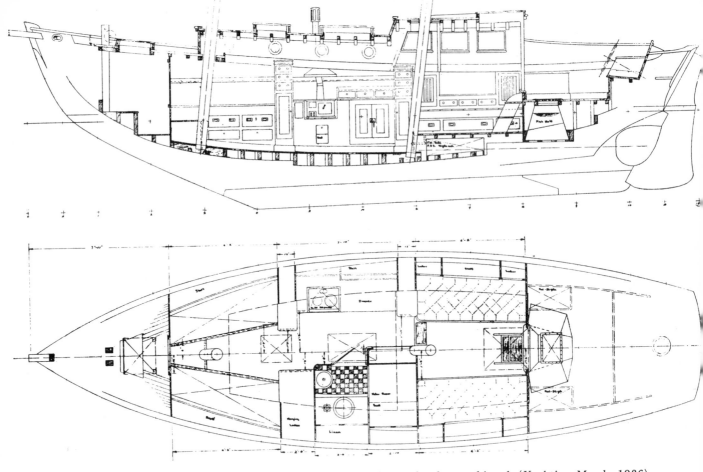

With the addition of the deckhouse, a more symmetrical layout has been achieved. (*Yachting*, March, 1936)

At one time in her career, the *Vamarie* was given an extra mizzenmast, thus making her a wishbone ketch-awl, or whatever. (*Yachting*)

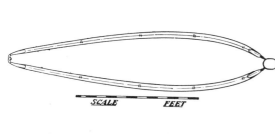

WISHBONE GAFF
SCALE   FEET

VAMARIE
SCALE   FEET

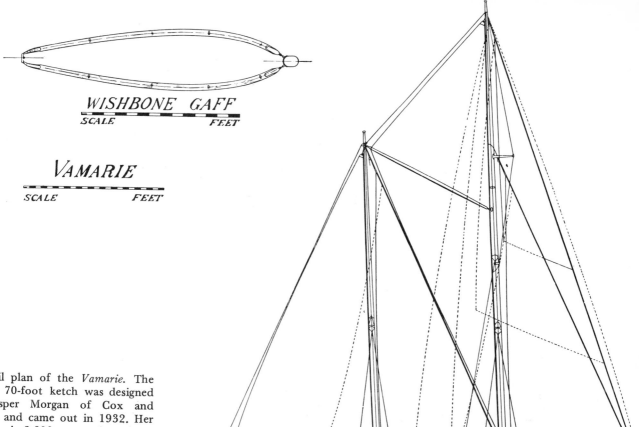

The sail plan of the *Vamarie*. The famous 70-foot ketch was designed by Jasper Morgan of Cox and Stevens and came out in 1932. Her sail area is 2,300 square feet. (*Sailing, Seamanship and Yacht Construction* by Uffa Fox. Reproduced by kind permission of the Executors of Uffa Fox Deceased.)

SCALE   FEET

WISHBONE.
SCALE   FEET.

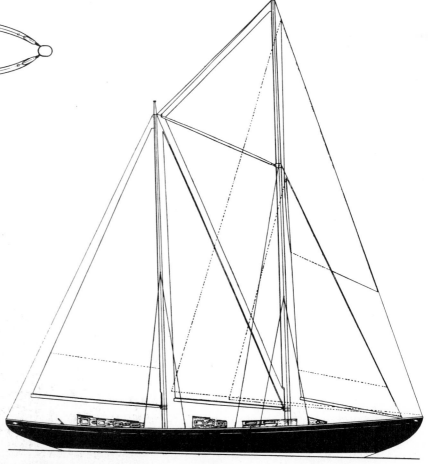

The sail plan of the 83-foot, double-ended, welded-steel ketch *Wishbone*, designed by Uffa Fox in 1934. Her sail area is 2,794 square feet, with 789 square feet in the main trysail. (*Uffa Fox's Second Book* by Uffa Fox. Reproduced by kind permission of the Executors of Uffa Fox Deceased.)

21/ The *Jedediah*

> Length on deck: 27 feet
> Length on waterline: 25 feet 3 inches
> Beam: 9 feet
> Draft: 3 feet 6 inches
> Sail area: 616 square feet
> Displacement: 8 tons
> Designer: Walter John Skinner

For chasing away before the wind, nothing can beat the old-fashioned square rig. Here is a true little squarerigger. Walter John Skinner designed the twenty-seven-foot hermaphrodite brig *Jedediah* some twenty years ago, and he made her a real squarerigger, not just a fore-and-after with a yard or two crossed as an afterthought. The *Jedediah* would appear to have some of the attributes—and some of the drawbacks—of her much larger seagoing ancestors of a century ago. For a man who likes to sailorize and wants a romantic vessel under his feet, she'd have to rate mighty high.

Walter Skinner designed this boat to take square rig. The lines show a hull with great initial stability—one that would support the weight of the spars aloft and that would provide a stable working platform. She has much bearing in the quarters and her bow is full enough to prevent a tendency to root under the pressure of the squaresails.

Because of her moderate draft, her ballast is not low, and her stability would not be great at large angles of heel. Certainly it would be prudent in this boat to reduce sail early as it breezed on.

With her heavy displacement, low freeboard, and high initial stability, there would undoubtedly be a bit of water on deck in rough going. The top of her rail at the bow is 3½ feet above the water, while the deck level aft at the freeing ports is only eighteen inches from the waterline. But then, a bit of ocean sloshing around on deck is perfectly normal to the squarerigger man.

Like a bluff-bowed Dutchman, she probably has enough weight to carry her through a chop as long as there is enough wind to keep her going, but in a nasty bobble left by a dying breeze, she might be stopped short when working to windward and hit the same sea twice. No matter. That's when the squarerigger man turns the wheel over to the cook and drops below for a mug-up.

The *Jedediah* is 27 feet long on deck, 25 feet 3 inches on the waterline, with a beam of 9 feet and a draft of 3 feet 6 inches. Her displacement is a bit over eight tons, with two tons of outside ballast, and one or two tons inside, depending on

The *Jedediah*'s sail plan with its 616 square feet broken up into nine working sails, the largest, her mainsail, having a scant 174 square feet. (*Rudder* Magazine, © June, 1955, Fawcett Publications, Inc.)

other installed weights. Her sail area is 616 square feet.

The construction specified calls for steam-bent, white oak frames, 1⅝ inches by 1⅝ inches, on 11-inch centers. The planking is 1⅛-inch white pine; the deck is half-inch teak laid over half-inch plywood. Fastenings are galvanized, wrought iron nails.

A tempting notion when studying this design is the wild scheme of giving her tandem center-

boards. A pair of shoal boards, perhaps increasing her draft by no more than 18 inches, might give her just enough additional lateral resistance to really help out when going to windward. Moreover, they would give the squarerigger man the ability to shift his center of lateral resistance forward or aft in order to achieve self-steering under many conditions. This could be a real asset when sailing the little brig shorthanded.

What a great boat for anybody who likes

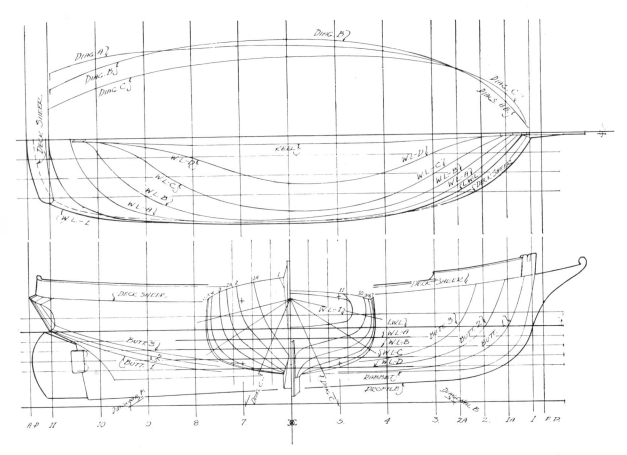

Her lines show a heavy hull with great initial stability and plenty of bearing and buoyancy in the ends to support her square rig. (*Rudder* Magazine, © June, 1955, Fawcett Publications, Inc.)

running rigging and blocks! One need never be bored in the *Jedediah*, and there are plenty of places to climb around on.

Walter Skinner points out that she can be handled by two people:

When the wheel is put over to begin the change of tack, the member of the crew who is forward will attend to casting free the old weather fore course, tack and sheet, and will carry the old lee tack and sheet forward and make them fast, and then move to what will be the new lee and trim the tack and sheet there. After this operation, the crew forward will tend brace winches to trim the yards as required for the given tack.

Taking in squaresails may be performed from the deck by casting free the clew lines and hauling on the bunt lines. This will bunch the sail close to the yard, not a neat furling job, but it is enough to reduce sail. The sail may then be furled neatly at leisure, with a member of the crew going aloft to do it.

This vessel would need her squaresails to do well to windward. A mistake sometimes made with a boat like this is for the squarerigger man to believe he can have the best of both worlds, namely, that he will use his squaresails when running or reaching but will revert strictly to fore-and-aft sails when beating to windward, thus avoiding the complications Mr. Skinner describes above. But getting good at these very complications would be the fun of sailing this vessel. And she really couldn't be expected to go to windward very well with her squaresails furled.

Her sail area is generous, as it needs to be to drive her heavy hull in light and moderate weather. As it breezed on, the first sails to come in would be the main topsail, main topmast staysail, and fore topgallant. Taking in these three upper sails would reduce her sail area from over 600 square feet to a bit less than 500 square feet. Clewing up the foresail would get rid of another 100 square feet, bringing the rig down to about 390 square feet. Taking in the jib and reefing the mainsail would shorten the rig down to a snug 280 square feet.

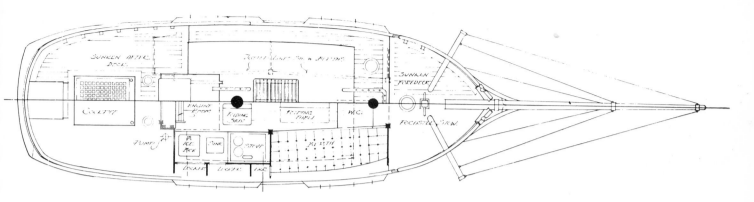

Her deck and arrangement plan shows how her raised deck and trunk cabin give space where needed below, while her sunken decks forward and aft provide protected working areas on deck. (*Rudder* Magazine, © June, 1955, Fawcett Publications, Inc.)

The versatility in these nine working sails can be seen to be considerable. And in spite of her large sail area, the biggest sail—the mainsail—has only 174 square feet. In a hard breeze, she could be run off under her foretopsail alone, or perhaps with her forestaysail set also, sheeted flat to keep her from rolling. Her main staysail would make a good riding sail for lying to. The squarerigger man in the *Jedediah* would have plenty of sail combinations to choose from in order to get just the right rig to suit the conditions.

The designer recommends a Bentinck boom to spread the foresail clews when running. This was a spar sometimes used on the big squareriggers to improve the set of the courses, especially in light weather.

Wouldn't her catheads be handy for anchor work? And why not put enough netting between them under the bowsprit, ostensibly to keep the headsails out of the water when hauled down their stays, but also to form the world's greatest hammock on a lazy afternoon or a moonlit night?

Her deck amidships is raised and is surmounted by a low trunk cabin. Her headroom is 4 feet 6 inches, except under the booby hatch, where the squarerigger man can stand up straight to wash his dishes. The seat in the galley makes a fine arrangement, especially when doing any serious cooking underway.

There is room for an engine under the bridge deck, but in our opinion, anyone who had enough time to take care of and sail this vessel

The 16-foot hermaphrodite brig *Vision*, with a beam of but 4′10″ and a depth of 2′9″, was lost on an attempted transatlantic crossing in 1864. (*Traditions and Memories of American Yachting* by William P. Stephens, © Hearst Corporation, 1945)

would probably have enough time to do so without an engine. The *Jedediah* is not for a man in a hurry. The greatest satisfaction would come from handling her smartly and well, and in arriving at her ports of call using the power of wind and tide alone.

Before leaving this most instructive little vessel, it may be of interest to note that 100 years ago men set out to cross the Atlantic in diminutive squareriggers. The sixteen-foot hermaphrodite brig

The 26-foot Ingersoll lifeboat *Red White and Blue*, converted to a full-rigged ship, crossed the Atlantic from New York to Margate, England, in 39 days in 1886. (*Traditions and Memories of American Yachting* by William P. Stephens, © Hearst Corporation, 1945)

Vision left New York for Liverpool on June 26, 1864. She was sailed by her builder, John C. Donovan, accompanied by a friend and a dog, Toby. After nine days, she put into Boston, leaking. When she was repaired, she put to sea again, and went missing.

A more successful venture was that of the *Red White and Blue.* This vessel was a converted Ingersoll "improved metallic lifeboat." Built of galvanized iron, she was 26 feet long over-all, with a beam of 6 feet 1 inch and a depth of 2 feet 8 inches. She carried the sails of a full-rigged ship. Her crew also was two men and a dog, Captain J.M. Hudson, Francis E. Fitch, and Fannie.

The *Red White and Blue* sailed from New York on July 9, 1866, and arrived at Margate, England, on August 16, after a passage of thirty-nine days. Although there is some speculation that the little squarerigger may have been carried part way across the ocean by the ship *William Tapscott*, most authorities agree that she did indeed sail across.

The purpose of the *Red White and Blue*'s voyage was to exhibit her at the Paris Exhibition of 1867. The little ship created no great sensation, however, despite the fact that she had sailed across the Atlantic.

22/ The Admiral's Cutter

> Length on deck: 41 feet 6 inches
> Length on waterline: 36 feet 6 inches
> Beam: 12 feet
> Draft: 4 feet 10 inches
> Sail area: 810 square feet
> Designer: John G. Alden

The designs for a surprising number of good cruising boats have been conceived by sailors dreaming during wartime about what they were going to do when the fighting was all over. It's natural during a long, quiet night at sea in a man-of-war or combat-loaded cargo ship to dream of sailing the same seas on the same sort of night, but on a mission and in a vessel of your own choosing.

This able cruising cutter was so conceived. On North Atlantic convoy duty during World War II, Vice-Admiral Sir Lennon Goldsmith, Royal Navy, DSO, a past commodore of the Royal Cruising Club, dreamed of getting a boat after the war in which he and his wife could live for extended periods and in which they could cruise wherever they wanted to go without necessarily taking on board additional crew. During brief turnarounds in Boston, he asked John G. Alden to design him a boat that would meet these requirements. Through Alden, he put many of his own ideas into the craft, with the result that while the boat has a definite Alden look to her, she also has a distinctly English appearance.

Admiral Goldsmith combined a lifetime of big-ship experience in the Navy with plenty of messing about in small boats. The combination shows in some of the practical arrangements in this vessel, like the large amount of working space around the engine; the two chart tables, one on deck and one below; and the use of chain instead of wire for bowsprit rigging and lifelines. There is about as much foolishness about this design as you would have found in the average British battleship. Look at the arrangement of heavy, basic equipment lined up as though for daily inspection right down the middle of the boat: a 200-gallon watertank under the main cabin table; the galley stove precisely on the centerline; and the diesel engine, placed so no speck of dirt or suggestion of rust could escape the Admiral's eye.

The boat has a husky, heavy hull, yet one that would be reasonably easy to drive. Her waterline forward is straight, not bulbous; she has quite easy buttock lines throughout; her bilges are powerful, but not really hard; and she has a reasonably low wetted surface. There is enough deadrise and curve in the transom to keep it from dragging and from being ugly. Her outboard rudder is back where it has maximum leverage and where it is relatively easy to inspect and repair.

The cutter is 41 feet 6 inches long on deck,

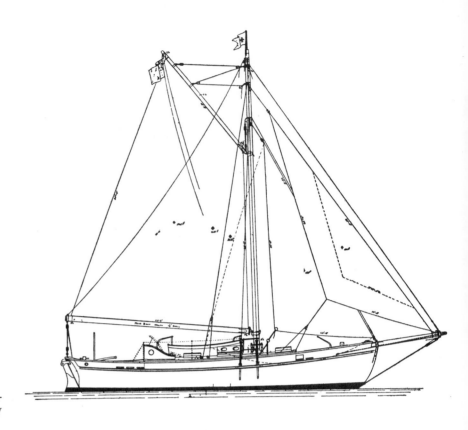

Admiral Goldsmith's cutter is definitely an Alden, yet unmistakably English. (*Yachting*, August, 1944)

with a waterline length of 36 feet 6 inches, a beam of 12 feet, and a draft of 4 feet 10 inches. Her sail area is 810 square feet, with the mainsail having 505 square feet.

The boat should have an easy motion and keep her decks dry at sea. She would not be a particularly good performer to windward, with her shoal draft and high freeboard. In a hard chance, or when it was necessary to make good distance to windward in a reasonable time, she would doubtless need help from her engine. Nor does she have enough sail to do well in light weather. She is, in fact, a fine example of the motorsailer type, or 50-50 cruiser. Of course most vessels so labeled today are really powercraft with rather generous steadying sails, but this vessel strikes me as the true motorsailer.

If you don't mind the expense and maintenance of using an engine a lot, or the very idea of having an engine running in the boat, this kind of design is very practical. With help from the propeller when needed, she could make fast passages and could take full advantage of good sailing conditions—and of course a long-distance cruise is usually planned to be sailed in a fair wind most of the way. (Did you ever want to make a cruise by simply putting your boat on a broad reach, or whatever point of sailing might be most appealing on a given day, and just go wherever the wind took you?)

One reason Admiral Goldsmith chose the gaff rig for his vessel was that he wanted to fly his ensign at the peak. As he said, "Early years in a sailing man-of-war give a man prejudices." He chose the traditional English cutter rig as being more efficient than two-masted rigs, especially to windward, though it must be admitted that that quality is somewhat wasted on this particular hull. Nonetheless, there is just no substitute for the drive of a single-sticker's big mainsail. The dark side of the compromise is the loss in versatility; in a squall, for example, you'd probably want to handle her under forestaysail alone, but she'd be rather out of balance. But again, if you accept this boat as a motorsailer and run her that way, in a squall you'd handle her under forestaysail and engine, and she'd be under fine control.

The sail plan shows the traditional English balloon forestaysail and very modest storm jib, both invaluable cruising sails. It might be well to add a smallish main trysail hoisting on the throat

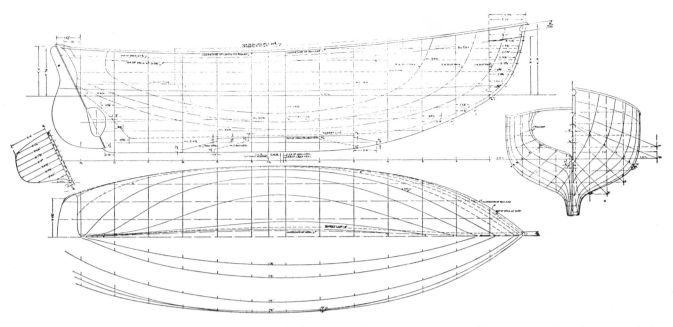

Her lines show a hull that should be able, seakindly, and as buoyant as a cork. Her strong points do not include windward ability or good performance in light weather. She is a fine example of the true motorsailer. (*Yachting*, August, 1944)

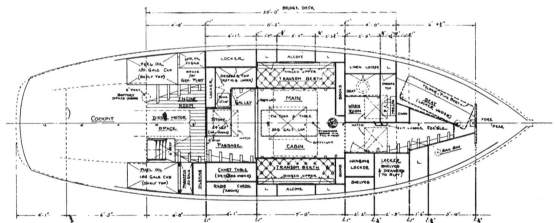

The cutter's arrangement plan shows a spacious layout to accommodate two people for long cruises or living on board, and up to five people for short trips. (*Yachting*, August, 1944)

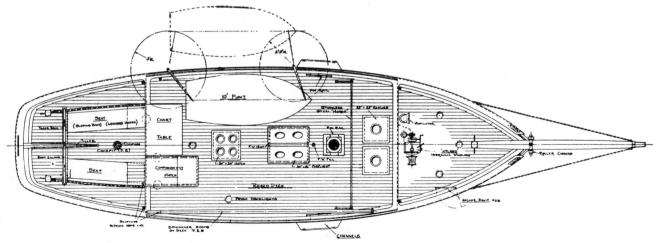

Her deck plan has a number of unusual features, starting with a 20-foot-long area raised to the level of the rail cap. With the 10-foot dinghy swung out on her davits, you could hold a dance up there. (*Yachting*, August, 1944)

halyard and with a double sheet rigged to the quarters. Such a sail would be a handy substitute for the close-reefed mainsail in a real breeze.

It would also be tempting to add a huge jackyard topsail to the boat's equipment as a toy for light weather days in mid-ocean or as a show-off sail when on soundings among traffic. For appearance' sake, however, I'd like to see the gaff peaked up a bit more, at least parallel to the headstay.

The boat has roller-reefing gear of the heavy, galvanized variety. Some folks may say roller reefing won't work on a big, gaff mainsail, but the Bristol Channel pilot cutters that used to sail shorthanded in all weathers operated it successfully on sails up to twice the 500 square feet we see here. One great advantage of the gear is that the sail can be reefed with the boom broad off.

Admiral Goldsmith wrote, "The secret of reefing with roller-reefing gear is *never* to start the peak halyards till the reef is down. Ease the throat halyards, roll up, and *then* set the sail properly by settling the peak. This ensures a taut leech."

She has a boomless forestaysail sheeting to a horse that runs right across the boat. Compared to the usual American, self-tending forestaysail on a club, this sail sets better and is much quieter. It probably cannot be made really self-tending when working to windward, though some folks claim it can be done.

The jib sets flying and tacks down to a traveler around the bowsprit, in typical English style. When the sail is set or handed, it can be handled from the bow rather than from the bowsprit by running the traveler in to the stem. Of course the sail needs a luff wire, and you still can't get as straight a luff as you can when the sail is set on a permanently set-up headstay.

The boat has twin spinnakers for long runs.

The shrouds are set up with deadeyes and lanyards making down to channels to give the rigging a better spread (she has no crosstrees aloft). An additional benefit is that the channels keep the shrouds clear of the deck, giving a bit of extra working space in way of the mast.

She has a raised deck amidships. Since it only comes to the rail, she looks like a flush-decker,

yet there is considerable gain in headroom below. And if water should come aboard amidships, there are no deep bulwarks to trap it. She has high, stout lifelines to give security on the raised deck. The raised deck ends just abaft the windlass, so there is a well deck forward to use for handling headsails and anchors.

One feature of the deck plan that may raise eyebrows is the off-center companionway. Well it should, for small, oceangoing vessels generally should have all their deck openings on the centerline. There is always the danger of a knockdown. Of course this vessel, with her great buoyancy, would have to be suffering indeed to put her companionway hatch under water. And, in any event, any hatch in a seagoing vessel ought to be built with the idea that someday it will be underwater.

She has real live davits for the dinghy, a luxury allowed by the spaciousness of the raised deck.

Having to traipse through the engine room to get to the main cabin may not appeal to some, but it would have its advantages, particularly in heavy weather or a cold climate. In such conditions, the engine room would become a sort of Down East "mudroom," a place to throw off wet oilskins and boots or a snowy pea coat and then shut the mess behind you when you go through the door to a snug galley.

The cutter's accommodations are really laid out for two people who would live and sleep in the main cabin. There are, however, two additional swinging upper berths in the main cabin, plus a pipe berth in the fo'c's'le.

The whole forward bulkhead of the main cabin from deck to overhead is taken up with bookcases. Now there's an arrangement to delight the heart of any publisher of marine books, though this one is the first to admit that even the best-made volume just won't stand up to the dampness it encounters at sea. While there's no use going to sea without good books, they really should be considered expendable. But there's just no better place to read Conrad, Kipling, and Melville than when you're making a sea passage in a well-designed cruising vessel like Admiral Goldsmith's cutter.

23/ The Falmouth 26

Length on deck: 26 feet 6 inches
Length on waterline: 21 feet
Beam: 8 feet
Draft: 5 feet
Sail area: 410 square feet
Displacement: 4.4 tons
Designer: Falmouth Boat Construction Ltd.

"Falmouth for orders" was the destination of many a British deep-water sailing ship bringing in cargo. The vessels would put in at this nearest large port to Land's End to learn where their owners had found the best market for whatever they were carrying and to which further port they would sail to discharge.

In Falmouth, the big wind ships would be tended by a type of small craft specially developed for the purpose and for other harbor and coastal chores. These were the Falmouth quay punts, plumb-stemmed, transom-sterned yawls whose squared-up ends belied the clever underwater curves that made their heavy hulls handy, seaworthy, and fairly fast. The quay punts were always bald-headed, since a topmast would have fouled the lower yards of a squarerigger when the punt was luffed alongside.

A fine example of a Falmouth quay punt is shown in the plans drawn by Uffa Fox of the *Twilight*, designed and built by W. E. Thomas of Falmouth in 1904. Fox describes a six-day passage in the *Twilight* from Kristiansand, Norway, to Cowes, much of it in a northerly

North Sea gale, which demonstrated the ability of the type. The *Twilight* is 28 feet long on deck, 27 feet 6 inches on the waterline, with a beam of 9 feet and a draft of 5 feet 10 inches. Her displacement is 7 tons, and her sail area, 670 square feet.

It was with the general requirements and characteristics of the Falmouth quay punt in mind that the Falmouth 26 was developed. The boat was designed by her builder, Falmouth Boat Construction Ltd. (now Merthen Trust Ltd.), in consultation with Nigel Warington Smyth.

Some of the general characteristics of the Falmouth quay punt have been retained in the Falmouth 26. She is short-ended, of rather heavy displacement, deep draft, and with a generous sail plan. Of course there are important modifications. She is not as heavy as her ancestor was, her bow is longer and much fuller, and her transom has been raked more. The rig has been simplified by eliminating the bowsprit and mizzenmast with their sails.

The Falmouth 26 is 26 feet 6 inches long on deck, with a waterline length of 21 feet, a beam

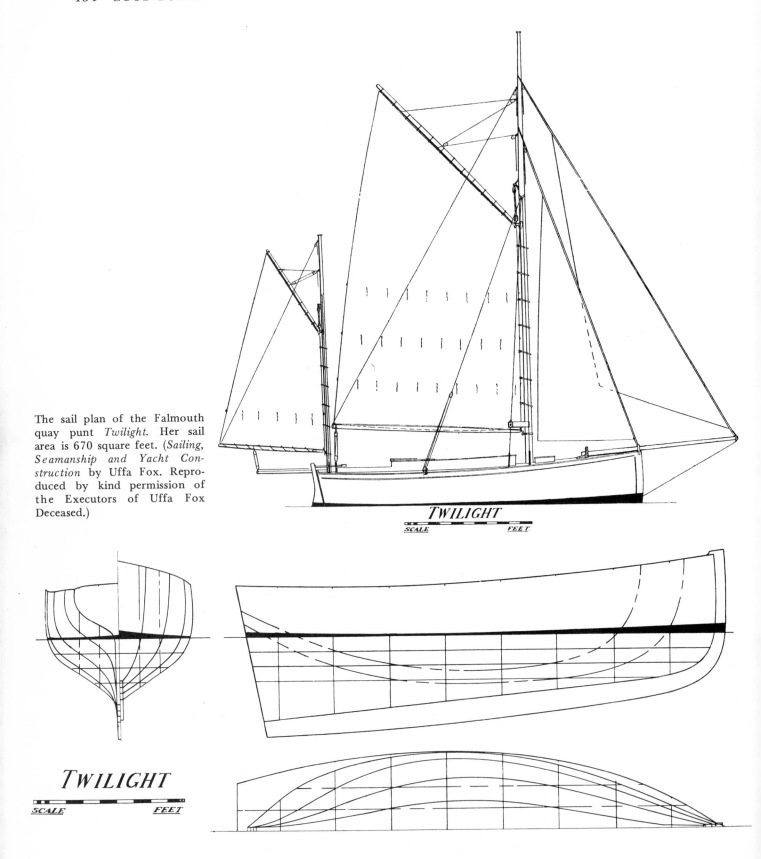

The sail plan of the Falmouth quay punt *Twilight*. Her sail area is 670 square feet. (*Sailing, Seamanship and Yacht Construction* by Uffa Fox. Reproduced by kind permission of the Executors of Uffa Fox Deceased.)

TWILIGHT

SCALE   FEET.

TWILIGHT

SCALE   FEET

The *Twilight*'s lines. She is 28′ long on deck, with a waterline length of 27′6″, a beam of 9′, and a draft of 5′10″. (*Sailing, Seamanship and Yacht Construction* by Uffa Fox. Reproduced by kind permission of the Executors of Uffa Fox Deceased.)

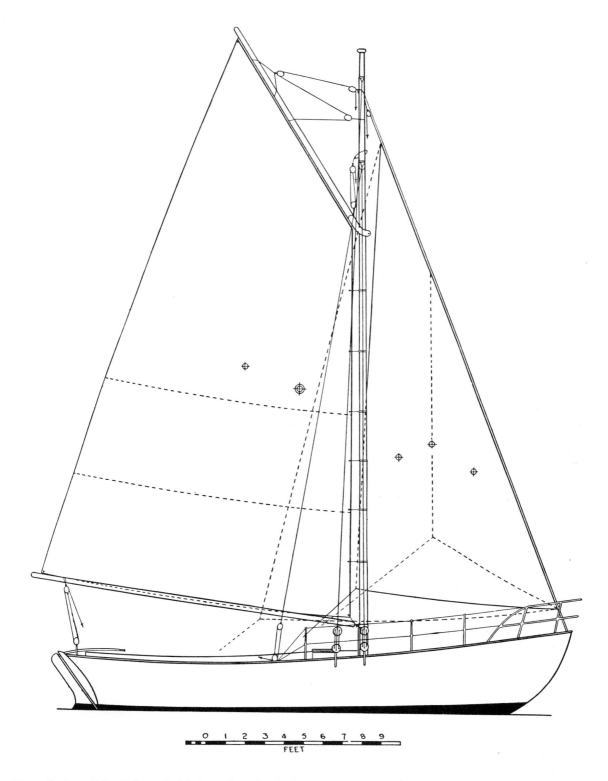

The sail plan of the Falmouth 26 shows her simple, jib-and-mainsail rig. (*Yachting World*, October, 1948)

of 8 feet, and a draft of 5 feet. Her displacement is 4.4 tons and her sail area is 410 square feet. The ballast-to-displacement ratio is 37 percent.

This boat, clearly no slavish reproduction of a Falmouth quay punt, nonetheless appears to be well suited for the same kind of sailing and general requirements around which the punts were developed. Here is a case of a yacht being

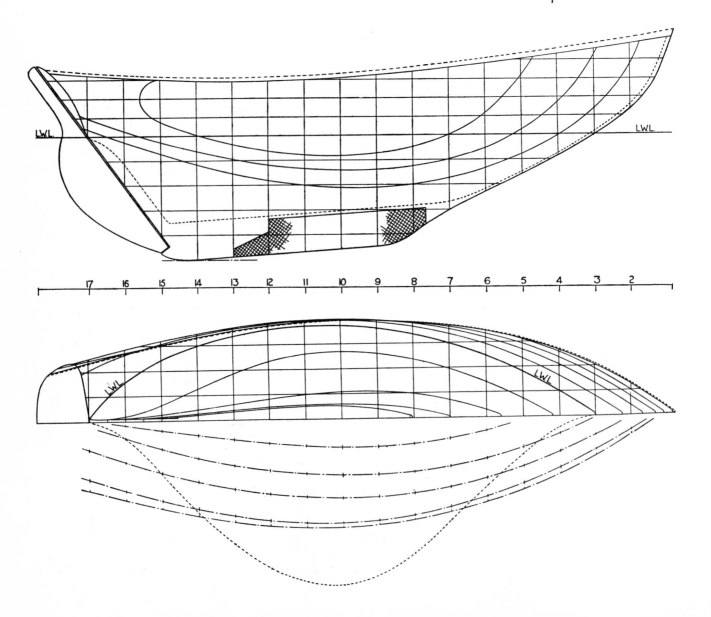

In the Falmouth 26, the Falmouth quay punt's forefoot has been cut away and the bow rounded up into a short, forward overhang, and the transom has been well raked. (*Yachting World*, October, 1948)

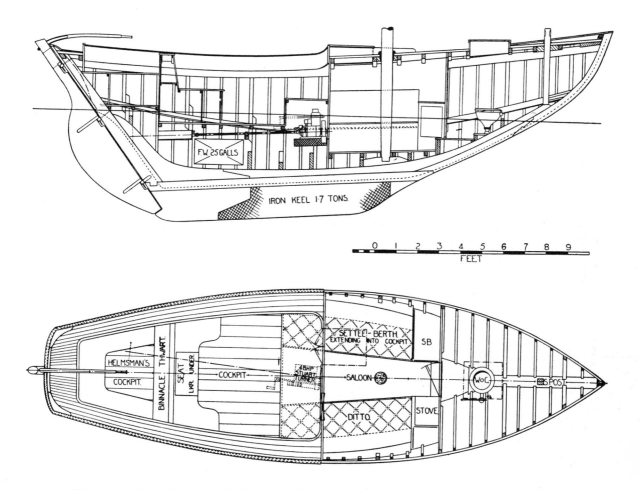

Her layout shows her huge, divided cockpit and snug cuddy. (*Yachting World*, October, 1948)

developed from a workboat with the workboat's requirements, rather than her specific design, in mind. The result seems to me to be a boat that looks mighty suitable for daysailing either short-handed or with rather large parties aboard, one that can cruise along the coast if she wants to, and one that need not fear being caught in unprotected water in a breeze of wind.

There is, of course, no disputing the fact that if the boat were to be sailed on a lengthy passage offshore, the prudent seaman would at least raise the level of the cockpit floor above the waterline and make the cockpit self-draining, or, at most, enclose the cockpit with a flush deck or a small, strong trunk cabin. But before closing in that big, deep cockpit, a man would do well to consider realistically how he would use the boat. Is he

really going offshore? How much will he really sail in early spring or late fall? How much time will he really spend below in the larger cabin area? Is there any real chance he will have this boat in unprotected water in a gale? If he is going to do a lot of daysailing and the kind of cruising where he anchors in a harbor at night, and not much of any passagemaking, then he will find that big, open cockpit one of the best features of the boat.

Here is a *Yachting World* editor's comment on this point:

We once owned a boat similar to the Falmouth 26, specially built with a large, open cockpit for fishing, or carrying parties of half a dozen or more on picnics or other day excursions, yet having a small cuddy which provided shelter in the event of a shower, conveniences

A **Falmouth 26** hustling along on the wind. (Falmouth Boat Construction Ltd.)

for mixed parties, as well as weekend sleeping accommodations for two people. We had more fun in her and she gave us more pleasure than any other boat we have ever owned.

From her great cockpit we fished, trawled, hauled up lobster pots, towed mackerel lines, and bathed. Parties, often with a dozen children, returned after a day in the sun, with empty picnic baskets and wet bathing suits, singing for the sheer joy of it. At one time we used her as a tender to a racing yacht, and even as a club boat.

The Solent was her home port, but we hoisted our tanned gaff mainsail and set sail for the west country, without a qualm about the weather.

Our family grew up, and then we extended the cabin, leaving only a self-draining cockpit aft, but she was a different boat, and although we cruised far and wide in her, we never had such real fun.

It seems to be a truism that in a small boat you live in the cockpit.

One feature that would add comfort to the cockpit of the Falmouth 26 would be a spray hood that could stow folded down just abaft the mast and be pulled up and slid aft on a track along the coaming, so that people could sit in the cockpit and be protected from the weather. Of

course, such a hood should be low enough so that the helmsman can see over it.

The separate helmsman's cockpit and the binnacle thwart make an especially happy arrangement.

I think the transom stern of this design bears close study. It's handsome, would provide plenty of buoyancy in a following sea, and would drag but little, yet provide some bearing in the quarters. It has enough tumblehome to keep the main sheet from fouling on the quarters and to look well, yet enough width to provide reasonable space on deck. Another desirable feature of this stern is the simplicity of the rudder arrangement it allows.

To American eyes, the gaff should probably be peaked up more. I also feel a tendency to raise the spitfire jib up off the deck two or three feet, although the very buoyant bow of this boat would probably keep the sail well up out of a head sea.

The interior arrangement looks very practical. The space under the bridge deck is used for the feet of the bunks, and the head, if you prefer it to the cedar bucket in a boat of this size, is where it should be.

The engine seems well placed. But anyone considering a boat of this type ought to think about a pair of sweeps or one of those wonderful Chinese sculling oars, a yuloh. I had a yuloh on a boat of this general size and found it was easy to get the knack of moving her along with it at two knots in a calm. A yuloh for the Falmouth 26 would be perhaps twelve feet long, with a crook of something like eight degrees at the point where it pivots on a "universal" ball securely fastened to the taffrail.

The key to the invention is the lanyard from the inboard end of the oar to the deck. It is attached to the oar on a long eyebolt extending down three to four inches from the oar. The yuloher yulohs with one hand on the oar and one hand on the lanyard. By leading the stroke with the lanyard hand, the oar is automatically twisted into sculling position. With medium effort back and forth, after a little practice, an amazingly heavy strain can be put on the lanyard. This is an indication of the considerable propulsive force of the device.

24/ A Twenty-Three-Foot Sloop

> Length on deck: 23 feet 1 inch
> Length on waterline: 18 feet
> Beam: 7 feet
> Draft: 4 feet 2 inches
> Sail area: 285 square feet
> Displacement: 5,789 pounds
> Designer: Arthur C. Robb

Bill Thon, an artist of note who makes his home in Port Clyde, Maine, told me one time that one of the things he really enjoys about having his little Friendship sloop, the *Echo*, on a mooring right off his dock is that when he feels like it, he can just go out on board, duck down into the snug cuddy, make himself a cup of coffee, stretch out on the transom, and think about things.

The diminutive cruising sloop shown in this chapter strikes me as just that kind of boat. Of course she, like Bill Thon's *Echo*, can provide her owner much more than a momentary retreat from the world. If need be, she can provide him a permanent home and take him to any part of the world in which he might want to become involved, as long as it is washed by a bit of water. At any rate, whether at sea or at anchor, there is something like the perfection of a jewel in a small, fully found boat that has all the basic characteristics and abilities of far larger vessels.

Such craft used to be called tabloid cruisers. The term was borrowed from the world of journalism, and, of course, it indicated something that was half the normal size.

This able-looking tabloid cruiser was designed by Arthur C. Robb in 1933. The requirements were for the minimum size boat in which two people could cruise extensively. She had to be able to survive a gale offshore, and she had to be able to carry her dinghy on deck.

Robb drew a well-balanced little hull with a nice sheer line. The little sloop has a handsome look to her, despite the necessity to give her quite a lot of freeboard for her length. Her lines are a bit finer than those of many such tabloid cruisers, especially at the entrance, and she should sail reasonably well for a boat only eighteen feet on the waterline that has to be able to carry full cruising gear and survive heavy weather at sea. The sloop has quite an easy turn to her bilge, yet with her low outside ballast, she should be quite stiff.

Her hull is very buoyant, and she might have a rather tiring motion in a short, steep sea. But if a small cruising boat is to be safe in rough water, she has to be plenty corky, and you just have to hang onto your teeth.

This tabloid cruiser is 23 feet 1 inch long on deck, with a waterline length of 18 feet, a beam of 7 feet, and a draft of 4 feet 2 inches. The

designer gives her displacement as 5,789 pounds, of which 2,100 pounds is in outside ballast.

Her mainsail has 166 square feet, the staysail, 78 square feet, and the jib, 41 square feet, for a total working sail area of 285 square feet. As to construction, the frames are specified as 2¼ inches square, taking 1⅛-inch planking. To make her easier to build, the garboard was kept flat rather than drawn hollow.

Arthur Robb specified iron rather than lead for the outside ballast on the keel because of its relatively greater strength and rigidity.

The rig is very snug, perhaps even too snug. What might be wanted would be a light-weather rig in which a larger gaff mainsail might be set with the gaff jaws coming just below the forestay and lower shrouds. The permanent backstay would have to be unrigged and runners set up to the masthead. She could even carry a small club topsail! To go with the increased sail area aft, you'd want a portable bowsprit to take a good-size overlapping jib. The jibstay could be set up to the end of this bowsprit with a tackle. Such a rig would give considerably more sail area and get

Above: The sloop's sail plan looks a trifle modest for light weather. (*Yachting*, July, 1933)   **Below:** Despite a waterline length of only 18 feet, Arthur Robb's sloop has a handsome and corky hull that would be stiff, dry, and able. (*Yachting*, July, 1933)

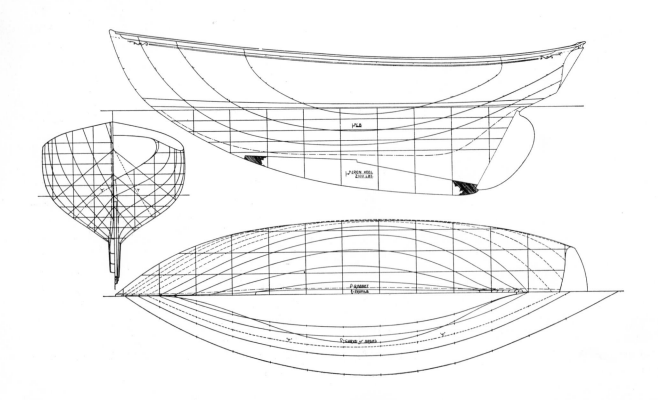

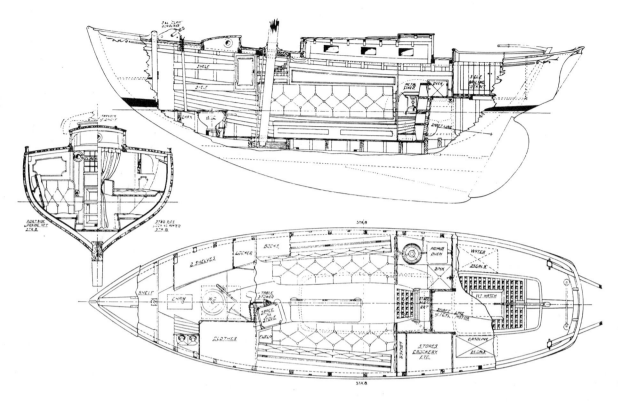

The arrangement of her little cabin is very well thought out. (*Yachting*, July, 1933)

the boat along better in light going, yet the big sails could quickly be struck if it breezed on, and she'd be right back to the snug sail plan shown, with the upper running backstays set up together to the end of the boomkin.

The sloop's raking mast makes the spar easier to stay, gives the sail lift when off the wind, and keeps the boom up out of the water when she rolls when running. The raked mast also looks well.

Mr. Robb wrote: "The rig is arranged to balance under reduced sail. With one reef in, the jib would be stowed. With two down, a smaller stays'l on a boom would be used, or a reef taken in the working one. With three reefs, the mainsail should suffice."

This little boat has room to work on deck, all too rare a feature in many small cruising boats. (While you are visualizing walking around on deck, note how high the lightboards appear in such a tiny vessel.) The deck plan was conceived around the requirement that the dinghy must be carried on board.

Robb wrote: "What most small boat men do with their tenders in a bad sea, I would like to know, for towing under such conditions is impossible." There is enough to think about when running a small boat off before a big sea without worrying about the tender turning battering ram.

The sloop's dinghy is seven feet long. The upper part of her transom folds down against her stern seat, so she will fit down snugly over the companionway hatch and not obstruct the helmsman's view. The sloop's trunk cabin is very narrow so that the dinghy will fit down over it, again with the visibility of the helmsman in mind. Headroom below has been sacrificed for the ability to carry the dinghy on deck and still be able to see where you're going all the time—not just when you bestir yourself to stand up. Few designers of modern boats would argue verbally with the sailor's maxim, "Eternal vigilance is the price of safety," yet time and again they defy it when they place high structures between the helmsman's eyes and the water through which he will soon direct his vessel.

But I preach. Back on board our nice little sloop, note that the running backstay makes a fine hoist-out for the dinghy, especially with a longer tackle on it.

The cockpit coaming is separated from the cabin house. This would allow a folding hood over just the cockpit, if wanted. There is a breakwater at the aft end of the house to turn water running aft on deck out over the rail. The cockpit itself is small and self-bailing, so it is no liability to the vessel. It's the kind of cockpit you can snuggle down into on a rough, cold day. It has no room for seats, other than the helmsman's at the after end, but there would be no reason not to keep a folding canvas armchair at hand. Now there would be solid comfort!

Down in the cabin, the boat has sitting headroom under the side decks and enough headroom under the narrow house to permit one to stand up briefly to move about or put pants on.

The transoms are seats, and the bunks fold down over them. When the bunks are folded down, they come nearly to the centerline, as can be seen in the inboard sectional drawing. Not bad sleeping arrangements, I say. The bunks could be joined to form a double or kept separate, but in any case, you have the great luxury of being able to sit up in bed and look out the cabin window to see who is making all the hullabaloo across the harbor. At sea, you'd likely use the port bunk for whoever's off watch, leaving a clear passage forward on the starboard side.

The head is up in the eyes of her, where it belongs in a little boat.

The top half of the companionway steps folds down against the bottom half to form a seat for the cook. With the ladder thus temporarily removed, the cook has some protection from the deck gang (probably a gang of one) tumbling below.

There is space abaft the cabin steps for an engine with an off-center shaft.

This little tabloid cruiser would certainly make an admirable singlehander. Or, with two aboard, standing watch-and-watch in such a perfect little vessel would be close to luxury.

25/ The *Andrillot*

Length on deck: 25 feet
Length on waterline: 21 feet 6 inches
Beam: 7 feet 2 inches
Draft: 4 feet 5 inches
Sail area: 366 square feet
Displacement: 4¼ tons
Designer: John Laurent Giles

R. A. Kinnersly of Guernsey came to John Laurent Giles, the great British naval architect, in 1936 with the request that he design a small cruising boat in which Kinnersly and his wife could set forth from their Channel Isle and cross the often-boisterous waters that separated them from their favorite anchorages. The 25-foot cutter *Andrillot* was the result. She was built by A. H. Moody and Son of Bursledon, up the River Hamble off Southampton Water.

The *Andrillot*'s waterline length is 21 feet 6 inches, her beam is 7 feet 2 inches, and she has a draft of 4 feet 5 inches. Her displacement is 4¼ tons, and her sail area is 366 square feet.

Some years after he had designed the *Andrillot*, Jack Giles wrote that she was "shaped to maintain the general outward character of the pilot-fishing boat, but having the benefit of the concentrated thought on the design of seagoing yachts that the activities of the Royal Ocean Racing Club had by then fostered. The result was a straightforward little boat with a modest forward overhang, full displacement, outside ballast, moderate beam, and a reasonably cut-away profile."

Though she does bear a very general resemblance to such traditional English craft as, for example, the Itchen Ferry smacks, many of which were built at the village of that name on the River Itchen (up Southampton Water from the Hamble), the *Andrillot* does have some marked differences. The nearly plumb bow of this sample ancestor has been given more overhang, and the deep forefoot has been cut away. The transom has been given both rake and tumblehome. The *Andrillot* is a narrower, deeper, heavier boat than were the Itchen Ferry craft, for she is to work out in the Channel rather than in the more protected waters of the Solent, and so she must inherit these basic characteristics from other deepwater ancestors, such as the Bristol Channel pilot boats. But here again there are differences, for the garboards have been well hollowed out to give the *Andrillot* a lighter, more responsive hull than the pilot cutters had.

As to rig, the *Andrillot*'s mast has been stepped quite far aft compared to most traditional English cutters, giving her a relatively small mainsail and relatively large forestaysail. Rather than having a separate topmast, she has a tall pole mast. Her

Right: One of the ancestors of the *Andrillot* is probably the Itchen Ferry smack, many of which plied the waters near where the *Andrillot* was designed and built. (Drawing by R.C. Leslie, *Thoughts on Yachts and Yachting* by Uffa Fox. Reproduced by kind permission of the Executors of Uffa Fox Deceased.)

Below: Though the *Andrillot*'s sail area is quite generous, none of her four working sails is large. (*Racing, Cruising and Design* by Uffa Fox. Reproduced by kind permission of the Executors of Uffa Fox Deceased.)

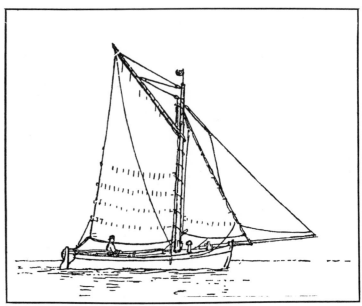

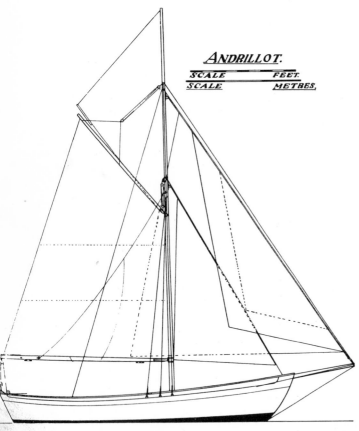

ANDRILLOT.
SCALE   FEET.
SCALE   METRES.

bowsprit is rather short and well steeved by comparison with older English cutters, and the jib topsail has been eliminated.

Later in 1936, a near sister to the *Andrillot* was built by Napier at Poole in Dorset. This was the *Wanderer II*, and her first owner was Eric Hiscock. She was a foot shorter than the *Andrillot*, but she had seven inches more draft and carried 129 square feet more sail. The Hiscocks sailed the *Wanderer II* from England to the Azores and back in 1950. With later owners, she went out to Tahiti and returned singlehanded to Victoria, British Columbia.

In 1952, the Hiscocks had built for them the *Wanderer III*, a thirty-foot version of this design rigged as a Marconi sloop. They sailed this craft over 100,000 miles, including two circumnavigations.

Soon after the *Andrillot* and the *Wanderer II* were built, Jack Giles turned out a design for a forty-six-footer of this same type. This was Roger Pinckney's *Dyarchy*, whose plans are in the next chapter.

Because of the great success of the *Andrillot* and her followers, the firm of J. Laurent Giles and Partners used her design as the basis for a twenty-five-foot cruising class that they developed soon after World War II. There seemed to be demand for greater accommodation, so by 1949 this class had increased freeboard amidships, giving less sheer than the *Andrillot* had. The modest little cabin house had grown until it extended well forward of the mast, was higher, and had sprouted a doghouse at its after end. (The lee window of one of these doghouses was smashed in when the boat took a knockdown on an Atlantic crossing.)

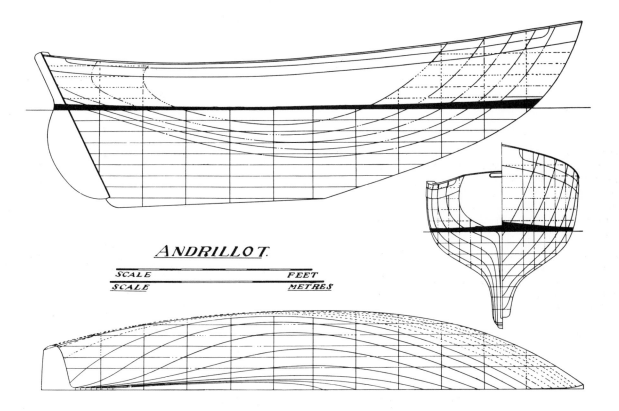

ANDRILLOT.

SCALE   FEET
SCALE   METRES

Above: Her lines show a handsome hull with plenty of lateral resistance for weatherliness and plenty of buoyancy for seaworthiness. (*Racing, Cruising and Design* by Uffa Fox. Reproduced by kind permission of the Executors of Uffa Fox Deceased.)

Below: Her cabin is snug and comfortable, but where do you sit when the boat is on the starboard tack? (*Racing, Cruising and Design* by Uffa Fox. Reproduced by kind permission of the Executors of Uffa Fox Deceased.)

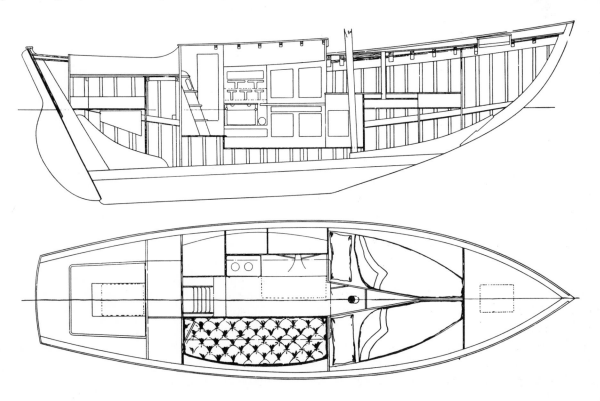

Eric Hiscock's *Wanderer II*, a near sister to the *Andrillot*. (*Voyaging Under Sail* by Eric Hiscock, Oxford University Press)

The *Wanderer II* at Honolulu just before she was sailed singlehanded to Victoria, B.C. (*Sea Quest* by Charles A. Borden, Macrae-Smith)

This class was named the Vertue class, after Michael B. Vertue, the honorary librarian of the Little Ship Club. The Vertue class boats had the same waterline length and beam as the *Andrillot*, were three inches longer on deck, and had an inch more draft. Their modest Marconi rig spread 68 square feet less sail than the *Andrillot*'s gaff rig.

In his book on the class, called *Vertue*, Peter Woolass reported that by 1972 the Vertue class numbered 128 boats, five of which had been built by their owners. Woolass records sixty-six major ocean passages made by Vertues. In 1927, Michael Vertue presented a trophy to the Little Ship Club, and this became known as the Vertue Cup. It was to be given annually for the best log of a cruise of at least a week made under the Club burgee during the year preceding the award. The award was not only for the way in which the cruise was described in the log, of course, but also for the competence with which the cruise was carried out. The Vertue Cup was twice won by Vertue-class boats, in 1950 by the *Vertue XXXV*, in which Humphrey Barton and Kevin O'Riordan crossed the Atlantic from east to west, and in 1960 by *Cardinal Vertue*, in which Dr.

David Lewis finished third in that year's single-handed transatlantic race.

Jack Giles said that in all his later versions of the *Andrillot* he didn't change the basic lines, because he couldn't improve on them. He has certainly created a handsome hull with an able and weatherly look. It is not surprising that many of the boats built to this basic design have made so much cruising history.

The *Andrillot*'s rig is handsome and practical. Such a small boat should certainly be a one-master, yet the *Andrillot* has four working sails set from her one mast to use in various combinations to meet different weathers. Her topsail would probably be stowed first as it breezed on, and then the staysail. Next you would probably reef the mainsail, reset the staysail, and either go to the small jib or leave the bowsprit bare of sail. She could use a storm forestaysail in combination with the double-reefed mainsail for a hard chance. Her deep reefs are most appropriate to her small size.

The *Andrillot*'s small cabin house allows only about 4½ feet of headroom in the cabin. I find that limitation less frustrating than the feeling you

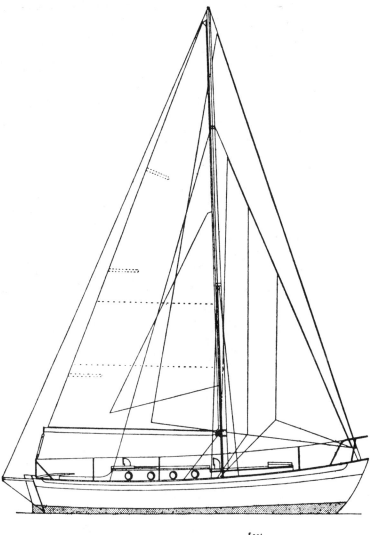

Feet
1 0 1 2 3 4 5 6

Left: The *Wanderer III* has a sail area of 423 square feet in her mainsail and working jib. (*Around the World in Wanderer III* by Eric Hiscock, Oxford University Press)

Below: The *Wanderer III* is 30′4″ long on deck, with a waterline length of 26′5″, a beam of 8′5″, and a draft of 5′. She displaces 8 tons and has a lead keel weighing 3½ tons. (*Around the World in Wanderer III* by Eric Hiscock, Oxford University Press)

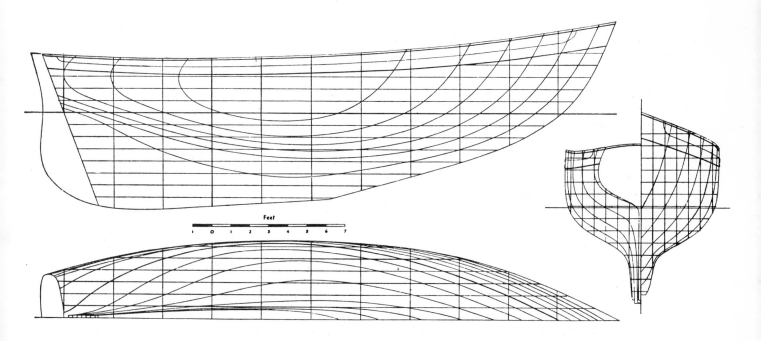

Feet
1 0 1 2 3 4 5 6 7

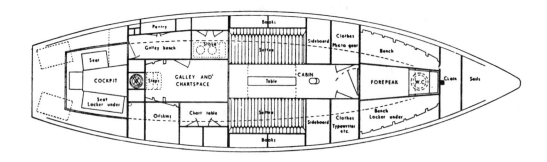

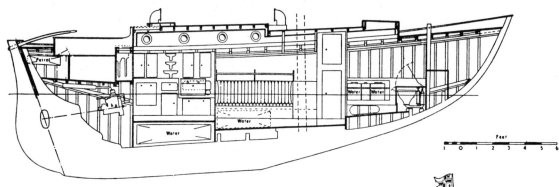

Above: The *Wanderer III* is laid out for two people. (*Around the World in Wanderer III* by Eric Hiscock, Oxford University Press)

By comparison with the *Andrillot*, the *Vertue* is three inches longer on deck, has the same waterline length and beam, and draws one inch more. Her Marconi rig, at 300 square feet, has 66 square feet less area than does the *Andrillot*'s gaff rig. (*Vertue XXXV* by Humphrey Barton)

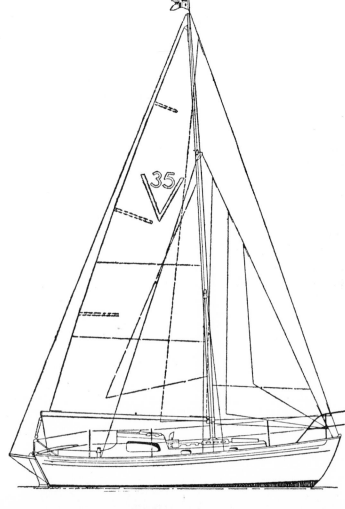

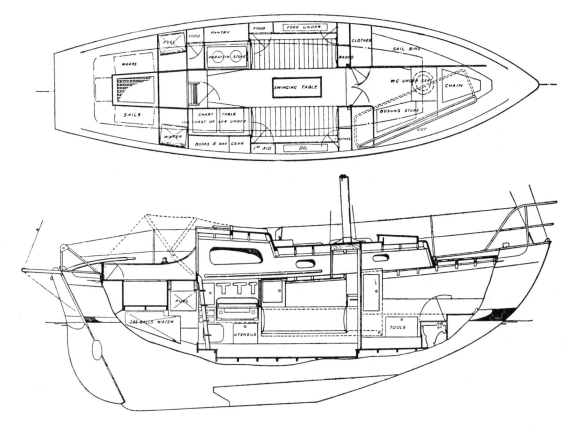

The *Vertue* has a good arrangement for two or three people. (*Vertue XXXV* by Humphrey Barton)

get—on a boat whose large cabin house blanks out your view of rail and deck—that you can't really sense her shape as she moves through the water. The *Andrillot* would be a constant joy to watch go, but at the helm of the Vertue, you would always be trying to imagine the full sense of her motion, since you wouldn't be able to see her whole shape on deck.

The *Andrillot*'s cockpit floor is a bit low for a self-draining cockpit, but this fault has been corrected in the Vertue. On both craft, the rudder could be unshipped relatively easily for inspection, cleaning, painting, or repair, a great advantage to the cruiser who would be self-sufficient.

I would prefer the arrangement plan of the Vertue to that of the *Andrillot*. The basic problem in the *Andrillot*'s cabin is that there is no place to sit comfortably when the boat is on the starboard tack.

The *Andrillot* is a fine design for a small cruising boat, in my opinion. The successful exploits of the Vertues have proven the worth of her design. But perhaps the happiest fact about the *Andrillot* is that she is still sailing on the beautiful coast of Cornwall.

26/ The *Dyarchy*

> Length on deck: 45 feet 10 inches
> Length on waterline: 38 feet
> Beam: 12 feet 3 inches
> Draft: 7 feet 6 inches
> Sail area: 1,410 square feet
> Displacement: 24.2 tons
> Designer: John Laurent Giles

Despite a name that implies she is a ship with two captains, the English cutter *Dyarchy*, designed by Laurent Giles in the mid-Thirties, has cruised a great many miles, with eminent success, around the coasts of the British Isles and the Continent. She is a boat that is well suited to the rough waters and tide rips of the leeward side of the Atlantic, but she would also be perfectly capable of extended passages offshore. She is a big, able boat.

The *Dyarchy* is 45 feet 10 inches long on deck, 38 feet on the waterline, with a beam of 12 feet 3 inches and a draft of 7 feet 6 inches. Her displacement is 24.2 tons and her sail area, 1,410 square feet.

She is a handsome vessel; the curves of her sheer line and stem profile, the rake of her transom and steeve of her bowsprit all seem to go together harmoniously. She looks to be a real sea boat. The outside wale gives extra strength to the topsides and accentuates the sheer. As may be seen in the drawing, the *Dyarchy*'s topsides are painted black, and the wale is varnished.

The full, deep sections of this boat give her plenty of body to hang on with in a seaway and also allow lots of room below. Looking at the waterlines, one sees she is somewhat full forward. To my knowledge, all who have sailed in the boat have praised her, but I wonder if her rather full bow wouldn't slow her down unduly when punching into a short head sea. There are few things more frustrating when beating along a coast under such conditions than having the seas slow the boat right down when she hits them. There's a good breeze, and you feel as if the boat should be working to windward nicely through the chop, but just when she seems to get going, she hits three in a row and seems to heave herself to for a moment. Meanwhile, that next point of land seems just as far to windward as it was an hour ago. A full, buoyant bow is nice when running off in a seaway, for she keeps her head up and her decks dry when running down the seas. But when working to windward under the same conditions, such a bow is another story.

The flat transom is curved enough in section to keep it from appearing clumsy. The great drawback to the transom stern is that, unlike a fine counter stern, it can disturb a following sea and cause it to break and perhaps come on board in

DYARCHY.

SCALE ———— FEET
SCALE ———— METRES

Jack Giles based the *Dyarchy*'s rig on that of the traditional English cutter, but gave her a smaller mainsail, taller topsail, and broader forestaysail than her ancestors had, all of which modifications add to the boat's efficiency and ease of handling. (*Thoughts on Yachts and Yachting* by Uffa Fox. Reproduced by kind permission of the Executors of Uffa Fox Deceased.)

Eric Hiscock called the *Dyarchy* a "great powerful creature." (*Thoughts on Yachts and Yachting* by Uffa Fox. Reproduced by kind permission of the Executors of Uffa Fox Deceased.)

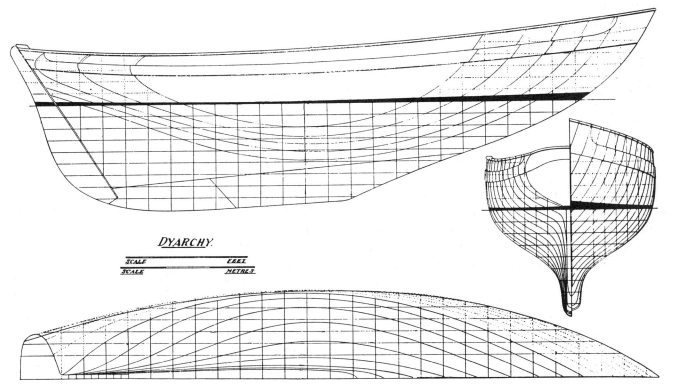

DYARCHY.

SCALE ———— FEET
SCALE ———— METRES

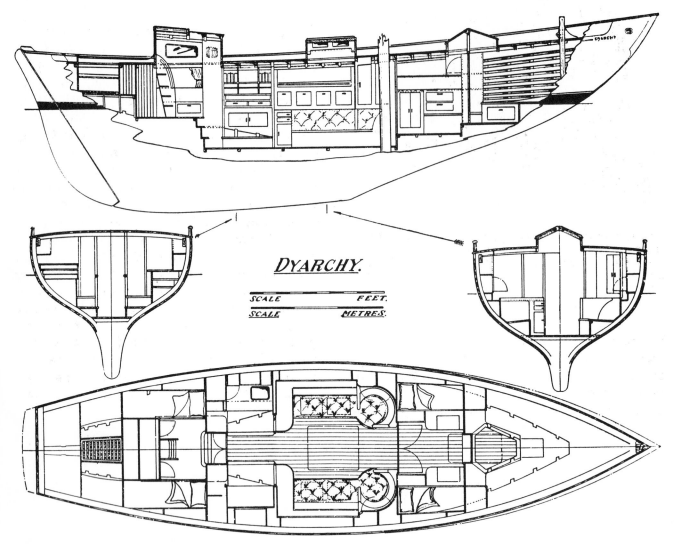

As fine a boat as the *Dyarchy* is to sail, it might be tempting to stay at anchor just so you could supervise harbor activities from her deckhouse, plan the next cruise in her chart room, or just relax in her armchairs and cruise vicariously by swapping lies. (*Thoughts on Yachts and Yachting* by Uffa Fox. Reproduced by kind permission of the Executors of Uffa Fox Deceased.)

the process. Uffa Fox often wrote of this danger, one example of which follows:

Once in a square-sterned boat we were driving her far too hard when chasing away before a gale of wind, and she pulled the sea in over the stern, which, besides filling her self-bailing cockpit, filled her cabin up to the bunk level, but immediately we took sail off her and let her drive along at a speed to suit the seas, she showed no tendency at all to pull them in over the stern. So it would seem that the point to remember with short-sterned boats is that there is a limit to the speed at which they can be driven before a gale and steep breaking seas, and that this limit is reached earlier in square-sterned boats than in those with well-designed counters, which do not disturb the following sea so much and so tend to pull it aboard.

This is the way of the world, and all things have their advantages and disadvantages, and only the owners of

vessels can decide what advantages they want and what they will endure to get them.

The *Dyarchy*'s cockpit is small, and her bridge deck is substantial. Although it doesn't show in the plans, the *Dyarchy* has a small engine installed under the floor of the deckhouse. It has seldom been used, since it is only big enough to move the boat into or out of the harbor in a calm. With any breeze at all, the cutter would move along nicely with her topsail set and her big, light headsails pulling her along. Her biggest jib has an area of 770 square feet.

Her rig is Laurent Giles' characteristic modernization of the traditional British gaff cutter. He

Dent's drawing of the *Dyarchy*, based closely on a photograph of her, shows her sailing fast on a close reach. (*Yachting Monthly*, January, 1974, drawing by William Dent)

the gaff mainsail quite short. The result is a small, manageable mainsail (610 square feet on the *Dyarchy*), a tall main topsail—which, in combination with the mainsail, gives the effect of a Marconi sail—and a very large headsail area, broken up into moderate-sized sails. There is no reason why she couldn't carry a working jib topsail, though it is not shown in the sail plan.

Thus the cutter has a sail plan that should be quite efficient to windward—one with generous area, yet one that can be shortened down to many different sail combinations to suit the weather. With her small jib, small forestaysail, and a close-reefed mainsail (she has roller-reefing gear), she would be snugly rigged indeed. The foot of each headsail is high enough so that the helmsman can see under them and also high enough so that they won't be struck by seas spitting off the lee bow. This headsail height is partly achieved by the well-steeved bowsprit, a welcome departure from the traditional and dangerous British practice of setting the bowsprit parallel to the water.

has made the lower mast and topmast into one spar (on the *Dyarchy,* the mast is solid up as far as the peak halyard blocks and hollow above them), shortened the bowsprit and main boom, moved the mast aft a bit, and left the hoist on

This slightly longer version of the *Dyarchy* has a bit less sail, with an area of 1,183 square feet. (*Le Yacht,* December 11, 1948)

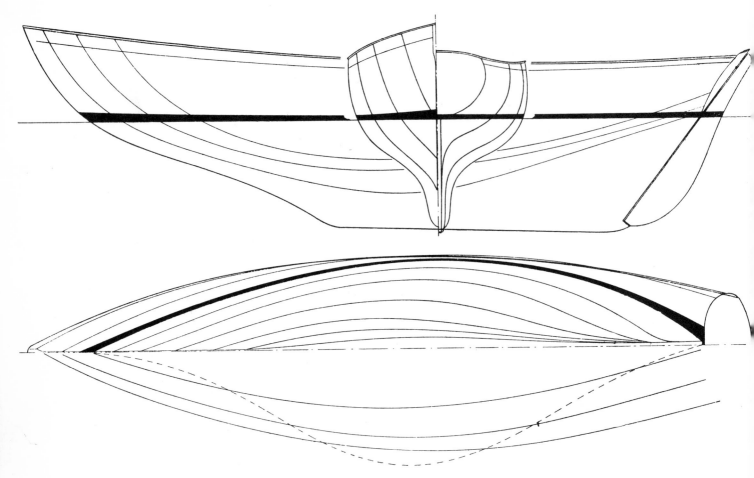

This version of the type is 49'3" long on deck, with a waterline length of 41'5", and the same beam and draft as the *Dyarchy* at 12'3" and 7'6". (*Le Yacht*, December 11, 1948)

The lower end of the jib stay on the *Dyarchy* slides on a bowsprit traveler so that the tack of the sail may be brought to the stem head, supposedly for ease of setting or handing the sail. Americans generally seem to prefer to leave the stay where it is and rig a downhaul to the head of the sail so it can be hauled right down the stay. And the end of the bowsprit is not really such a bad place to work. It's high and out away from the water thrown by the bow, and it has a pair of shrouds and a bobstay forming angles with the spar into which legs may be jammed to keep one from deserting his work. The end of the bow itself has no such amenities. Perhaps the biggest advantage of being able to bring the jib stay inboard is that a space is cleared for passing through a big jib topsail when tacking.

The *Dyarchy* has a most interesting arrange-

ment below decks. Her deckhouse would make a fine place to cork off during an easy watch, while remaining handy to the deck. Forward of this is the galley to port and a generous chart room to starboard. In the saloon are two real armchairs, and the transoms extend aft under the sideboards so that they can be used as full-length bunks. The bunks in the forward stateroom are set high, with much storage space below them. There is also a small seat on each side of the stateroom. The forward hatch serves both the stateroom and the fo'c's'le, to which place the head has been relegated.

Eric and Susan Hiscock made more than one cross-Channel cruise in the *Dyarchy* when she was owned by Roger Pinckney. Recounting one of the passages returning westward across the Channel, Eric Hiscock wrote the following, which

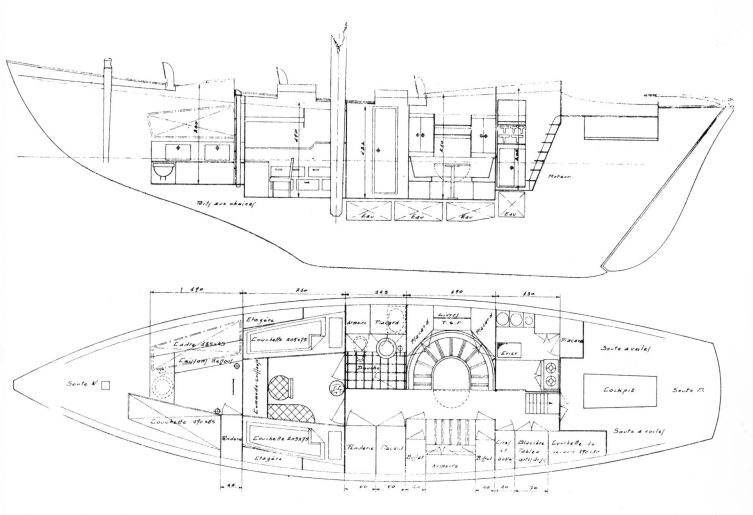

Her curved settee in the saloon and convenient chair at madame's dressing table forward may give away the fact that this boat was designed for French sailors even before you notice that in the head there is a bidet. (*Le Yacht*, December 11, 1948)

pretty well sums up what it was like to sail in the *Dyarchy*:

Clear of the breakwater, we found a large and rather confused sea on our beam. Once or twice a playful crest leaped over the weather rail and down the necks of those of us who happened to be in the cockpit at the time, but *Dyarchy* went rejoicing on her way, rapidly dropping Alderney over the horizon as hour after hour the patent log recorded a steady 7½ knots. Susan and I, who do most of our sailing in our own four-tonner [this was written in 1948], were much impressed by the ease and grace with which the great powerful creature surged buoyantly along, for we had expected a wet, tiring, and uncomfortable passage. But this was completely the opposite, and, having prepared for the worst, it turned out to be a quite delightful sail. Mrs. Pinckney (age 82)

spent the entire day on deck, but for those of us who were less hardy, there was always the glowing Courtier stove round which to sit down below.

And so, as the wind moderated, they added more sail and kept her going, so that they had her home to Lymington by 8:30 that evening. Eric Hiscock continues:

She had averaged 7½ knots for the round cruise, and that included the long struggle against the foul tide in the Ortac Channel when outward bound. We had experienced some magnificent sailing in a very fine vessel, and we had had some anxious moments, but all of us will remember that last cross-Channel passage for as long as we live.

27/ The *Coaster*

Length on deck: 36 feet 5 inches
Length on waterline: 29 feet 8 inches
Beam: 11 feet 2 inches
Draft: 5 feet 9 inches
Sail area: 900 square feet
Designer: Murray G. Peterson

Upon looking around the anchorage off Burr's Dock, New London, Connecticut, after we had dropped the hook there many years ago, I was delighted to see the little schooner *Coaster* tied up at the wharf. I had often admired Murray Peterson's plans of her, and here was a chance to see the vessel herself.

Inspection from alongside in the dinghy and then from the dock showed her to be just what the plans indicated: every inch an able and handsome vessel. Finer lined than her big cargo-carrying ancestors, she was nonetheless beamy enough to have plenty of stability and full-ended enough to rise to a steep sea without making much fuss over it.

But would she sail fast? Her nicely hollowed entrance said so, but then it came out to form an almost bulbous shoulder, well forward; her straight run said so, but it was more steep than flat.

The fellow on deck who was delivering her someplace for the owner answered my question. "She's nothing spectacular in light going," he admitted, "but give her a breeze o' wind and she sails like a fool, just like a fool."

Judging by the bone in her teeth in Edwin Levick's fine photo of her sailing full-and-by under plain sail in a gentle breeze, she's no slouch.

The *Coaster* is 36 feet 5 inches long on deck, with a waterline length of 29 feet 8 inches, a beam of 11 feet 2 inches, and a draft of 5 feet 9 inches. Her sail area is 900 square feet, with 796 square feet in the four lowers.

What a wholesome design this is for a cruising boat. First off, she's pretty. Some say the Peterson schooners (for there were later variations on the theme of this design) are too pretty. I guess they mean that if she's supposed to resemble a coasting schooner, then she ought to look more like one.

The *Coaster* certainly resembles the workaday schooners of the past, but she has her own style and grace—and why not, since her good looks don't compromise her ability. Capable of a good turn of speed, especially when she gets her favorite weather, she is also eminently seaworthy and seakindly. She'd be easy on her crew, an important attribute in a cruising boat, though one not always achieved in today's designs.

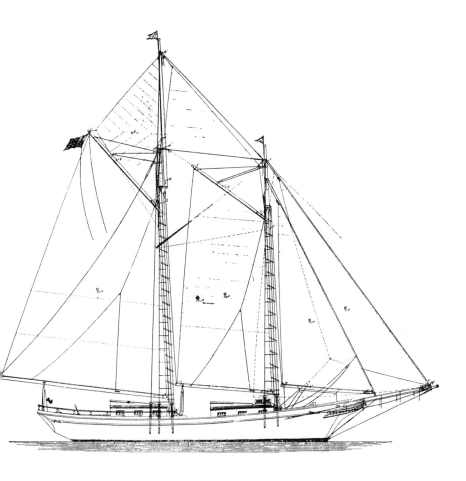

The *Coaster*'s rig can be handled easily by two people without need of winches. (*Yachting*, November, 1931)

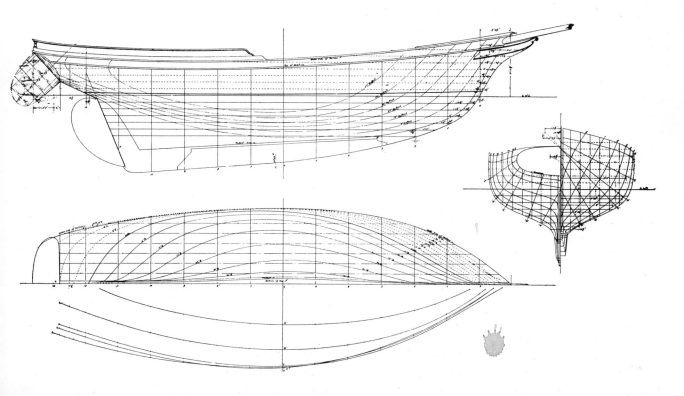

Her lines show her to have a deep body, considerable drag to the keel, and a long run. (*Yachting*, November, 1931)

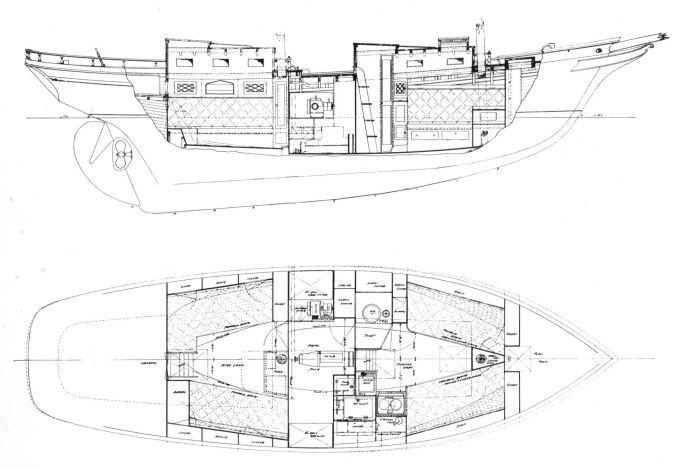

Above: The *Coaster* has comfortable accommodations for four. (*Yachting*, November, 1931)

Below: The original *Coaster* slipping along nicely. (Edwin Levick Collection, Mariners Museum, Newport News, Virginia)

Easy on her crew, with all those sails, spars, and pieces of running rigging? Absolutely.

Four working sails to set with rope halyards that are easy on the hands and enough purchase so that winches aren't needed. Light sails that are fun to play with and that set far enough aloft to really catch the best of a small breeze, but enough sail area without them so there is no need for a big overlapping headsail with its heavily straining single-part sheet. A stiff enough boat (note the fairly hard turn of the bilge just below the waterline) so that reefing wouldn't be necessary until there was real weight in the wind. (And reefing that overhanging gaff mainsail in a breeze with the boat jumping isn't all that hard, provided you keep the boom under control with sheet, topping lift, and gallows frame, and keep the clew earing rove off so you don't have to climb out on the boom.)

With jumbo, foresail, and a reefed main, she'd stand up to plenty. And she'd run off in a gale under foresail and jumbo. If her people needed rest, she could be brought up with just a reefed foresail to lie with her head tucked under her wing.

It's the very complexity and versatility of her rig, the many ways she can be sailed to suit the weather and the wants of her crew, that make her, in the end, an easy boat to handle when cruising.

The *Coaster* has good accommodations for four people. The two pairs of bunks are well separated for privacy. The after cabin makes a comfortable saloon immediately handy to the cockpit, and its house protects the cockpit. The weight of the engine, a 25-h.p. Falcon, is in the middle of the boat, and in this position, the motor can be low enough so its shaft can be nearly level, yet the wheel will be well submerged.

The galley doesn't interfere with saloon-to-cockpit traffic, yet it is immediately accessible from the deck. Looking back on this boat forty years after she was designed, perhaps the most notable feature of her layout is that she has plenty of room for four people, rather than not enough for more.

The *Coaster* was built by Goudy and Stevens at East Boothbay, Maine, and was initially sailed by her designer. She is still going strong on the West Coast, having been cruised to Alaska via the

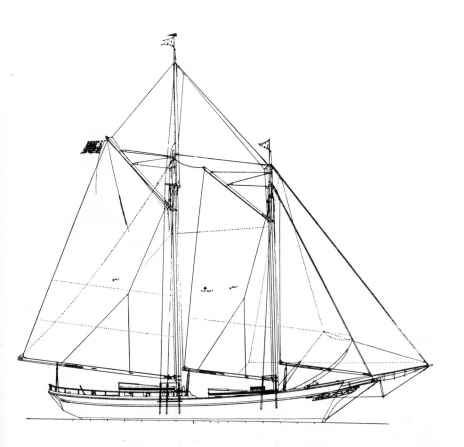

The *Coaster II* is big enough for a dolphin striker. (*Yachting*, December, 1933)

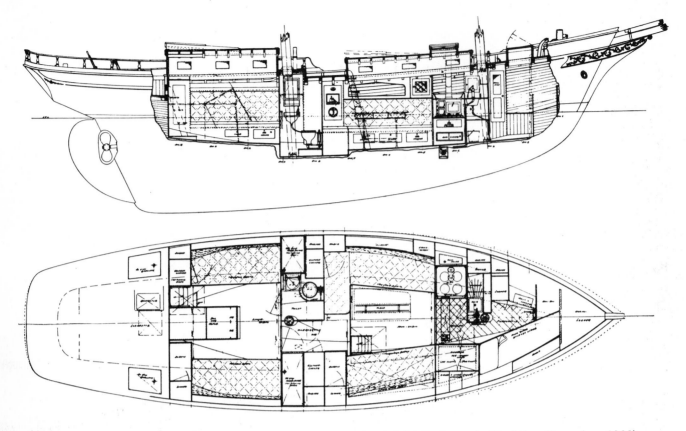

Above: In the *Coaster II*, the engine is aft and there is a single-berth fo'c's'le forward. (*Yachting*, December, 1933)

Below: The *Coaster II*, now renamed the *Quissett*, with her light sails set. Notice the channel for the main shrouds. (*Sailing*, February, 1974)

The *Coaster III* is 41'2" long on deck, 33'8" long on the waterline, with a beam of 12' and a draft of 6'3". (*Yachting*, June, 1937)

Panama Canal and Hawaii by Dodge and Layle Morgan a few years ago.

At least two sisterships have been built: the *North Star*, by the Camden (Maine) Shipbuilding Company in 1962, and the *Serenity*, by Malcolm Brewer at Camden, Maine, in 1964.

In 1933, Peterson designed a larger version, the *Coaster II*. Her dimensions are: length on deck, 42 feet 7 inches; length on the waterline, 35 feet 2 inches; beam, 12 feet 3 inches; draft, 6 feet 6 inches; and sail area (four lowers) 1,005 square feet. Two years later came the *Coaster III*, a similar model 41 feet 2 inches long on deck. The *Silver Heels*, built by the Camden Shipbuilding Company in 1963, was a near sister to the *Coaster III*. Peterson also designed an interesting

offshoot, a ketch-rigged version of the original *Coaster*.

A larger successor to these craft was the *Don Quixote del Mar*, a modified fifty-seven-footer that Peterson designed in 1937 for Frederick R. Rogers for ocean cruising. As can be seen in her plans, she is shoaler and a little fuller than the *Coasters*, her additional dimensions being: length on the waterline, 47 feet; beam, 15 feet; and draft, 6 feet 10 inches.

The *Don*'s rig is intriguing, the traditional schooner sail plan having been broken up into smaller units for ease of handling. The main boom has been cut off and a leg-o'-mutton mizzen added. The jib has been given a full club so it can be self-tending; this rig is reminiscent of that on some of the biggest of the coasting schooners. The jib topsail sets low and well forward, to keep it clear of the square foretopsail that has been added. The triangular foresail, set from the yard, won't be blanketed as much by the mainsail as it would if it were square, doesn't require sheets and tacks on the clews, and, in any case, preserves the most efficient part of a square-sail. This sail is reminiscent of the laborsaving mizzen of some of the later four-masted barks.

Her layout below looks just as practical as her rig, with spacious charthouse aft and galley amidships where the motion is least. She even has a piano in the main saloon! Who wouldn't sell his farm and go to sea?

All in all, it is instructive to look back on these designs of Murray Peterson. They represent a distinctive type of cruising boat, a type that never seems to go out of style, a type that borrows good looks and seagoing ability from traditional American working vessels and makes the most of them.

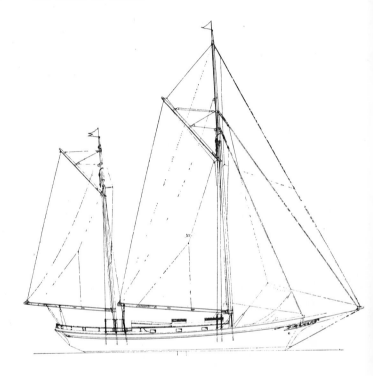

The ketch-rigged version of the *Coaster* sets 737 square feet of sail in her four lowers. (*Yachting*, May, 1935)

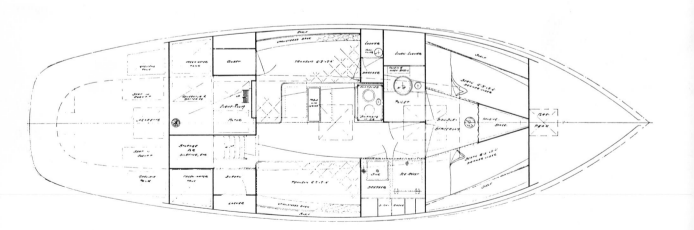

The ketch is laid out for four people. Her hull dimensions are identical to those of the original *Coaster*. (*Yachting*, May, 1935)

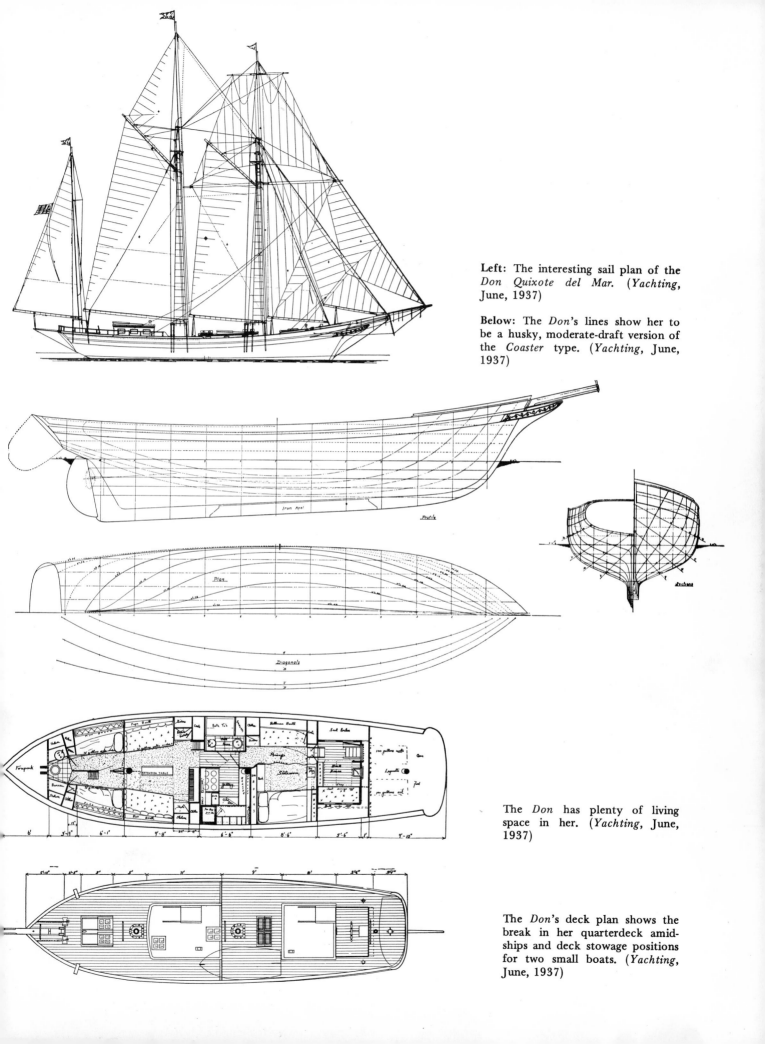

Left: The interesting sail plan of the *Don Quixote del Mar*. (*Yachting,* June, 1937)

Below: The *Don's* lines show her to be a husky, moderate-draft version of the *Coaster* type. (*Yachting,* June, 1937)

The *Don* has plenty of living space in her. (*Yachting,* June, 1937)

The *Don's* deck plan shows the break in her quarterdeck amidships and deck stowage positions for two small boats. (*Yachting,* June, 1937)

28/ A Fast Schooner

> Length on deck: 50 feet
> Length on waterline: 42 feet
> Beam: 12 feet
> Draft: 7 feet
> Sail area: 1,560 square feet
> Displacement: 15 tons
> Designer: William Douglass

Among fore-and-aft sailing rigs, the gaff schooner takes top honors, as far as I am concerned, for seamanlike good looks. This example of the type, designed by William Douglass of Moncton, New Brunswick, in 1946, seems to capitalize on the aesthetic possibilities. She has a slender, rakish look that would appeal to marine artists and sea poets. She ought to appeal to sailormen as well, for she would be fast and able.

This schooner's hull should be very easily driven. She would have a much better turn of speed than would be immediately apparent to the skippers of more modern boats sailing today; they might be surprised when they found they couldn't stay ahead of "the old gaff schooner" astern. Can you imagine the shock of seeing her bow lift out of a head sea to expose, instead of a deep forefoot, just nothing at all?! That might be the first clue that this "old character boat" has plenty of character all right—most of it aimed not at quaintness but at speed.

Of course, like some other slippery hulls, she would not be the easiest boat in the world to steer. Her rudder is fairly far forward due to the long counter, and the cutaway forefoot would let her yaw some.

Her bow is nicely proportioned above the waterline, and the stern is a beautifully sculptured affair, with its finely curved and somewhat delicate wineglass transom. The sections are nicely curved also, and her moderately hard bilges, tumblehome, and hollow garboards indicate a vessel that would have both power and grace in a seaway. Her buttocks have a fair, flat sweep from bow to stern; she'd leave the water almost the way she found it.

It's too bad a halfbreadth plan of this schooner is not available so we could see her waterlines.

The schooner is 50 feet long on deck, with a waterline length of 42 feet, a beam of 12 feet, and a draft of 7 feet. Her displacement is about 15 tons, with 3½ tons in outside ballast. Her frames are 1¼ inches by 3 inches, and the floors are sided 3 inches. The sail area is 1,560 square feet, broken down as follows: mainsail, 616; foresail, 236; forestaysail, 200; jib, 140; main topsail, 88; and fisherman staysail, 280.

If this schooner were to enter and win a race

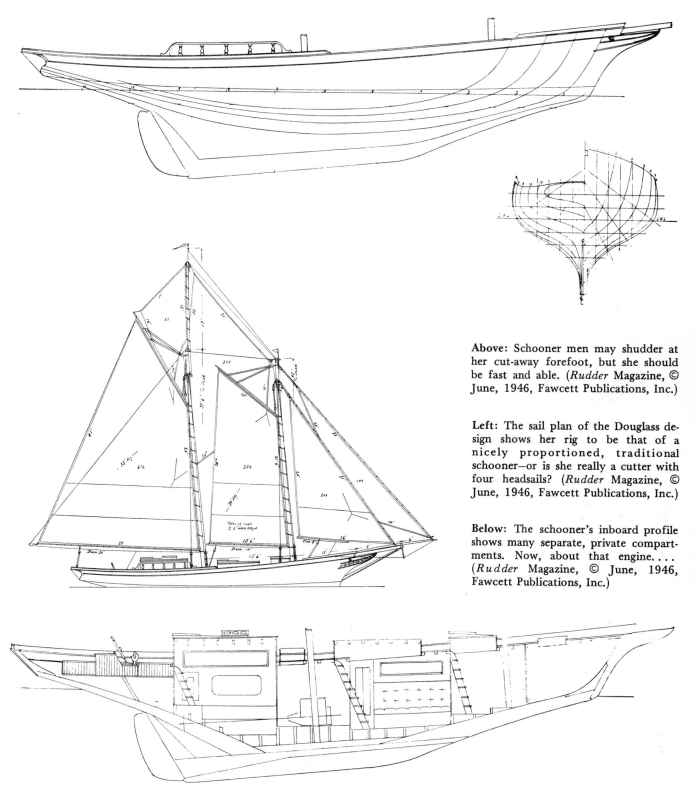

Above: Schooner men may shudder at her cut-away forefoot, but she should be fast and able. (*Rudder* Magazine, © June, 1946, Fawcett Publications, Inc.)

Left: The sail plan of the Douglass design shows her rig to be that of a nicely proportioned, traditional schooner—or is she really a cutter with four headsails? (*Rudder* Magazine, © June, 1946, Fawcett Publications, Inc.)

Below: The schooner's inboard profile shows many separate, private compartments. Now, about that engine.... (*Rudder* Magazine, © June, 1946, Fawcett Publications, Inc.)

in which a rig allowance were given, some sea lawyer would doubtless object that while technically she is a gaff schooner, in reality she is a Marconi cutter. She just happens to have a "foremast" propping up the middle of her topmast stay and a "gaff" splitting off the head of her mainsail. Perhaps the sea lawyer would have an argument that made some sense, for once.

Think of her as a cutter with a mainsail that can be reefed from the top (by taking in the main topsail) as well as from the bottom, and with four headsails (including the foresail and fisherman). A clever rig, what? She has the advantages of the cutter for efficiency to windward (especially with a vang to keep the fore gaff from sagging off), but she also has the versatility of the many sail combinations of the schooner. For instance, she would balance very nicely under foresail alone, and the true cutter has no such ability.

Her masts are well raked, and the topmast is sprung well forward in the traditional manner, to eliminate the need for backstays. The shrouds are set up with deadeyes and lanyards, simple and reliable gear that looks seamanlike because it *is* seamanlike.

Her jibboom passes forward on the left side of the forestay and then curves to starboard to bring the jibstay to the centerline.

It would be a great temptation to make for this boat a huge ballooner that would tack down to the end of the jibboom, hoist on both fisherman staysail halyards, putting its head to the main truck, and sheet to the end of the main boom, with the clew perhaps directly above the wheel. It would be a sort of balloon jib and balloon main topmast staysail combined into one bold sail of some 1,200 square feet. Anytime there was enough air to fill it, the boat would move. Having succumbed to the first temptation of making the thing, one would find it all too easy to succumb to the second, hanging onto it too long as the breeze increased from light to gentle. It might just be a good idea to put a preventer backstay on that main topmast. Uffa Fox had such a sail on his schooner, *Black Rose*, a miniature North Sea pilot schooner of about this same size and with the same straight line from main topmast head through foremast head to jibboom end. He was inordinately proud of that sail, as he had a right to be.

The short monkey rail on this schooner looks a bit odd at first, but her stern is too delicate to take a full rail, and besides, the protection is needed mostly where you have to walk around the house. The more you explore this design, the more you realize that her details are very well worked out.

The placement of the steering wheel in the middle of the cockpit is governed by the position of the rudder post, but the arrangement should work out well. The helmsman would be more protected by the house than if he were farther aft, and cockpit passengers would be out of his way behind him, where they can handle the mainsheet nicely.

Of course it would be highly desirable to take the engine out of this vessel. She would be a smart sailer, quick in stays, and easy to maneuver under sail alone. She would slip along well in light weather. But what if it's calm and you have to get "back"? Well, "back" has a way of taking care of itself when that is necessary, and this vessel was designed to go to sea and use the wind.

It might be a mistake, however, to commandeer the empty engine room immediately for more accommodations. The space could be extremely valuable as a convertible area. That midships compartment with its own hatch right under the main halyards could be used as (depending on the purpose of the cruise) a cargo hold, laboratory, dormitory, salvage gear locker, or photographic darkroom.

She has separate sleeping cabins for privacy. In addition, this arrangement keeps the watch below (sleeping amidships) from being disturbed by the watch on deck when they tumble below aft for a quick look at the chart or duck down into the snug galley forward to forget for a minute about cold spray or a biting wind.

This is a fine, fast schooner that would be a constant delight under sail. She might be the kind of rakish vessel that inspired Richard Hovey's "There's a schooner in the offing with her topsails shot with fire." That might just be this schooner seen waiting for her breeze at sunset. Admire her with your telescope while you can. With the darkness, the breeze will reach out to her off the land, and, by morning, she'll be well gone.

29/ The *Mahdee*

Length on deck: 53 feet 3 inches
Length on waterline: 45 feet 11 inches
Beam: 15 feet
Draft: 6 feet
Sail area: 1,500 square feet
Displacement: 29 tons
Designer: S. S. Crocker, Jr.

Alexander W. Moffat, better known in the boating fraternity as "Sandy," came into Camden, Maine, a couple of years ago in what has to be the ugliest powerboat in the world. He said it was the twenty-sixth boat he had owned. Number 26 may not be pretty, but she certainly is practical, and she proved well suited to her intended use: a home afloat in which Mr. Moffat could, with the aid of a single crewman, cruise between one mooring at Manchester, Massachusetts, and another at Crockett's Cove, on Vinalhaven Island.

Sandy Moffat is a realist. He plans his boats for the use to which he intends to put them. Some forty-five years ago, he planned a boat to serve as a summer houseboat, be a weekend cruiser, and be able to sail coastwise during his two-week summer vacation. For these purposes, he wanted an able and roomy vessel, and one that had an auxiliary powerplant that would be a pleasure to operate, rather than the opposite. Mr. Moffat sought safety, comfort, and silence. The result was an interesting schooner, the *Mahdee*, believed to be the first gasoline-electric-drive auxiliary built. (A *mahdee* is a pretty woman in eastern India.)

To design the boat, Mr. Moffat turned to S. S. Crocker, Jr. The vessel was built at Dorchester, Massachusetts, by G. F. Lawson and Son. She was launched in April, 1931. Sandy Moffat described her fully in an article in the February, 1932, issue of *Yachting* magazine.

The boat's length was determined by the fact that Moffat wanted 6 feet 4 inches headroom (he needs it) under a flush deck in a boat with a pleasing profile and sheer line. Given this requirement, the length on deck worked out to 53 feet 3 inches. The draft was to be limited to 6 feet. Her waterline length worked out to 45 feet 11 inches, and her beam, 15 feet. She displaces 29 tons, with 10 tons of lead ballast, eight outside and two inside.

Mr. Moffat describes the *Mahdee*'s hull as that of a shoal-draft Brixham trawler. She certainly has a powerful hull of the type that stands up to her sail. She has hollow waterlines forward and a nice run, so she should have a good turn of speed in a breeze. Her limited draft would keep her from being a star performer to windward, but that was not one of Sandy Moffat's objectives. There is no doubt she can sail, given her conditions; she has logged 9½ knots reaching.

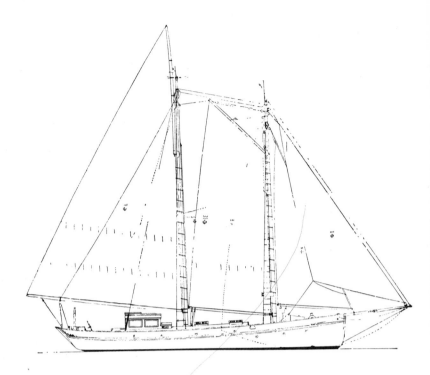

Right: The *Mahdee* is rigged as a schooner with a sliding gunter mainsail. (*Yachting*, March, 1931)

Below: Sandy Moffat called Sam Crocker's design for his summer house and cruising boat "a shoal-draft Brixham trawler." His objectives were safety, comfort, and silence. (*Yachting*, March, 1931)

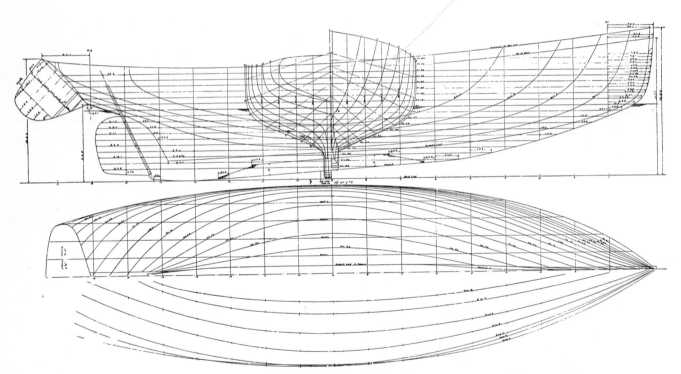

The schooner can steer easily with her long, straight keel and her big rudder set well aft. Yet her forefoot is cut away enough so that she can turn fairly easily.

The *Mahdee*'s working sail area is 1,500 square feet. She has a moderate rig, Mr. Moffat's intention being to start with a rig that already had the equivalent of a single reef tied in so as to avoid reefing the boat except in a real breeze. This makes her a bit slow in light weather, but her owner planned to use his auxiliary power as frequently as necessary. And she has a huge, deep-footed balloon jib that overlaps half of the foresail.

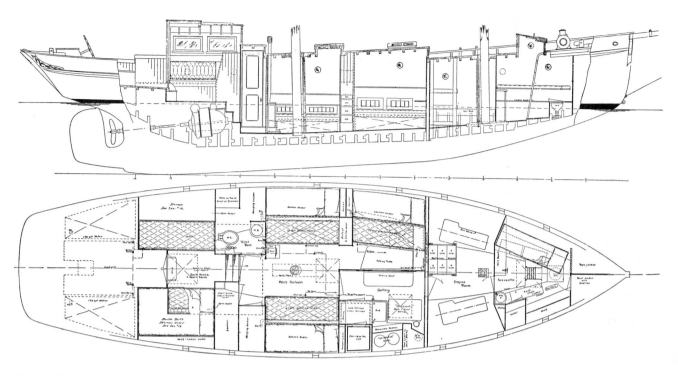

Above: She has plenty of room for from six to ten people and for her interesting power plant, a gasoline-electric-drive installation with the generator sets forward and the propulsion motor under the big deckhouse. (*Yachting*, March, 1931)

Below: Close-hauled with a single reef in the mainsail. Note how the main yard reefs down with the sail to reduce mast height, in effect, and how the vang keeps the fore gaff from sagging off. (*Yachting*, February, 1932)

Her tall, narrow foresail has a vang to take the twist out of the sail. But it is the gunter mainsail that is perhaps the most interesting feature of the *Mahdee*'s rig. Sliding gunters are usually relegated to sailing dinghies. Yet, if a gaff rig makes sense in a large sail, surely the gunter does also, for it is merely a high-peaked gaff. You get the advantage of the shape of a Bermudian sail together with the advantage of the gaff rig, namely, that the gear is more simple and reliable and that the mast height can be kept moderate.

Sandy Moffat wanted a quiet powerplant, so quiet that it would not have to be shut down to listen for fog signals. He achieved this objective with electric drive and an unusual exhaust system, with the nice by-product that he could put his engines wherever he wanted them. The propulsion system was expensive, of course, partly because it was a pioneer installation and partly because it is a twin-engine system, and one that requires extra equipment, such as an electric propulsion motor and an unusually large set of batteries. The *Mahdee*'s powerplant cost $9,200 installed. Mr. Moffat wanted the best of everything; he says he could have gotten by for perhaps half the price. It must be remembered, though, that these were Depression dollars.

To achieve quietness and not interrupt the

The *Mahdee* under power. The generator sets supply power to the motor and maintain the battery charge with a zero float. The engine exhaust runs up through the foremast. (*Yachting*, August, 1931)

accommodation, Sandy Moffat had his engines installed forward. He says they are "well back from the bow," but they are really pretty well forward, and, together with the batteries, they weigh 3,800 pounds. They are Winton engines hooked to 10-kw generators. The propulsion motor, located beneath the deckhouse, was made by General Electric.

Normal operation takes power for the propulsion motor directly from the running generators, carrying the batteries at a zero float. With both generators turning at 1,350 r.p.m., she makes 7.6 knots and burns 4½ gallons of gasoline per hour. On one generator, and with half the fuel consumption, she has made 5.7 knots. She can be run, of course, on the battery alone. Starting with a full charge, she can make 5.7 knots on the battery for a few minutes, or three knots for an hour.

At first, the *Mahdee* had a solid, three-bladed propeller, but Mr. Moffat soon went to a two-bladed, 28-inch-by-18-inch feathering wheel to reduce drag.

Much attention was paid to achieving a silent exhaust. The *Mahdee* has a hollow foremast with a 2½-inch copper pipe built into it to take the exhaust from both engines. The exhaust exits just below the truck of the mast.

Sandy Moffat says if he were working out the *Mahdee*'s propulsion system today, his only change would be to make her entire electrical system 110 volts, thus eliminating the 12-volt system for the sake of simplicity. All the other details of the system worked out fine, he says.

The *Mahdee* has a flush deck with a break abaft the foremast. This arrangement gives her plenty of headroom below and a large, clear, working space on deck. Her cockpit extends the full width of the boat, giving plenty of room. In wet or hot weather, it can be protected by a huge awning set on a track and slides on the bottom edge of the main boom. The awning is lashed forward to the main rigging and aft to arms that swing out from the gallows frame.

Ventilation was planned carefully. For example, her skylights are square so they can be turned to funnel air in from any of four directions.

The schooner has no fewer than ten berths, if you count her four transoms. There are permanent bunks for six. In the deckhouse, the starboard seat folds back when the double berth is used.

The *Mahdee* would certainly make a comfortable home afloat and would be a most interesting vessel in which to cruise under both sail and power. Her many unusual details are well worked out.

The achievement of creating this fine schooner is the result of the efforts of a team consisting of a practical-minded owner who knew what he wanted, an extremely able designer who could translate the owner's wishes into plans, and an excellent builder who could transform all the ideas into a sound vessel.

In commenting on the design and building of the *Mahdee*, Sandy Moffat wrote, "We adhered to the three mottos that anyone building a boat should swear faithfully to follow: the best is none too good; the most expensive is generally the cheapest in the end; if you are going to sea and going in safety, you've got to be particular."

30/ The *Mildred IV*

Length on deck: 34 feet
Length on waterline: 33 feet
Beam: 9 feet
Draft: 4 feet 2 inches
Sail area: 240 square feet
Designer: John G. Alden

What a joy is an able power launch that can be gotten underway quickly to take her owner wherever he wants to go in any reasonable weather. Such a craft makes a most useful and versatile boat. Here is an example of the type large enough for four people to cruise in for short periods, or for two to make lengthy trips in.

When this boat went on trials nearly a half century ago, she proved to have an easy motion and keep her decks dry in rough water, hold her speed of eight knots in most any conditions, and be very steady on her helm.

Jere Wheelwright, her owner, knew just the kind of boat he wanted and turned over rather specific requirements to John G. Alden, who produced the design. The boat was built by Goudy and Stevens in East Boothbay, Maine.

She is 34 feet long on deck, with a waterline length of 33 feet, a beam of 9 feet, and a draft of 4 feet 2 inches. Her freeboard forward is 6 feet. Her mainsail has 170 square feet and her jib, 70 square feet.

The rather deep sections, outside ballast, and hard bilges of this design should give her excellent stability; she wouldn't roll uncomfortably, especially with her steadying sails set. Her hull lines show the fine, rather than flat, run of the nonplaning boat. No speedster, she would still be very easily driven. Her ease of steering is doubtless a product of the long, straight keel.

The outside ballast on the launch's keel is 1,500 pounds of iron. In addition, her bilge is filled with concrete. Pouring cement in the bilge of a wooden boat seems to be a practice that all boatbuilders rave about, some one way and some the other. My preference would have been to add the weight to the iron on the keel.

Mr. Wheelwright wanted a big, heavy, reliable engine in his powerboat, and in 1926 he chose a 40-h.p. Lathrop. A somewhat smaller diesel might be selected today. The Lathrop swings a twenty-six-inch wheel with a twenty-two-inch pitch. She cruises at a little better than eight knots and can do 9½ when buttoned up at 700 r.p.m.

The gas tanks are on either side of the engine, holding sixty-five gallons each. Aft is a 150-gallon water tank. All this weight is pretty much amidships, leaving the ends of the vessel light and buoyant.

If she were mine, I'd put a rather lengthy plank bowsprit on her to take a long, skinny jib,

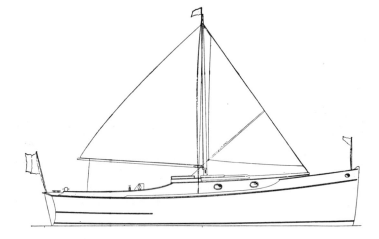

You'd live outdoors in this boat, and it would be a hard breeze and rough sea indeed that would make you run for shelter. (*Yachting*, July, 1927)

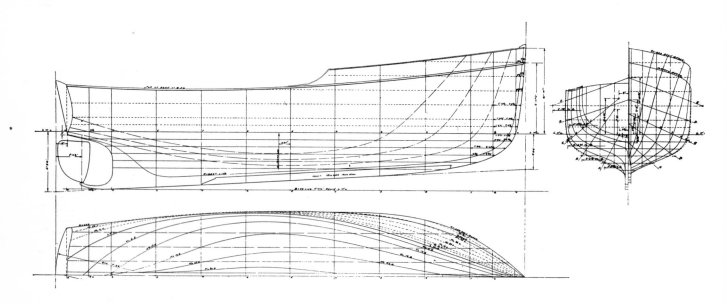

Above: The lines of this low-speed but easily driven power launch show the value of the motto, "Moderation in all things." No element is exaggerated; nothing "sticks out." (*Yachting*, July, 1927)

Below: It's the head that's tucked away in a corner in this layout, not the engine; both features make good sense. (*Yachting*, July, 1927)

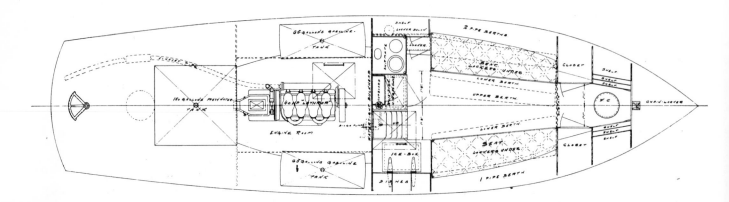

A picture to set a fellow to thinking. (*Yachting*, July, 1927)

and also for anchor handling. Of course it would have to have a pulpit so you could lean right out over the water, or turn around and admire the little vessel running along through it. It wouldn't do any harm to bring lifelines aft from the pulpit at least as far as the main rigging.

Her headsails could well be roller furling for ease of handling. As a matter of fact, so could her mainsail. The boom ought to have a very stout topping lift, and the sheet blocks on deck should be spread one at each gunwale. That would keep the boom under good control all the time. Then the mainsail could roll up on a luff wire and could be set in a twinkling by releasing the furling line and trimming the sheet. The sail could also be taken off just as quickly.

The boom might be lengthened a bit so it could double as a boat derrick for bringing the dinghy on board. A nine-foot tender would stow quite nicely athwartships on the stern deck.

It would be kind of fun to have a light but strong crow's nest aloft on a boat like this. Of course that would mean doubling up on the shrouds and rattling them down. With all this rigging fitted, it would be a crime not to carry a harpoon or two and spend some time pretending you didn't care whether or not you saw a swordfish.

One of the owner's requirements was a pair of good quarter bitts, so that the inevitable towing chore would be a pleasure rather than an embarrassment. I used to spend some time in a boat something like this one, and one of her very best

features was a huge oak towing bitt that stood right up in the middle of the cockpit. When you held a turn or two on that post, you had not a care in the world, and the top of it was the best seat in the vessel.

The trunk cabin on this boat looks harmless enough today, but in the Twenties, this boat was launched among many sisters with raised decks and opinionated owners. Mr. Wheelwright's great friend and shipmate, John I. Sewall, addressed this point as follows: "Raised decks are dangerous to work on. It is a wonder to me that the first raised-deck cruiser did not annihilate the idea then and there. A gain in cabin space (to a degree) but no security for getting anchors, nor room to sit, stand, or move forward amidships, and of questionable appearance. As our plan worked out, the boat is certainly about as high forward as she would be with a raised deck; but she is unquestionably better looking, and the high rail forward makes this part of her a paradise in the eyes of any raised deck sufferer."

It takes but little discernment to see that this power launch was born in the era of the Great Raised-Deck Controversy! I would have sided with Mr. Sewall.

An important feature of this design is her watertight, self-draining cockpit. A good part of the advantage of such a craft is that she can put to sea safely in rough weather, an advantage that would be largely lost with an open cockpit that drained into the bilge. She has a watertight bulkhead right across the boat at the forward end of the engine room. This is another worthwhile safety feature and also keeps the engine smell out of the cabin.

The engine is not hidden away in this boat. If you're going to depend on one engine to get home, it's good to have plenty of working space around it, including some headroom. This design provides just that, with the result that the engine gains the preeminence and attention it ought to have in a powerboat.

The large engine room and spacious cockpit mean that the cabin cannot be gigantic. In fact, by today's standards, it looks a bit cramped. That's just fine. What is wanted is a snug place to get out of the cold and wet and do some eating and sleeping and such-like. But you'd live on deck in a boat like this.

The layout of the cabin seems excellent. The head is away forward where it should be, and the galley is far enough aft to avoid most of the vertical traveling when the boat is pitching.

Incidentally, there are windows in the after end of the house to help ventilate the engine room and to let the helmsman watch his engine. (I don't really trust the things, so it's comforting to be able to look right in there and see if it's on fire or anything.)

Looking at this design today, my natural tendency is to want to put a big glass house over the forward end of the cockpit. Of course, the climate in which the boat is to be used would be an important factor here. Such a structure would make great good sense in Seattle, but it would probably be much better left off in Florida. In Maine, there's no outguessing it.

Another factor would be the age of the captain. I remember chortling a bit when an uncle traded his schooner for a motorsailer with a glass house amidships. But he said, "I'm getting too old to take a drubbing in an open cockpit." And he had sailed enough miles to rate a wheelhouse—and have a radiator in it if he wanted to.

I'd leave the house off this boat but put a canvas spray hood over the companion hatch and another one over the forward end of the cockpit, low enough for a standing helmsman to see over. Both could fold down when not wanted. Another possibility would be to move the steering stand to the forward end of the cockpit and fit a scoop windshield across the top of the house. It's a curved metal shield just a few inches high, so you can easily see over it. The shield deflects the wind up over your head rather than letting it blow in your face. It really works very well.

Looking at the photo of this able power launch lying quietly at her mooring in a Maine cove is enough to set a fellow to thinking.

31/ The *Iris*

Length on deck: 18 feet
Length on waterline: 17 feet 4 inches
Beam: 5 feet
Draft: 1 foot 4 inches
Sail area: 193 square feet
Designer: J. A. Akester

Some twenty years after John MacGregor began popularizing the canoe yawl, this lovely little specimen of the type, the *Iris*, was built (the year was 1886) by J. A. Akester of Hornsea, near Hull, England, for H. Munroe. Forty-six years after that, in 1932, A. W. Barlow, of Providence, Rhode Island, wanting an able and fast small boat for sailing on Narragansett Bay, discovered the plans of the *Iris* in a book called *Canoe and Boat Building: A Complete Manual for Amateurs*, by W. P. Stephens, the fifth edition of which was published in New York City by the Forest and Stream Publishing Company (Stephens was then the canoeing editor of *Forest and Stream* magazine) in 1891. Barlow was intrigued with the old design and felt the *Iris* might meet his needs very nicely. He and his son built a replica of the original from the plans and offsets that Stephens provided. At least they took her up through the planking stage and then she was finished off by a professional builder, Herbert Salisbury, of Pawtuxet, Rhode Island, in a sensible reversal of the usual procedure.

Happily, the *Iris* herself can still be examined by anyone, for she is among the utterly fascinating fleet that makes up the small craft collection of the Mystic Seaport, at Mystic, Connecticut.

The *Iris* is a fine little sailing and rowing vessel and would make an admirable daysailer and camping cruiser for protected waters. For some reason, poring over this design, I visualize her chiefly on a tidal river, perhaps beating down with a good ebb helping her grab every foot she can on each tack, or maybe running up from cove to cove with the last fresh puffs of the day.

There is something about river sailing in a little boat like this. I suppose I have beat down one particular river (the Pawcatuck, mentioned in the Prologue) hundreds of times in little boats. It's different every time. Will she make it to the house with the blue trim on the first leg out from her stake or won't she? And coming back across—say it's low tide—will she fetch to the deep hole just below the boatyard so we can go right in to the shore, or will we have to tack short of the oyster bed? All this little-boat river stuff has an appeal equal to—though admittedly far different from—cruising to the South Seas or

Right: The pretty, little *Iris* with her fully battened sails. (*Yachting*, December, 1933)

Below: W. P. Stephens suggested giving the canoe yawl a centerboard; he was, of course, right. (*Yachting*, December, 1933)

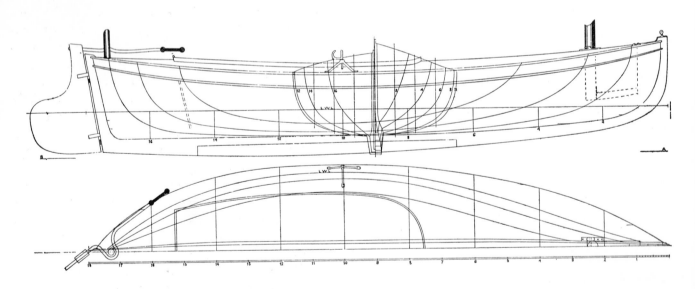

coasting down to Labrador, but the point is the rivers and the *Irises* are readily available from the points of view of geography, time, and money.

The *Iris* is 18 feet long on deck, with a water-line length of 17 feet 4 inches, a beam of 5 feet, and a draft of 1 foot 4 inches. Her least free-board is 1 foot 1 inch. She carries 450 pounds of lead ballast outside on her keel and an additional 225 pounds of lead inside. Apparently the inside ballast was not used in the Barlow replica.

A relatively short mainmast stands 15 feet 3 inches above the deck, and her little mizzenmast is only 7 feet high. Her sail area is 193 square feet, with 168 in the mainsail and 25 in the mizzen.

When A. W. Barlow built his *Iris*, he added four inches to the depth of the keel, giving his boat a draft of 1 foot 8 inches. Neither version carried a centerboard, though W. P. Stephens commented: "A centerboard could readily be fitted to work entirely beneath the floor, and would be a great aid to the boat in windward work." I agree heartily. When Stephens said the board could work beneath the floor, he was probably thinking of a metal fan board whose thin leaves came up side by each when the board was raised, so that when the board was up it had the height of just one leaf.

The canoe yawl has a fine, hollow entrance, and quite flat buttock lines fore and aft. By her passage, she would disturb the water but little, and she should be a fast little boat. She has a good spread of sail, and with her original Chinese, or battened, lug rig, she could be shortened down quickly in a breeze.

She would depend a good deal on her outside and inside ballast for the stability to carry her sail, for though her midsection shows a flat floor, she is quite narrow. Of course the ability of her crew to get their weight out to windward when it is blowing would enhance her sail-carrying power—nor would a half-dozen sandbags be amiss in a boat like this.

The *Iris* should row reasonably well and could even be rowed a short distance to windward in a breeze, an ability that can be most convenient on occasion for an estuary cruiser that needs to shift berths in the middle of the night when the cold front comes in. Of course she would be a rather heavy boat to row and would take some time to get going, but then she would carry her way well and would not be stopped by a bit of a bobble. If used as a pulling boat, her inside ballast should be left ashore.

A. W. Barlow kept the *Iris'* basic sail plan intact, but he rigged his mainsail as a sliding gunter rather than lug. On the leg-o'-mutton mizzen, he dispensed with the sprit batten that extended the leech of the sail on the original *Iris*. I'd prefer the lug rig, chiefly because of those full-length battens. They work well on a sail whose luff is free-standing, and they make reefing a picnic. On the other hand, W. P. Stephens

wrote that Warrington Baden-Powell, an early British sailing canoe enthusiast (and brother of the founder of the Boy Scouts), after analyzing eight different ways of rigging a sailing canoe's mainsail, including four variations of the lug rig, chose the sliding gunter as best. On the *Iris'* original rig, the sprit batten on the mizzen suggests that the sail could be brailed right up against the mast when taken in and stopped off with a few marling hitches taken with the end of the topping lift, since it would be no trouble at all to reach right to the top of the mast! The chief use of this tiny sail would be to balance a close-reefed mainsail in a breeze of wind.

A problem to be solved in a little yawl whose mizzenmast interferes with her tiller is how to shape that implement to dodge the obstruction. On the halfbreadth plan of the *Iris*, the designer shows his notched metal tiller hard aport, as if to prove to the skeptic that his solution will work.

The little yawl's open cockpit could be covered by a light wooden hatch for keeping the rain out at anchor to save bailing, and also as a shelter to sleep under. For sleeping, I'd prefer to lift the boom to a nice angle with the topping lift and fit a tent over it.

After sailing his replica of the *Iris* for two seasons, A. W. Barlow reported that she was "quite fast, has good windward qualities, carries her sail well, and is very dry for so small a boat." Statements like this have a good ring to them, and none of these comments is particularly surprising, yet subjective comments about a boat's speed, windward ability, and so forth, always seem both intriguing and a bit frustrating. How did she really go?

Depending upon one's experience with other boats, one might think that when the *Iris* was able to sail at, say, four knots under a given set of conditions that she was "remarkably fast," or again, "surprisingly slow."

Perhaps what is needed is some sort of standard or guide for the use and edification of those of us who are interested in the way boats sail. For example, it might be most interesting if we all made a practice of recording certain performance data about our own boats for present and future comparisons. We're talking about simple craft without instrumentation, and we're talking about getting down enough data to be able to come up with some reasonably objective

TABLE OF OFFSETS—CANOE YAWL IRIS.

Stations.	HEIGHTS.			HALF BREADTHS.						
	Deck	Rab't	Keel.	Deck	No. 1.	No. 2.	L WL.	No. 4.	No. 5.	Rabbet
0..	3 4	.....	.....	0^2	.....	.....	.....	.....	.....	1
2..	3 0^2	11^6	8	1 0^7	8^4	7	5^2	3^2	.....	1^5
4..	2 9	9^4	5^2	1 9^1	1 6	1 4	1 1^2	9^4	4^6	2^5
6..	2 7^1	7^7	3	2 2^2	2 0^6	1 11^1	1 8^6	1 5	11^3	3^1
8..	2 6	7	1^4	2 5^3	2 4^4	2 3^4	2 2	1 11^2	1 6^1	3^2
10..	2 5^6	7	0^4	2 6^2	2 5^6	2 4^7	2 3^4	2 1^2	1 8^4	3^2
12..	2 6	6^6	.....	2 5^5	2 4^7	2 4	2 2^4	1 11^6	1 7^2	3^1
14..	2 7^4	6^6	0^2	2 2^2	2 0^6	1 11^5	1 10	1 7^1	1 2^1	3
16..	2 9^7	6^6	1^1	1 5^5	1 3^3	1 1^7	1	9^4	6^5	2
18..	3 0^4	.....	2	0^3	.....	.....	.....	.....	.....	1

Stephens' offsets of the *Iris*. (*Canoe and Boat Building* by William P. Stephens)

Above: A. W. Barlow's replica was rigged with a gunter mainsail and leg-o'-mutton mizzen. (*Yachting*, December, 1933)

Below: On a reach, she comes on strong. (*Yachting*, December, 1933)

comparisons, rather than an exhaustive analysis that might discourage many of us from the effort. What is needed is a recording system that could become popular, so that the many comparisons that are and will be made from boat to boat inevitably will be a bit more objective than they have been.

We might start by writing down the general weather conditions, since sailing in a steady southwest breeze is quite a different thing from sailing in a fluky northwester. Then record wind strength and sea state. Put down the sails that were set at the time of the trial and record any unusual conditions, such as loading, that would affect the speed of the boat.

Now put her up close-hauled and record the estimated speed in knots and the number of points off the wind she was steered. Do the same with the boat one point free of close-hauled. Estimate and record the boat's leeway, using the terms *unnoticeable, slight,* or *marked.* Put the boat on a beam reach and record her estimated speed. Do the same on a broad reach, with her headsails just filled, and do the same on a dead run, stating whether or not headsails were filled.

Finally, indicate how long you have sailed the boat. If this is your tenth year with her, she's probably going better (and you can estimate her speed more accurately) than if you've only had her two years.

This "system" obviously would be no panacea for obtaining perfectly accurate records of the performance of sailing craft; it would, however, be quite an improvement on the owner's statement that such and such a boat is "quite fast," or has "good windward qualities."

It would be mighty interesting to see how the *Iris* would sail under various conditions. I'll bet she would be "quite fast," but there we go again.

32/ The *Eel*

Length on deck: 21 feet
Length on waterline: 19 feet
Beam: 7 feet
Draft: 2 feet
Sail area: 200 square feet
Displacement: 3,000 pounds
Designer: George F. Holmes

When the English canoe clubbers on the river Humber wanted more substantial boats than their canoes to cope with the steep chop their river could throw up, they developed the lovely little double-enders that became known as canoe yawls, and their club became the Humber Yawl Club. Here is, in my opinion, an excellent example of the canoe yawl. The *Eel* was designed by her owner, George F. Holmes, a marine artist whose etchings delighted English yachting magazine readers for years.

In a description of the *Eel,* Uffa Fox said that while most of us don't know why we like the appearance of our various favorite objects, the artist has to know why what he sees is attractive (or not so) and has to be able to put on paper the essence of that attractiveness. Thus, Fox comments, an artist usually has the ability to design a most handsome boat. Of course some nonartist boat designers are also most concerned with the appearance of the craft they turn out and know exactly what they like about the looks of a boat, and these designers can create vessels that are handsome as well as able. Fox went on to comment that artists sometimes soften the lines of a boat too much, and he said he believed the *Eel* might have had firmer bilges. I agree. She would be quite tender initially, though her flare would keep her rails dry unless she were pressed hard.

The *Eel* would make a snug singlehander or an ideal cruiser for two close friends. She would also be a relatively easy and inexpensive boat to ship foreign, thus opening up all sorts of wonderful cruising grounds, such as the islands of Japan or the Aegean Sea. Moreover, she would be relatively easy to move over land, so that her owner could cruise on whichever coast of his continent he chose, or launch her in lake or river. She'd be a fine boat in which to spend a week on New Hampshire's Lake Winnepesaukee or to explore the bayous of the lower Mississippi.

The *Eel*'s lines are easy and fair; she has a sweet little hull. One could almost be tempted to apply that terrible word *cute* to her, with her high-peaked gaffs, her good-looking double-ended hull, and her short house with the single oval deadlight, but she is meant for and fully able to carry out extended coastwise cruises.

This canoe yawl should be quite fast and have

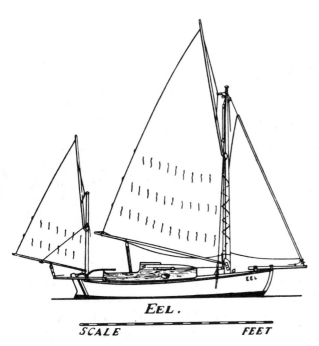

EEL.

SCALE   FEET

The *Eel*'s slightly forward-raking masts, high-peaked gaffs, and well-lifted booms give the little cruiser a perky look. (*Sailing, Seamanship and Yacht Construction* by Uffa Fox. Reproduced by kind permission of the Executors of Uffa Fox Deceased.)

an easy motion. Her hull would be very easily driven, and she would be sailed in a hard breeze under a much-reduced rig, such as a close-reefed mainsail by itself, a partially rolled-up jib and close-reefed mizzen, or, if she had to be driven to windward in a hard chance, all three of these tiny sails.

The boat would certainly be easy to steer, with her big rudder placed well aft.

The *Eel* is 21 feet long on deck, with a waterline length of 19 feet, a beam of 7 feet, and a draft of 2 feet. She has a sail area of 200 square feet and displaces about 3,000 pounds.

Her L-shaped centerboard has the advantage that you can force it down with the lever if it is jammed. Also, the board's hoisting gear is in full view for easy inspection and replacement; there is no hidden pendant that is hard to see and get at. It should be noted that this board cannot be dropped farther than is shown in the drawings, or it will have too little bearing in the trunk.

Her roller jib would be handy, for her bowsprit would be wet and precarious at times. Some steeve to the bowsprit would be practical and would certainly look better to American eyes. (Why did the British insist for so long on setting their bowsprits parallel to the water?) Note that both the bowsprit and boomkin have no stays, for they are relatively short spars, and the sails they spread are small. The boomkin is fitted on the starboard side, canted so as to bring its after end to the centerline. The tiller has an oval in it for working around the mizzenmast.

The *Eel*'s mast is in a tabernacle so it can be lowered to go under bridges or for travel other than under her own rig. Her mast is 18 feet long, so it should be no great chore to raise and lower it. This arrangement adds to her versatility and

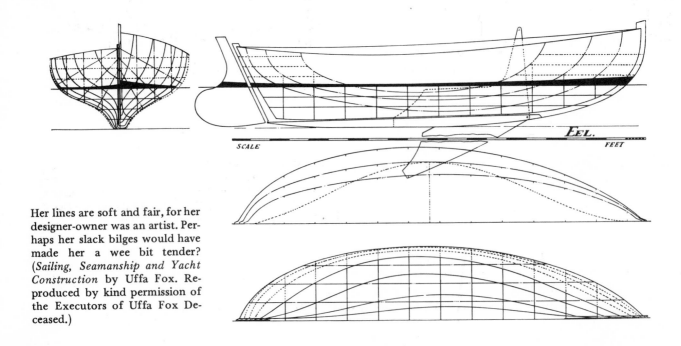

EEL.

SCALE   FEET

Her lines are soft and fair, for her designer-owner was an artist. Perhaps her slack bilges would have made her a wee bit tender? (*Sailing, Seamanship and Yacht Construction* by Uffa Fox. Reproduced by kind permission of the Executors of Uffa Fox Deceased.)

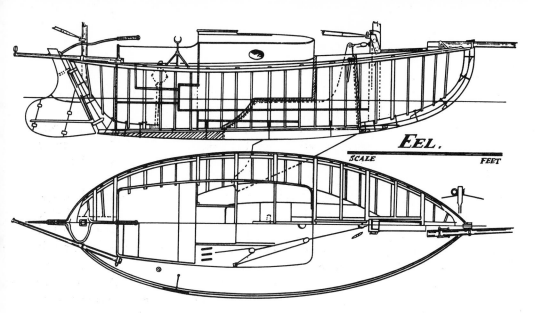

EEL.

SCALE　　　　　　　FEET

Besides showing her scantlings and the placement of her timbers, the construction drawing shows some interesting details of centerboard, boomkin, and tiller. (*Sailing, Seamanship and Yacht Construction* by Uffa Fox. Reproduced by kind permission of the Executors of Uffa Fox Deceased.)

her ability to wriggle in and out of tight places.

You'd want a longish pair of oars in a boat like this to move her along in a calm or work her right to the very head of the creek you were exploring. She would also need a short, sturdy pair of legs to keep her upright if she were to ground out. These would be a bit of a bother, but, again, they would further widen her owner's choices of how she could be used.

That the *Eel* proved indeed to be a highly successful little cruiser is perhaps best attested to by the fact that George Holmes had fifteen boats in fifteen years, culminating in this canoe yawl, which he then kept for the next fifteen years. The *Eel*'s next owner kept her for twenty years. For, in truth, how could a man part with such a lovely little lady in the spring, or summer, or fall, or even winter? She's too handy not to be always sailing in some interesting watery corner of the world.

The *Eel* nested snugly on the deck of the S.S. *Eemstroom* returning from a cruise in Holland.

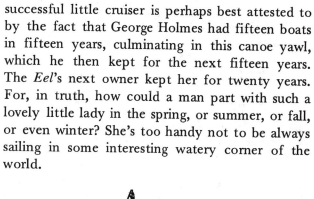

Nearly all of the Goud Zee was less than a fathom deep, so when the wind failed, out came the quant. (These sketches of the *Eel* on her Dutch cruise were made by George F. Holmes during the trip and appeared originally in *Yachting and Boating Monthly* for May, 1907.)

While in Holland, she crossed the Zuider Zee under a press of sail.

33/ The *Escapade*

Length on deck: 37 feet
Length on waterline: 30 feet
Beam: 10 feet
Draft: 3 feet 9 inches
Sail area: 480 square feet
Displacement: 6 tons
Designer: Walter Stewart

There must be something about sailing a canoe that stirs the imagination. It was Frits Fenger's canoe sailing that got him going on self-steering and eventually led to his development of the main-trysail-ketch-rigged, dhow-type yacht. The designer and owner of the unusual double-ender *Escapade* was also a canoe sailor. As a matter of fact, Walter Stewart came from Britain to win the New York Canoe Club's international challenge cup in his sailing canoe, the *Pearl*, in 1886, and then repeated the feat in his *Charm* two years later. It was not until 1930 that he designed the *Escapade*, but he was certainly influenced by his canoeing in the design, for she is—like a canoe—light, strong, and buoyant.

In designing this cruising boat and having her built, Walter Stewart, like most of us, was limited by economics to a "compromise between the ideal and the possible." The way Stewart wrote about the situation seems to indicate he would have exceeded the limitations imposed on the design had he had the money. In any event, he was restricted to "small displacement (six tons) and weight of keel (4,300 pounds); small sail area (480 square feet); solid instead of hollow spars (except the boom); simplicity of construction; limited accommodations; no auxiliary power."

Now that's what I call proof-positive that money is the root of all evil. Had Stewart been a rich man, he evidently would have ruined this design quickly. Be that as it may, Stewart went about creating the design for his ideal cruiser, within the limits of his pocketbook, with great good sense and a lively imagination.

In thinking about his craft's windward ability in heavy going, he considered not only the sail area, fine underbody, and lateral plane to make her go, but also the minimization of windage of hull and house to keep her from being stopped. Some designers of today seem to overlook this last factor. Stewart wanted the *Escapade* to be able to work to windward in rough water with the wind at Force Eight and her sail area cut to 220 square feet. (Force Eight, Mr. Beaufort reminds us, is a "fresh gale," a breeze of 34 to 40 knots. At sea, you can tell it is blowing Force Eight by the following signs: "Moderately high waves of greater length; edges of crests begin to break into spindrift; foam is blown in well-marked streaks." Ashore, the symptoms are: "twigs and small branches broken off trees; progress generally impeded.")

In addition to wanting this kind of ability in hard going, Stewart wanted his boat to be able to

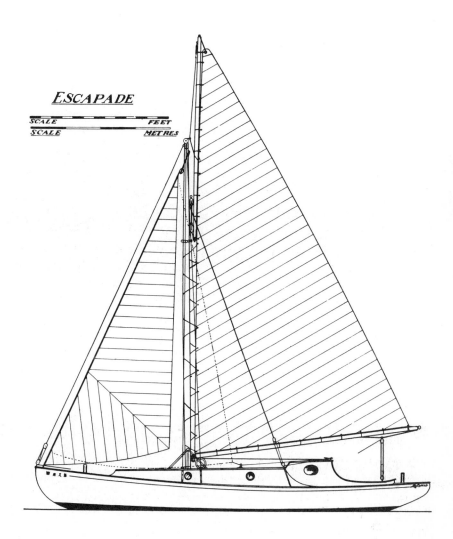

ESCAPADE

SCALE   FEET
SCALE   METRES

The sloop's sail plan shows her gunter mainsail laced to a mast that can be counterweighted and lowered in its tabernacle by the headstay. (*Sail and Power* by Uffa Fox. Reproduced by kind permission of the Executors of Uffa Fox Deceased.)

sneak into unfrequented harbors and ascend smallish rivers. He hoped to get away with a draft of 3 feet 6 inches, but he had to settle for 3 feet 9 inches. Stewart wanted a boat that would have accommodations for three men, but one that two men could handle easily and that he could sail by himself if need be. All of these objectives were achieved, and Stewart evidently didn't go broke over the boat.

Uffa Fox wrote of the *Escapade* that her sections made for "a very easily driven and fast hull, one that will gain power immediately it is listed, but one that will roll very easily at anchor because of its narrowness on the waterline." It is certainly true that she has little initial stability.

Evidently she was quite fast. Stewart wanted a boat with a good turn of speed, and he was not disappointed with what he wrought. Indeed, there is little to her under the water to hold her back, and though she would not need to be driven

hard, she has more power to carry sail than appears at first glance, for we are used to seeking such power below the waterline. In this boat, the very bilge is not immersed until she starts to heel.

The *Escapade* is 37 feet long on deck, with a waterline length of 30 feet and a beam of 10 feet. She is deceptively big. A fairly long-ended boat with a waterline length of 30 feet is a big boat where I come from, yet this sloop always seems quite small when you look at her plans and pictures.

She was built with mostly steam-bent frames, 1 inch by 1¼ inches, spaced 6 inches apart, but she also has four sawn oak frames in her. She is planked with ⅞-inch Honduras mahogany. There are two heavy, longitudinal stringers on each side, and she has four diagonally planked bulkheads tied to the sawn frames and to the adjacent deck beams by galvanized steel plates. Her deck beams are rather widely spaced wide planks; they are 4½

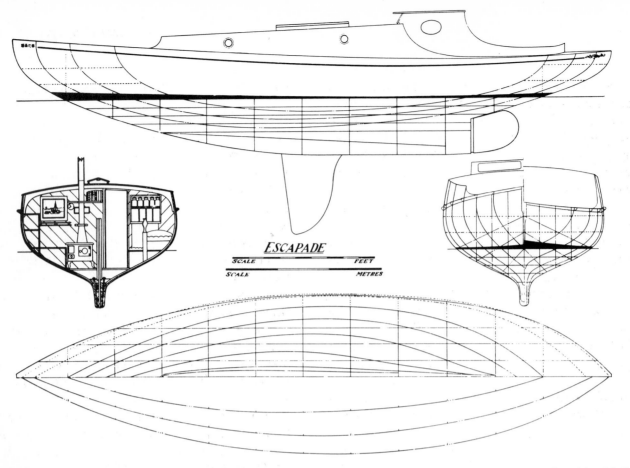

Above: Like a canoe, she is light, buoyant, and easily driven. (*Sail and Power* by Uffa Fox. Reproduced by kind permission of the Executors of Uffa Fox Deceased.)

Below: You can see many interesting innovations in the *Escapade*'s construction drawings—from her diagonal deck strapping to her standing-headroom "tiller house." (*Sail and Power* by Uffa Fox. Reproduced by kind permission of the Executors of Uffa Fox Deceased.)

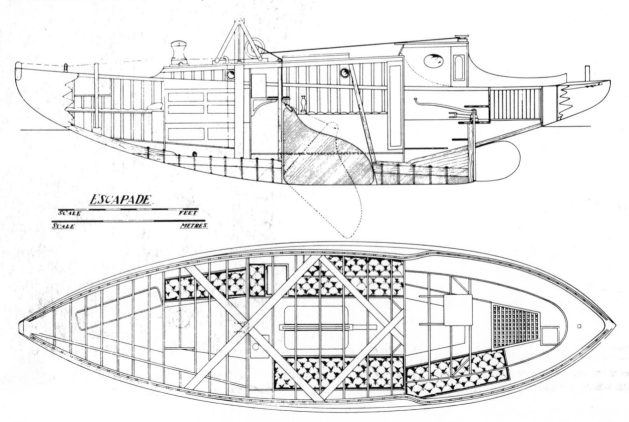

inches by 1¼ inches, spaced 24 inches apart. The deck itself is double diagonal planked with a total thickness of ⅞ inch. The deck also has diagonal strapping of 4½-inch-by-⅞-inch Honduras mahogany. It can be seen that Walter Stewart was intent on having a strong boat without going to heavy scantlings.

The *Escapade* has a bronze centerboard weighing 200 pounds. As may be seen in the inboard profile drawing, the power to raise it was derived from the difference in diameters of the sheaves on the hoisting gear.

The after portion of the inboard profile of the *Escapade*, drawn by Walter Stewart, shows the slot in the cockpit sole through which the dinghy's centerboard could be lowered to reduce weather helm. This slot also drains the cockpit, but I wonder if it wouldn't create a small fountain when she is overtaken by a big following sea. Perhaps the slot is plugged in such conditions.

An outboard motor well may be seen at the after end of the cockpit, just off center on the port side.

The *Escapade*'s mast is of British Columbia pine. Since Stewart envisioned considerable river work, he wanted to be able to lower the spar, and the original requirements of the design that Stewart laid out for himself specified that the mast extend no more than thirty feet above its tabernacle. Hence the gunter rig, to get a fairly tall mainsail without a tall spar.

Actually, he got away with a mast only twenty-seven feet from tabernacle to truck. There is a horn on the lower end of the mast on which to hang lead weights to balance the mast when it is being lowered or raised. These weights are stowed in the bilge as ballast when sailing. The tackle on the lower end of the forestay is used when dropping the mast or setting it up.

The gunter yard is a stout piece of bamboo, five inches in diameter. Stewart wrote that this spar was "inclined to whip at times in strong winds, but this is accepted as a hint to shorten sail."

In reefing the mainsail, there is no need to touch the peak halyard, for as the sail is lowered to the reefing point by the throat halyard, the bridle on the yard slides through the shackle on the end of the peak halyard.

Note in the sail plan that the mainsail is laced to the mast using the back-and-forth, forth-and-

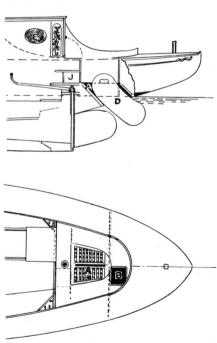

Walter Stewart's sketch of the boat's stern shows how he used her dinghy's centerboard for extra lateral resistance aft in order to decrease weather helm when necessary. (*Yachting*, July, 1934)

A sketch of the *Escapade* sailing under her winter rig, as a snug, leg-o'-mutton yawl. (*Yachting*, July, 1934)

The *Escapade* reaching along, guided by her helmsman seated in the companionway. (*Sail and Power* by Uffa Fox. Reproduced by kind permission of the Executors of Uffa Fox Deceased.)

back method, as Pete Culler describes it. This keeps the lacing from binding on the spar when the sail is hoisted or lowered.

It used to be a fairly common practice in England for a cruising boat to have a winter rig. This was a shortened rig designed for ease of handling in a strong breeze. The concept makes great good sense and makes a small cruising boat more useful than she otherwise would be at the early and late ends of her season, or it may extend her season year round. The *Escapade*'s winter rig may be seen in Walter Stewart's sketch of his boat. When converted to a snug, leg-o'-mutton yawl, she has only 300 square feet of sail.

Stewart copied the *Escapade*'s raised-deck amidships from the ketch *Alice*, designed by Commodore Ralph M. Munroe (see Chapter Nine). To add security on the raised deck, it

might be well to run a lifeline between the shroud and the running backstay on each side of the boat. The weather backstay would normally be set up, so that there would be a lifeline to weather to grab when going forward.

One of the most interesting features of this design is the boat's deckhouse. It does not extend the full width of the vessel, as does the raised deck. The boat's steering station is inside this structure, the idea being that you stand up (the headroom is 6 feet 2 inches) to the tiller and steer completely sheltered from the elements. There is a narrow windshield, which can be opened on hinges, across the forward side of the house, as may be seen in the body plan. The large, oval side windows may be slid open. You can also steer while sitting in the companionway hatch, using a line to the tiller.

This all looks very comfortable, but I wonder if the house is really quite high enough to give sufficient vision forward, especially since the photograph and sketch show that the skiff is stowed on deck forward of the windshield. It's tempting to think of cheating the elements by staying out of a bitter breeze, chilling rain, or even driving snow while steering from inside the boat, but it strikes me that anytime you try to combine sailing a small boat with cheating the elements, you're just asking for it. In any event, I feel the *Escapade* could use at least an alternate steering station out in the cockpit to good advantage.

The galley is just forward of the mast on the port side. For singlehanded work, it might make sense to put it where the quarterberth is in the deckhouse. The thought may be obsolete in these days of self-steering rigs, but the dream of every singlehander used to be to be able to steer and cook at the same time.

There is a heating stove in the saloon just abaft the mast on the port side. She is a snug little vessel below for two or three people. As a matter of fact, Stewart and his son lived aboard the *Escapade* for four years.

The design of this cruising boat is interesting and instructive, not only for the intriguing innovations Stewart incorporated into her, but also because of the versatility of her performance. Besides being a home afloat, the *Escapade* carried her designer and owner wherever he wanted to go.

On September 10, 1933, she crossed the English Channel in twelve hours, covering ninety miles in a rough sea under shortened sail. She once sailed a measured mile at slack water at a speed of just under nine knots. This was under her winter rig with a reef in her leg-o'-mutton sail and a small jib. Unfortunately, we don't have a description of wind, sea, and point of sailing on this occasion.

She regularly sailed into canal locks if there was any wind at all, and otherwise she could be maneuvered with a fifteen-foot sweep. She once sailed up the Rhine River, all the way to Cologne.

The results of canoeing, in terms of inspiration relative to boat design, are, I think, quite impressive. At any rate, I now have a canoe that I am using with some regularity. I can hardly wait for the inspiration to begin.

34/ The *Sheila II*

> Length on deck: 31 feet 6 inches
> Length on waterline: 24 feet
> Beam: 8 feet 6 inches
> Draft: 4 feet 11 inches
> Sail area: 545 square feet
> Displacement: 6.2 tons
> Designer: Albert Strange

Albert Strange was an English small-boat sailor, artist, and designer of cruising boats. He is best known for the lovely canoe yawls he created.

Strange was born at Gravesend in 1856 and lived until 1917. In 1891, he joined the Humber Yawl Club. This was a well-known group of small-boat enthusiasts, with skillful oarsmen, sailors, boatbuilders, and designers among the membership. The influence of the club and its activities was a strong factor in the products of Albert Strange's drawing board.

The Humber Yawl Club, according to W. P. Stephens, was formed in 1883. It was descended from the eastern branch of the Royal Canoe Club, begun ten years earlier. And that club, too, had an antecedent, in an organization called simply The Canoe Club. One of the founders of The Canoe Club was John MacGregor, the London lawyer who not only was sufficiently intrepid to go cruising in his little canoe yawl, the *Rob Roy*, but also was so sanguine about cruising in small craft that he wrote books about his watery adventures, thus creating something of a craze for messing about in boats.

Into this heritage came Albert Strange, who loved to sail and row, could draw and paint boats well, and so naturally turned to designing boats. He drew some 150 designs, from dinghies to sixty-footers. It is his designs for canoe yawls that have been preserved, and the *Sheila II*, built in 1911 by A. M. Dickie for Robert E. Groves, is the distillation of all such craft he designed. She is the prettiest one, and, I venture to say, the best performer under sail. In the next chapter, I'll take a look at some of her cousins, from a twenty-foot centerboarder, the *Cherub II*, to a powerful thirty-seven-footer, the *Seal*.

The *Sheila II* is 31 feet 6 inches long on deck, with a waterline length of 24 feet, a beam of 8 feet 6 inches, and a draft of 4 feet 11 inches. Her displacement is 6.2 tons and her sail area is 545 square feet.

Her lines show her beautiful curves throughout, and, of course, her most interesting feature is the canoe stern. There is no simpler, more symmetrical stern form than this, and, hence, none more difficult for the designer to shape exactly right. Albert Strange certainly hit the mark with the *Sheila*.

The overhang of the *Sheila*'s stern is greater

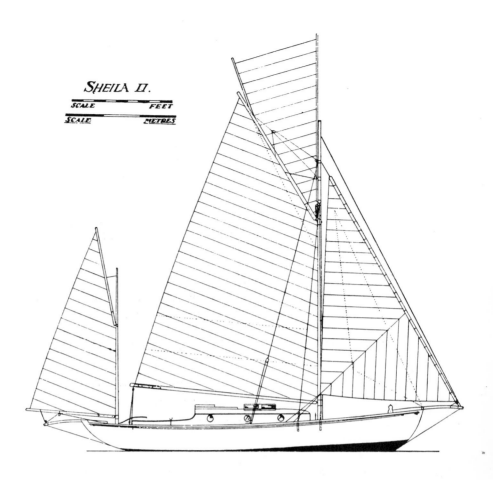

SHEILA II.

| SCALE | FEET |
| SCALE | METRES |

Right: The *Sheila*'s sail plan shows a jib that furls on a wooden roller, a storm jib that sets to the stem head, a topsail whose jackyards can stow lashed upright to the main shrouds, and a mizzen whose boom is a scant three feet off the water. (*Thoughts on Yachts and Yachting* by Uffa Fox. Reproduced by kind permission of the Executors of Uffa Fox Deceased.)

Below: Albert Strange, the marine artist, gave the *Sheila* a beautiful set of lines. (*Thoughts on Yachts and Yachting* by Uffa Fox. Reproduced by kind permission of the Executors of Uffa Fox Deceased.)

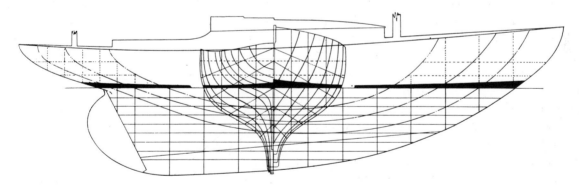

SHEILA II.

| SCALE | FEET |
| SCALE | METRES |

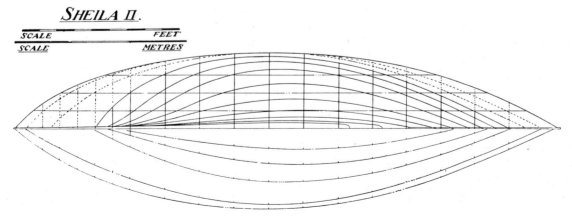

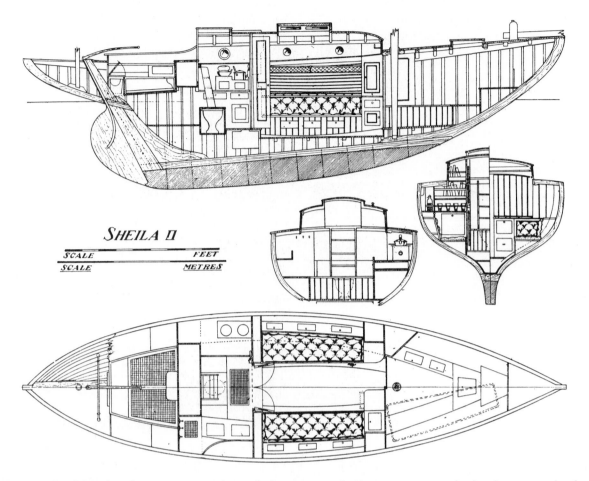

SHEILA II

SCALE   FEET
SCALE   METRES

Every detail of her interior arrangement is worked out to perfection except one: the head turns up in the middle of Grand Central Station. (*Thoughts on Yachts and Yachting* by Uffa Fox. Reproduced by kind permission of the Executors of Uffa Fox Deceased.)

than that of the bow, and this gives the boat grace and elegance where they can be afforded. The sections of the stern are flat enough near the centerline to gain some stability, yet this flatness is moderate and rather narrow, so the stern wouldn't slap or pound.

I once made a cruise in the *Hostess III*, Philip Chase's fine canoe-sterned yawl out of Horseshoe Cove, Maine, and I noticed that anytime we were rowing near the boat, my eye was always drawn to that well-proportioned canoe stern.

The *Sheila* looks deceptively dainty; her midsection is really quite powerful.

Her yawl rig is handy, with its jib set on a wooden roller. There would probably come a time, though, when you were working to windward in a hard breeze under the stem-head storm jib and close-reefed mainsail, when you'd want to strike down the rolled-up jib. That could be quite

a chore with the bowsprit plunging under now and then. And what do you do with it when you get it down?

The great feature of the yawl rig for cruising is the ability to sail the boat under jib and jigger in blowing weather. Of course she can't be expected to get to weather in a big seaway under that combination, when the reefed mainsail would be needed to give her drive, but the jib and jigger makes a fine rig when reaching in a strong breeze. The overhanging foot of the mizzen is a bit close to the water, though; when reaching, or even running, in a rough sea, a steep wave might reach it and do some damage. It would be good to give her a somewhat taller mizzenmast and raise the gooseneck. The *Sheila*'s jackyard topsail would be fun to play with; when it is not set, the yards stow up and down the main shrouds.

The yawl's saloon is snug and well appointed.

Robert Groves, for whom the *Sheila* was built, made this sketch of the yawl with her mizzen sheeted flat to keep her from yawing around an anchor dropped in the shelter of spray-covered rocks at Lunga, one of the Treshnish Isles on the west coast of Scotland. (*Thoughts on Yachts and Yachting* by Uffa Fox. Reproduced by kind permission of the Executors of Uffa Fox Deceased.)

It can be shut off from the fo'c's'le by a sliding door and from the galley by a narrow pair of swinging doors. The headroom under the carlins is 5 feet 7½ inches.

The water tank is under the sole in the galley, and the head is in a box at the base of the companion ladder. This latter arrangement just doesn't make sense. A number of ludicrous

Left: The *Sheila* sailing in Australian waters during a break in Adrian Hayter's long, singlehanded voyage in her from England to New Zealand. (*Sheila in the Wind* by Adrian Hayter)

Right: The *Sheila* on the hard for bottom painting. (*Sheila in the Wind* by Adrian Hayter)

scenarios—all of which I will spare the reader—come to mind. Far better to use that admirable box for firewood, and hang up on its becket in the fo'c's'le that versatile paragon of sanitation, the cedar bucket.

The *Sheila*'s lack of an engine means that there is plenty of storage space under her bridge deck and an abundance of peace and quiet throughout the ship.

Adrian Hayter sailed the *Sheila II* out to New Zealand from England via the Mediterranean and the Red Sea in the Fifties. He spent from 1950 to 1956 on the voyage, for along the way he had to stop and work to raise the money to continue. He wrote a book about his odyssey called *Sheila in the Wind: A Story of a Lone Voyage*, for he went singlehanded.

Hayter met his share of heavy weather on the voyage. He and the *Sheila* faced their toughest test on the last leg in the Tasman Sea—a cyclone:

By dusk on the second day it was blowing gale force, and still increasing. *Sheila* lay hove-to under storm canvas, but at 9 that night I struggled to take it in before the still

rising wind tore it to shreds or pulled out the stick. *Sheila* felt easier thereafter, steadied (without being over-burdened) by the tremendous wind in her rigging, and the only discomfort came with occasional breakers against which no small ship has protection.

Dawn came slowly through the dense rain, but at 10 a.m. the screaming wind stopped suddenly, the sky cleared overhead into bright sunshine, and we lay in the centre of the cyclone, enclosed by a huge beyond-horizon-wide circle of black clouds under which the storm still raged. There were only faint puffs of wind, but the seas were gigantic, rushing into each other, lifting into tall, top-heavy triangles and flopping back to cause more trouble. I could do nothing to steady *Sheila* without wind, the unrhythmic tossing and battering placing terrible strains upon her; during that day, the eye of the storm slowly passed over us and the other rim approached.

We entered the other side just after dark that night, and flew east before the screaming rush under bare poles. It eased to gale force near midnight when I got on storm canvas, and replaced this just before dawn (when the wind eased further) by the closely reefed main and storm jib. I reckoned we covered 100 miles in the next fifteen hours, and at times when *Sheila* was lifted high on a crest and the full force of the wind hit her, she was flung far over on her side until half the sail was flat in the water. It was bad seamanship to sail so hard in such weather; the short rations impelled it, but it imposed the great strains and discomfort that bad seamanship always does. And so I had my cyclone.

35/ Albert Strange's Canoe Yawls

Small-boat cruising men on both sides of the Atlantic owe much to John Macgregor and his followers for the development and perfection of the canoe yawl. While Macgregor's Rob Roy books tempted many to venture forth on ambitious cruises in small boats, they also demonstrated, to sailors already so attracted, a different and more wholesome type of boat than had previously been available to them. Prior to 1865, when Macgregor had built for himself the first of his small, able double-enders, a coastwise cruising man had to choose between light, delicate pulling boats designed to travel fast during an afternoon on a peaceful river, and heavily built fishing craft, designed to be stable, burdensome working platforms. The canoe yawl was a nice compromise that met a real and growing need.

One of Macgregor's later disciples, and the man who probably did as much as any other to bring the canoe yawl to the peak of its perfection, was the English artist and boat designer Albert Strange. In the previous chapter, we had a look at the *Sheila II*, perhaps the ultimate boat among the many canoe yawls that Strange designed. In this chapter are four earlier canoe yawl designs from the board of Albert Strange.

The little *Cherub II* was designed by Strange for his own use in 1893. She is 20 feet long on deck, with a waterline length of 17 feet 4 inches, a beam of 5 feet 10 inches, and a draft with the centerboard up of 1 foot 9 inches. Her sail area is 249 square feet. She has 284 pounds of ballast on the keel and another 680 pounds inside.

The designer's painting of the boat shows her simple rig, with lug mainsail, no headsail, and a tiny mizzen that is almost leg-o'-mutton shaped but has a sprit that gives the leech of the sail a little peak.

The cabin roof lifts to give headroom and also may be slid forward. She would be a snug, handy boat indeed and would make an admirable vessel for a singlehander to use for the exploration of any but the most exposed of coastlines.

Albert Strange wrote of her performance:

The boat actually proved to be a first-rate sea-cruiser, holding her own with cobles of much larger size, and only on one point of sailing—*i.e.*, turning to windward in a light breeze with short sea—was she outclassed by boats of similar length, but of greater draught of water and more power and sail. In a large sea and strong wind she performed very much better than could be expected, and was actually at her best under double-reefed sail and mizen, when her dryness was most noticeable, and was doubtless due to the long easy bow and sharp underwater sections forward. I do not remember any heavy water coming on board in sailing, except on one occasion in running through the Looe Channel, when one sea did fall on her forward deck with startling weight and volume.

The *Norma* is a more sophisticated canoe yawl and one of a size that would make an ideal cruising boat for two people. She is 25 feet 5 inches long on deck, with a waterline length of 20 feet, a beam of 7 feet 2 inches, and a draft of 3 feet 4 inches. Her displacement is 3.35 tons, and her sail area, 365 square feet.

Albert Strange designed the *Norma* in 1910, the year before he drew the plans for the *Sheila II.* By this time, his canoe yawls had some attributes of more "advanced" cruising boats,

Albert Strange at his drawing board. (*Traditions and Memories of American Yachting* by William P. Stephens, © Hearst Corporation, 1945)

The *Cherub II*, a sweet little canoe yawl that the English artist and small-boat man designed eighty years ago. (*Yachting and Boating Monthly*, March, 1908)

such as a fairly deep keel with considerable outside ballast, the distinctive overhanging canoe stern with the rudder totally submerged, a gaff-rigged mainsail and mizzen and a single headsail setting on a short bowsprit, a fixed trunk cabin, and, below, a cabin fitted out with almost all the comforts of home.

Evidently the *Norma* was thought to be too small for a topsail; in truth, is any boat too small for a topsail?

With the *Seal*, we see an apparent influence of the deep and narrow English cutter on a larger Albert Strange canoe yawl. The combination certainly produces a powerful and able-looking

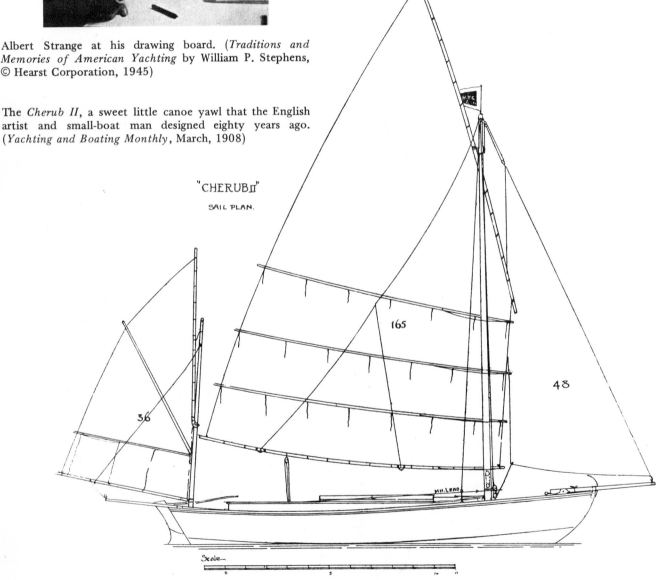

"CHERUB II"

SAIL PLAN.

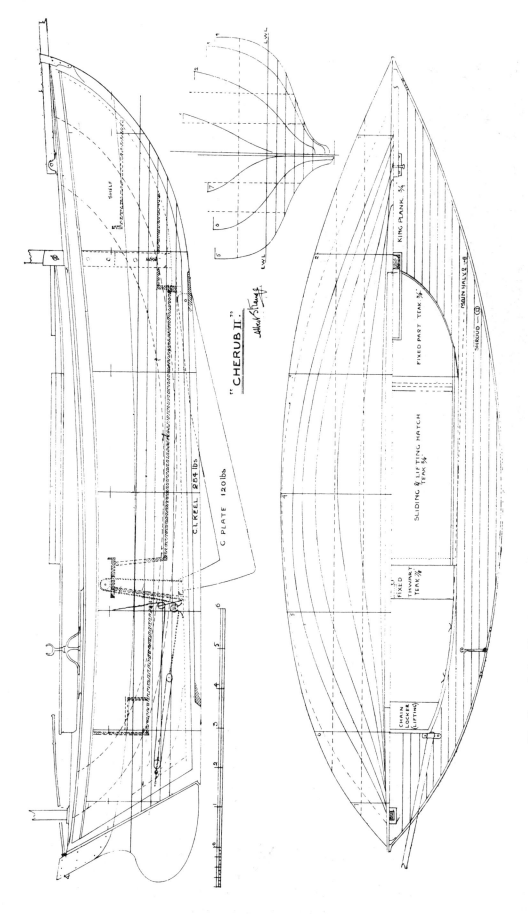

"CHERUB II."

The lines of the *Cherub II* show a dainty but able hull. (*Yachting and Boating Monthly*, March, 1908)

Albert Strange painted his *Cherub II* boiling along on a broad reach under shortened sail. (*Yachting and Boating Monthly*, February, 1908)

hull. Perhaps it is the cutter influence that has caused Strange to knuckle the *Seal's* stem profile around till it is vertical at the sheer line, and then repeat the process with an even sharper knuckle at the stern. Happily, none of this influence crept into the design of the *Sheila II*, nor are these knuckles so pronounced in others among Strange's canoe yawls.

The *Seal* is 37 feet 7 inches long on deck, with a waterline length of 30 feet 7 inches, a beam of 9 feet, and a draft of 6 feet. The sail area is 740 square feet, and her displacement is 11.68 tons, with over four tons of lead on the keel.

The *Seal's* timbers are of English oak; her floors are galvanized wrought iron; her fastenings are muntz metal and copper; her planking thickness varies from 1⅛ inches to 1⅜ inches.

She would make a fine cruising vessel. In the words of the marine historian and authority E. Keble Chatterton, "Such a craft as this would be able to be independent of the shore for a week, would be able to go through a fair amount of dirty weather, and would be dry in a seaway, plucky and strong." As a matter of fact, with proper gear and provisions, doubtless she could be independent of the shore for considerably longer than a week.

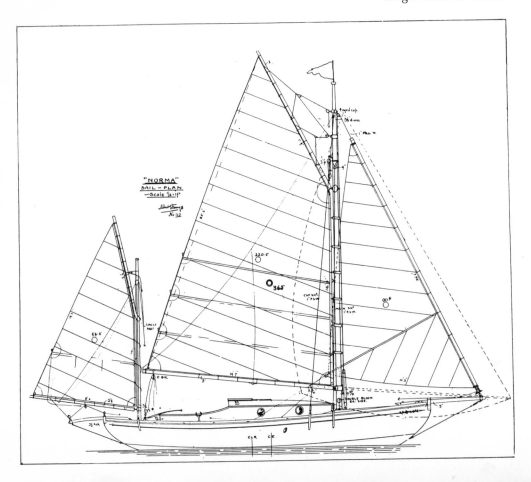

The sail plan of the *Norma*, a 25-footer. (*Fore and Aft Craft and Their Story* by E. Keble Chatterton)

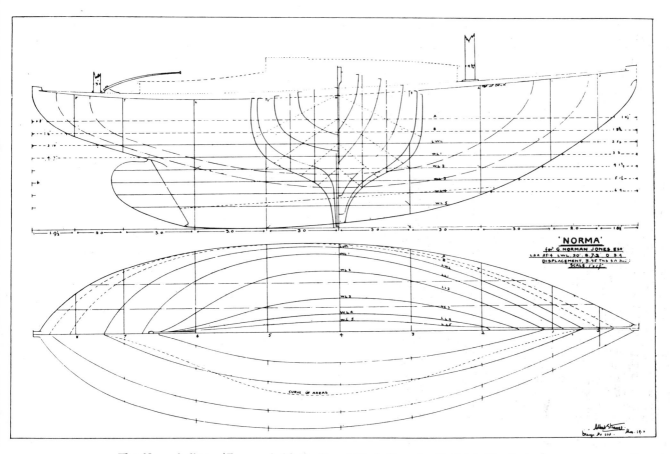

The *Norma*'s lines. (*Fore and Aft Craft and Their Story* by E. Keble Chatterton)

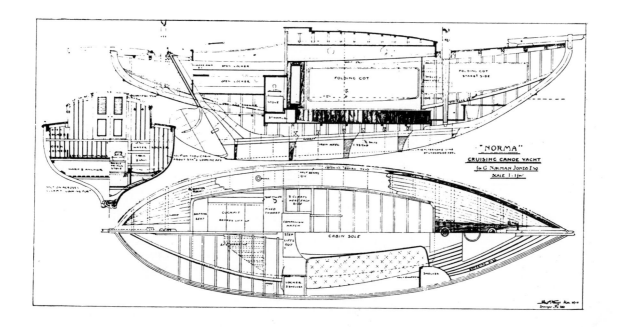

The *Norma* is laid out for two. (*Fore and Aft Craft and Their Story* by E. Keble Chatterton)

"SEAL"
SAIL-PLAN.

JIB.   130.
FORESAIL   100
MAINSAIL   330
TOPSAIL   105
MIZEN   75
TOTAL   740. SQ FT

(WORKING AREA 585)

Left: The sail plan of the *Seal*, a 37-footer. (*Fore and Aft Craft and Their Story* by E. Keble Chatterton)

Below: The *Seal*'s lines show a powerful hull. (*Fore and Aft Craft and Their Story* by E. Keble Chatterton)

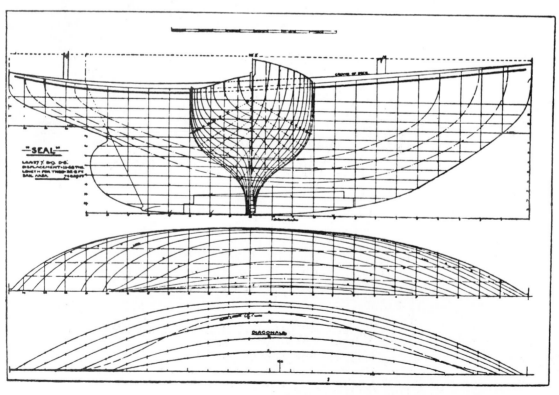

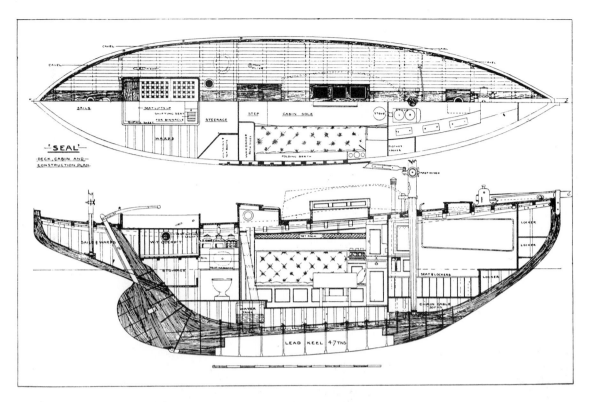

The accommodation and deck plan of the *Seal*. (*Fore and Aft Craft and Their Story* by E. Keble Chatterton)

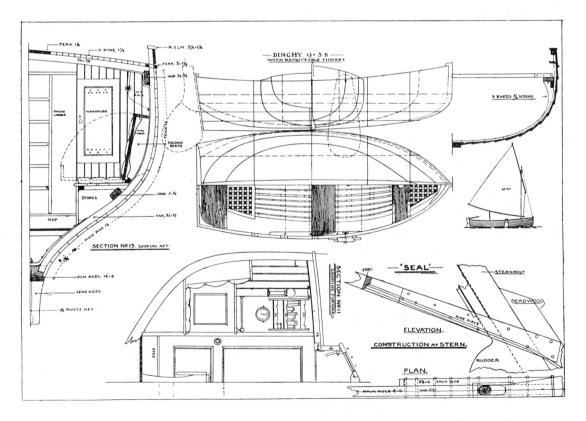

Some details of the *Seal* and the plans of her dinghy. (*Fore and Aft Craft and Their Story* by E. Keble Chatterton)

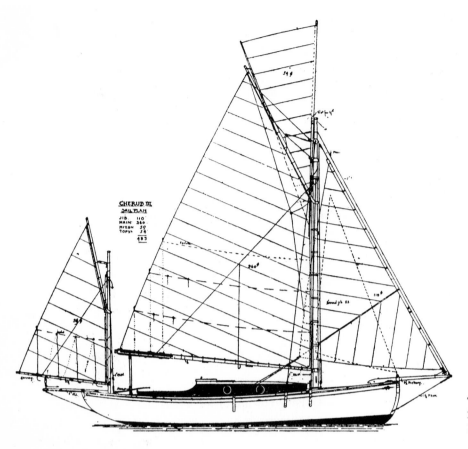

The sail plan of the *Cherub III*, a 28½-footer. (*Fore and Aft Craft and Their Story* by E. Keble Chatterton)

The *Cherub III*'s lines. (*Fore and Aft Craft and Their Story* by E. Keble Chatterton)

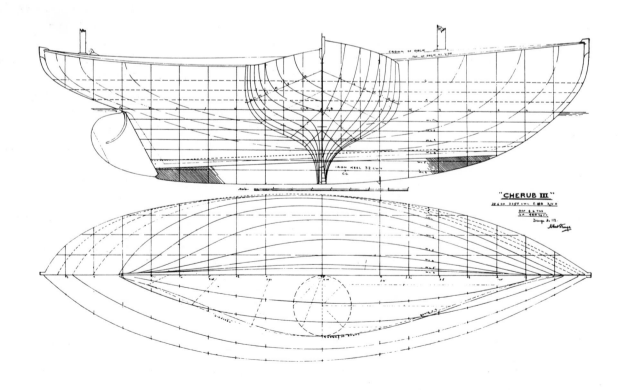

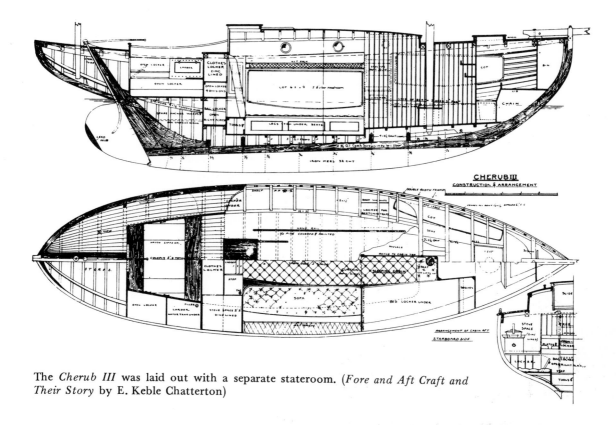

The *Cherub III* was laid out with a separate stateroom. (*Fore and Aft Craft and Their Story* by E. Keble Chatterton)

The *Seal*'s size enabled Strange to give her a versatile double-head rig, to make her flush-decked for extra strength and so a tender could be stowed on deck, to move the galley forward into the fo'c's'le, and to give her a real steerage under the bridge deck, one big enough to house the head. The *Seal*'s dinghy has a removable thwart and leeboards rather than a centerboard, so she could stow upside down over the skylight.

Albert Strange designed the *Cherub III* for his own use in 1910 and sailed her in 1910 and 1911. He had to sell her in 1912, for by then he was in declining health. In 1911 he made a long cruise to Scotland in her in company with the *Sheila II*. Would that we had a detailed log of that voyage kept by the great designer-artist, and as long as we're at the wishing well, why not throw in some nice full-page sketches by Strange of the *Sheila* sailing as seen from the cockpit of the *Cherub*, the two canoe yawls thrashing their way around some Scottish headland, or, say, both yawls at anchor behind a rocky island that was

all that stood between them and the great seas finishing their oceanic journeys. Alas, we have to be content with our own imaginings.

The *Cherub III* is 28 feet 6 inches long on deck, with a waterline length of 23 feet, a beam of 8 feet, and a draft of 3 feet 10 inches. She displaces 4.6 tons, and her sail area is 483 square feet. She is slightly smaller than the *Sheila* and is decidedly less delicate. Her plans were drawn with a specific cabin plan in mind, for there is a separate stateroom forward for Mrs. Strange.

These handsome, able double-enders of sixty and more years ago are interesting and instructive today. There are surely more choices of cruising designs open to us now than there were to those seeking a wholesome cruising boat before Macgregor made his breakthrough with the canoe yawl over a century ago, but we have to seek out these designs, for the ones thrust upon us are all of a kind. To get a real choice takes some digging, usually into the past.

36/ The *Brownie*

Length on deck: 31 feet 11 inches
Length on waterline: 23 feet 6 inches
Beam: 8 feet 6 inches
Draft: 5 feet 6 inches
Sail area: 590 square feet
Displacement: 5½ tons
Designer: S. S. Crocker, Jr.

A couple of years ago, when I was prowling the waterfront in Newport, Rhode Island, I saw a boat that gave me a real start. The little yawl looked somehow so completely familiar, yet at the same time so strange and small lying at the end of a float just beyond the usual lineup of stock plastic sloops.

It took me quite a few seconds of gawking to realize that here was a sistership of the yawl my father had owned during my growing-up years. I used to think of the *Brownie* as a very big boat indeed, and not having seen her in a couple of decades, it gave me a funny feeling to look over all the once so thoroughly familiar features of the boat, seemingly in miniature.

About four boats were built to the design, a creation of S. S. Crocker, Jr. Pop always said she was the best boat Sam Crocker ever turned out, and I have to agree with him. The *Brownie* was built by Goudy and Stevens at East Boothbay, Maine, in 1931. She is 31 feet 11 inches long on deck, with a waterline length of 23 feet 6 inches, a beam of 8 feet 6 inches, and a draft of 5 feet 6 inches. Her displacement is about 5½ tons and she carries 590 square feet of working sail area.

She has a sweet set of lines; hauled out on the railway we built for her on the Rhode Island bank of the Pawcatuck River, she was always pretty to look at.

We did all our own work on the yawl; everybody in the family knew every inch of the boat inside and out. I liked varnish work best myself, that is, until Pop discovered a holiday where I'd just been brushing. After one or two of those revelations, you made sure you had the light reflecting off the spar just right as you brushed, so you could see those little suggestions of bare spots and go back over them quickly.

Every seam below the waterline was red-leaded and puttied. She looked nice that way, with all the lines of her planks accentuated, but then somehow even better with the fresh copper paint on.

But all that took place after the bottom was sanded smooth. I remember uncles, who had boats of their own, coming around and feeling the yawl's bottom. They'd always say how smooth it was, but I never knew whether our bottom was really smoother than theirs or not. I guess Pop knew.

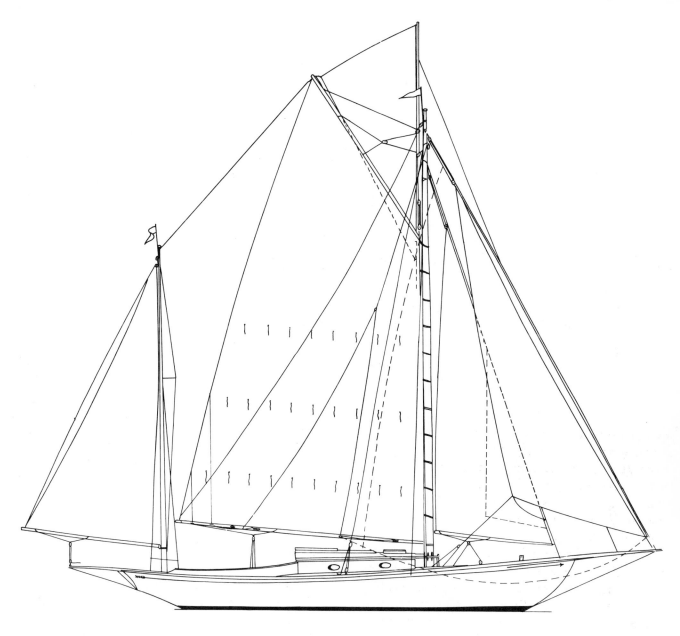

The *Brownie*'s sail plan is most versatile for cruising, and with nearly 600 square feet of working area, setting kites is more for fun than necessity.

I hated sanding the canvas-covered deck. Where the paint was chipped, you had to feather the edges, which meant bearing down hard. But you weren't to dig into the canvas on any account. This created a dilemma. You'd be working away and not getting anywhere, so you'd bear down impatiently and have a near miss with the canvas, so then you'd let up again and not get anywhere with the feathering. Pop never seemed to recognize this problem.

Of course, the great reward for all our toil was launching day, followed by rigging her up and going sailing. Launching was always quite an excitement, because to get from our railway across the River to the dredged channel and hence to the mooring, you had to thread your way through the so-called old channel, which included dodging some oyster beds. This could only be done at the top of a spring tide and took some tricky piloting. It was done in daylight, of

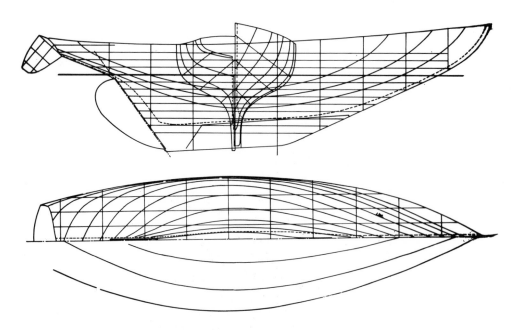

Her lines show an almost dainty hull, yet one with plenty of power and ability.

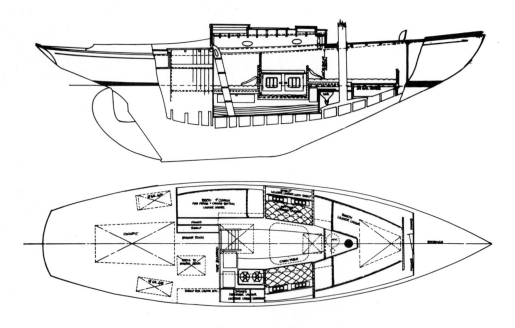

She could house three people comfortably, but cruising with two was real luxury; each one had his own seat at the table and you could keep junk in the quarterberth.

course, whenever possible, but I remember a couple of times when Pop buoyed the oyster beds and lashed lanterns to the buoys so he could hit the top of the tide after dark. To us, that put Pop way ahead of Columbus.

We had some fine cruising in the little yawl.

The *Brownie* would sail. A good friend of mine used to say that watching my father sailing this boat was a maddening experience: "He just sits there and sails by everybody."

The yawl goes especially well to windward, for she has enough ballast low enough to really stand

Pop leaving Block Island, Rhode Island, with a couple of his cronies. This is a rare photograph, for it shows Great Salt Pond in something less than a gale. (Photo by Edward Cabot)

up to her sail, enough lateral resistance to go where she looks, and a low enough hull and house so as not to have too much windage.

The heavy, low, iron keel gives her her only fault; she has a rather quick roll at times.

Her wide transom gives her extra bearing when heeled and also plenty of room on deck to handle the mizzen. In fact, there is room to stow a dinghy aft, as shown in the photo, and we used the mizzen boom as a boat derrick.

Her big rudder makes her maneuverable in light going and relatively easy to steer off the wind in a strong breeze and rough sea. The shape of the propeller aperture seems very practical and is a Crocker trademark. She has a two-bladed, feathering wheel.

The *Brownie* has a generous sail plan without having to resort to kites. One day in Block Island Sound we sailed right past the famous yawl

Dorade, in light going, with both boats under working sail. The *Dorade* needed her big overlapping headsails to get her going, and had she had them set, she certainly would have turned the tables on us.

The little yawl is heavy for her length; she has to carry sail to do well to windward in a breeze, but she has the power to do it. The rig is excellent for cruising, with many combinations of sail possible for different conditions.

Going to windward in a fresh-to-strong breeze, we would take the forestaysail and mizzen off her. She balanced better under mainsail and jib than she did under main and staysail, carrying a bit too much weather helm with the latter combination.

Staysail and mizzen was the standard rig for squalls. It was handy to be able to take the mainsail off and still have the boat be well balanced.

Running off the wind in a breeze, we used to let her go under mainsail alone. Pop sort of liked that; he'd been brought up in catboats.

One nice thing you could do with this boat due to her generous mizzen was to back her down in a straight line with just the mizzen set. That trick let us get underway under sail from a tight berth more than once.

Both main halyards were rigged on the port side, so you could grip them together and hoist the mainsail singlehanded. This rig makes good sense with a small gaff sail.

A most useful piece of rigging was a downhaul on the jib, so you could pull the sail right down its stay and hold the head down without having to go out on the bowsprit until you were ready to furl up.

Now it can be revealed whence came my great love of vangs. We had a vang on the mainsail running from the end of the gaff through a single block at the mizzen masthead and down to a cleat on the mizzenmast in easy reach of the helmsman. By adjusting the vang, you could really control the shape of the mainsail beautifully. It kept all the sag out of the gaff when going to windward, and also kept the gaff off the lee rigging when running with the boom well squared off.

One time when we were setting the mainsail, powering slowly into a head sea, the slack vang managed to cast a beautiful half-hitch over the top of the mizzenmast. The next fifteen minutes produced a good lesson in seamanship—to say nothing of quite a little new terminology. It all went to show that engines and sails don't mix too well; the vang probably couldn't have performed so diabolically without the engine pushing the boat right to windward into the head sea.

The *Brownie*'s mainsail had reef points as shown in the sail plan. One time we were beating up Narragansett Bay in the late fall, and since the northwester had some plenty heavy gusts, we just had the triple-reefed mainsail and the staysail on her. Pop said he thought the close-reefed main was a "modest little sail," which it certainly was. But it suited the yawl just right that day.

One of our favorite sails was a big balloon forestaysail. We'd often carry it reaching and pole it out when running. The English used to like this sail a lot; it was the handiest light sail we ever had for cruising.

The house on this boat was short and narrow, leaving plenty of room to work on deck. We never thought of lifelines, but I don't remember anybody ever falling overboard. The rule was simply to hang on and not fall overboard. I guess we were more afraid of what Pop would say about it than we were of drowning.

The cabin was hardly palatial, but it was big enough for a father to teach his son to play cribbage during a four-day layover at Duck Island Roads forced by a miserable spell of weather. The layout was designed for three people, which is probably enough to have on board when cruising in a boat this size for any length of time. The small seats in the cabin are not often seen today. They worked out very well. You can't design a seat that's really right for sleeping, nor a bunk that's really good for sitting. In this boat, the bunks were bunks and the seats were seats.

The head, I must say, was a miserable arrangement. It could only be used when the whole cabin was cleared. It would have been better to have had a bucket in the engine room.

The separate engine room under the wide bridge deck gave relatively good access to the engine and kept that piece of machinery and all that went with it properly separated from the nicer features of life afloat. The yawl had a little Redwing that you started by rolling the flywheel with your foot while standing in the engine-room hatch. It ran so smoothly you could hardly hear it. But when the Redwing finally packed up, it just sat there as ballast for a number of years and we sailed her without power, which worked out fine, for she was always smart and easy to handle.

The *Brownie* was a great boat to grow up in, and when you sailed around the coast in her with Pop, you learned a lot about how to do things on the water. Pop sold her in the fall of 1948, after what turned out to be his last sail. In a way, it seemed right that they both should go at about the same time, because you couldn't really think of the one without thinking of the other.

Epilogue — A Sail in the *Brownie*

When a certain gentleman had been piloted by his son through the intricacies of Hadley Harbor on Naushon Island, and brought to anchor in the Inner Cove, he peered about on all sides of his schooner and finally said, "Why, we're as safe as in God's pocket."

Pop and I, in our little yawl, were in the same snug harbor just off Buzzards Bay one grey September morning. We should have stayed there.

As a matter of fact, I was secretly looking forward to a layover in Hadley's, for that would mean a row over to the Forbes' red boathouse and a little deliberate trespassing, in spite of dark looks from the brusque boatkeeper. The sight and the smell of those old, varnished pulling boats with the perfect wineglass-shaped sterns hanging overhead in the boathouse made up for the sneaky feeling that goes with being uninvited. I'd stand as long as I dared, drinking in every fine feature of the big six-oared cutter, and then hurry back to my own dinghy, hoping to escape before the keeper challenged my expedition. Then, instead of rowing a little boat back to the yawl, I'd pull an oar in that cutter, rowing off in my mind's eye to some tremendous schooner yacht becalmed in Vineyard Sound.

But today there was to be no expedition to the boathouse, for Pop was anxious to clear away toward our home mooring to the westward, despite the leaden sky and falling glass.

As I transferred steaming oatmeal from its pot on the stove into tan enamel bowls set out on the oiled mahogany cabin table, Pop said he hated to waste a southeast breeze. Beating all the way home against the prevailing southwester was always a discouraging process to Pop. He was pessimistic about making long tacks and then having the wind shift to put him right back where he started. I never could understand why he would predict the wind's capriciousness with such accuracy and then sail off and get stung. But today, with the wind east of south, we could reach along to Cuttyhunk in the lee of the islands and duck in if it looked dirty. Or, if the weather improved, we could hang on for Point Judith.

The breeze was moderate to fresh, and Pop said we'd have all the sail we wanted without the jib and mizzen. So we hove up short on the anchor and then set the big gaff mainsail. It was on this cruise that I happily discovered that I was at last heavy enough to take advantage of Pop's both-main-halyards-on-the-same-side arrangement, and I could hoist away on throat and peak together and watch the gaff majestically climb the mast with no sound save that of the sail shaking itself awake and cheerily rattling its reefpoints. That morning in Hadley's, I proudly displayed my new-found strength, but Pop was unimpressed. He was probably wondering how I'd make out with the boat jumping a little, and some wind and water in the sail.

We coiled down, hung the halyards on the fife rail, and set the forestaysail. With the mainsheet slack and the staysail aback, the yawl payed off on her anchor and broke it out. I brought it aboard while Pop spun her around on her heel and headed out the entrance to the cove. When my foredeck was shipshape, I went aft and wanted to know why we hadn't hoisted the dinghy on board as usual. Pop ignored the question and told me to see what time we were getting underway. Eight o'clock went into the log. If Pop was towing the dinghy, I guessed that meant he was figuring to put into Cuttyhunk.

We had a grand sail up the islands, roaring along with a fresh beam wind and almost no sea. We sneaked inside Weepecket Island and watched the dull green hills and storm-gnarled trees of Naushon slide past. The sand beach at Kettle Cove looked cold and grey. We were glad the coal stove was humming along down below. The smoke bowling out of its little chimney cheered us.

Roaring along in the smooth water to leeward of Pasque, with the boat ticking off a healthy six knots and just as steady as a church, we felt that the yawl was a great juggernaut, compelled to forge ahead, heeled over just so, forever. This illusion was quickly shattered when the seas that were pouring through Quicks Hole started her rolling and plunging.

In the lee of Nashewena, I went forward to my favorite post, lying on deck with my head out over the rail watching the never-ending, rushing, curling bow wave. On the windward side, he was a tall, thin, dapper gentleman, sweeping back with just the proper curve, and not making too much noise about it. But on the lee side, he was a great burly fellow, crashing about in all directions and drowning out all other sounds with his roaring.

When the waves started rolling in and reaching for the bow from a new angle, I looked up to see that Pop was laying her off a couple of points to pass to leeward of Penikese. We were evidently going on. Tonight there would be no walk to the top of the hill at Cuttyhunk to watch the reds of Gay Head and the sunset combine, but instead a rough-and-tumble go of it to old Point Jude. I scrambled aft to see if I was right.

"It seems to be lightening up some," I said.

Pop made a face to windward. "Oh, I guess we'll get some rain," he said.

"Aren't we going to Cuttyhunk?"

"Pull the dinghy up under the stern and bend that new line onto the towing ring in the stem. Then cast off the painter and give her plenty of towline." I was right.

It was half-past-ten when I took the wheel. We were just leaving the protection of Cuttyhunk, and starting to feel the big seas the southeaster had been building up outside Buzzards Bay. "Keep her going west," Pop said, as he climbed out from behind the wheel.

"West it is," said I, grabbing the spokes and chocking my back up against the weather side of the mizzenmast. But west it wasn't, at least not for more than an instant at a time. A green roller would ease in under the quarter and send her rolling and dipping to west by south, no matter how much helm I could put on beforehand. Then the sea would roll on under her, pulling the bow off with it, and lower us gently down into the trough heading west by north with the helm hard alee.

Pop had disappeared below, to tamper with the stove, as I knew by the sounds of the grate grinding, the shovel thrusting in the bin, and the new coal crackling just before the lid was banged back into place. I didn't let myself get really hopeful, though, until I heard the double-boiler jump out of its locker, to clatter about on the cabin floor, the way it always does when you're in too much of a hurry about pulling out the big frying pan. Sure enough, in a minute there appeared on the bridge deck, just outside the cabin hatchway, a steaming fried-egg sandwich. Once that stout friend was safely stowed away, the steering was easier. Perhaps it was because we were leaving that evil spot south of Hen and Chickens, where the seas heap up as if possessed by devils.

We rolled past Ribbon Reef, and the melodious notes of the ship's clock striking eight bells momentarily diverted us from the woeful groaning of the whistle buoy. The breeze went light quite suddenly, we thought. The rain started just as we were setting the mizzen. The whitecaps disappeared almost immediately, but the high seas rolled us violently in the light air. We made slow, uncomfortable progress.

Out came the oilskins and slam-shut went the cabin hatch. Pop took the wheel, and we settled down to await developments, wondering when we would get to Point Judith.

Glancing to windward, I thought I saw white water, and was just going to remark on it when Pop said, "Main halyards—quick—get that sail down!"

I jumped forward, threw the halyards off the

pins, and had the mainsail half lowered when the squall hit us. For the first few seconds, all my senses were fully occupied trying to comprehend a new scale of wind force. There was nothing in my small experience with which to compare this sudden screamer. Never before had it been so nearly impossible to see and hear. Rain and spray together roared horizontally across the deck. Breathing was a conscious effort. When my stunned mind recalled that I was supposed to be getting the mainsail down, I saw that Pop had slacked away the mainsheet and had brought the yawl close enough to the wind so that I could pull the gaff down and pass a stop round the flogging sail. I clawed my way aft to take the wheel, while Pop finished tying up the mainsail.

She raced along rail down, with just the staysail and mizzen on her. The seas crashed forward—foaming—dropped down, and rose again—steeply—to hurl themselves on us in a seething rush that jolted the boat down to her beam ends and left us weltering in foam.

Pop peered into the binnacle. "Hey, where are you taking her?" I looked at the compass as we swung by northwest. Pop never had much use for a soldier at the helm, and he was angry. When he looked at me, though, I guess he realized I was just too excited to steer properly. Otherwise he would never have said, "Just keep her going west, fella. Let me worry about the boat." After that, I kept her near west and marveled at the way the little yawl stood up to her beating.

The squall soon left us, but the rain poured down, and the sea was high and confused. The dinghy, filled nearly to her gunwales, pulled heavily on her towline. The towing ring in her stem let go. The next steep sea rolled her over. We managed to wear the yawl around and head back for the capsized dinghy, but with so little wind and so much sea, we barely had steerage way.

Pop sent me forward to set the mainsail by myself. Was I proud! But with the boat's wild motion, I couldn't put all my weight on the halyards. The loosely furled sail was sodden and heavy with water. Pop seemed to take no notice of my futile efforts. I crawled aft to deliver the unnecessary report that I could not set the sail by myself, as I had in Hadley Harbor. Pop mumbled something to himself and went forward to set the sail.

With the mainsail on her, we worked alongside the overturned dinghy and retrieved her towline with the boathook. She righted herself as we took her in tow. We pulled her bow right up out of water under our stern and towed her thus, half full of water and snubbed up short.

We had just steered around to a westerly heading again, when another line of white water charged down on us from the south'ard. This time we lowered and lashed the mainsail before the squall hit. Again we thrashed westward, in the high, confused sea, with wind and water tearing at our staysail and mizzen. Again the squall left us to slat and bang in the endless rain. I had never seen it rain so hard for so long. Pop said he had, in Panama once.

Three more squalls struck us from the south'ard. When the last one blew over, Pop and I were pretty tired and wet. Some of the rain

The author sailing the *Brownie* at about the time of the Epilogue, but on a distinctly better day.

must have gone down the chimney, because the stove was out. At least there wasn't any sign of smoke.

Nonetheless, prospects were improving. The sky now showed definite signs of clearing. And we could still head west, where lay the haven of Point Judith.

At five o'clock in the afternoon, a good breeze sprang up from the northeast. Suddenly the rain stopped, the horizon cleared, and there was Point Judith fine on the starboard bow about six miles distant. The northeaster came breezing on, knocking down the old seas and building up its own regiments of marching columns of tumbling water. It was a rattling good breeze for the yawl.

Pop didn't drive a boat much. He liked to keep going, but when it was time to reef, he would shorten sail and ease the boat. I guess he was pretty fed up with this day's sail. When the northeaster started to breeze on, he seemed to take a diabolical pleasure in setting the jib and balloon staysail. We had a wild run of it that late fall afternoon.

I huddled low in the cockpit, marveling at how Pop could keep her always somehow within a point of her course, at how the wind could cut so quickly to the bone, and at how the yawl could stagger along so fast under her press of sail. As a big sea rolled under her, her stern dipped low and swung to windward. The next sea, piling up astern, looked as if it must certainly come right aboard, but as it foamed down on us, she lifted her stern and rolled to leeward so that only half the whitecapped crest slapped over the rail, making us hunch down under our sou'westers. Then away she shot on the crest of the sea, shuddering along at top speed and spreading a wide blanket of foam both sides as Pop spun the wheel far down to meet her. Then she dropped down into the trough, quietly ready to meet the next wall of water.

The yawl rolled westward in this symphony of motion until sunset found us under the first gleam of the lighthouse on Point Judith. We doused the balloon staysail, skirted round the rocks on the point, and gratefully bore up between the breakwaters.

As we rounded up to drop anchor in the Harbor of Refuge, Pop said: "Different nations, different customs, as the Dutchman said when he went aft to haul down the jib." I went forward to haul down ours, wondering what the Dutchman had to do with it. When the main and mizzen had been lowered, Pop looked around and allowed he was pretty tired and thought he'd go below. I furled up, but it wasn't what you'd call a real harbor furl.

Pop had the stove crackling by the time I tumbled below. He also fetched out the bottle of dark Jamaica rum, but by the finality with which the cork went back in after his second swallow, I knew I would have to rely on the abilities of the stove to dispel the effects of hard squalls, rain and spray, and a biting northeaster.

I never did find out about the Dutchman. I fell asleep in the middle of Pop's yarn.